Selected
Paintings
and Drawings
of
DAVID
DUBAL

Published by

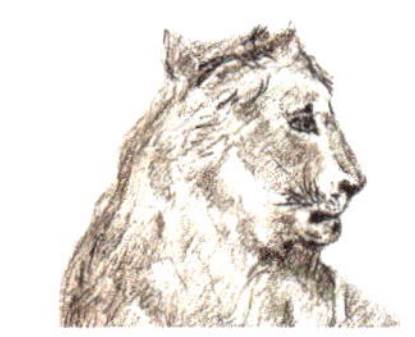

TIMP Universal
NEW YORK, NY

ISBN-13: 978-0-578-78636-0

Production by Jackson Kohl
www.jacksonkohl.com

Cover and interior design by Gary A. Rosenberg
www.thebookcouple.com

For Stella and Jax,
my great niece and nephew.
Hoping that this volume may
stimulate their creativity . . .

David Dubal:
A Personal Sketch

The Spanish philosopher José Ortega y Gasset wrote: "To be surprised, to wonder, is the sport, the luxury, special to the intellectual man. The gesture characteristic of his tribe consists in looking at the world with eyes wide open in wonder. Everything in the world is strange and marvelous to well-opened eyes. The faculty of wonder . . . is the one which leads the intellectual man through life in the perpetual ecstasy of the visionary. His special attribute is the wonder of the eyes, hence it was the ancients who gave Minerva her owl, the bird with the ever-dazzled eyes."

Perhaps the central event in prehistory is the magnificent cave paintings of thirty-five thousand years ago, before Homo sapiens appeared. Most likely these artists were exempt from the arduous tasks of hunting and food gathering, simply because their peers had discovered and valued their visual gifts. In a sense these were the very first art patrons, and the cave painters were the first professional artists who used their talents for the spiritual and symbolic that bound their cave homes together, enveloped in the light of beauty. These paintings predate sophisticated language and music, telling us that the aesthetic visual sense was appreciated by their fellows. Their renderings of many kinds of animals and hunters are as beautiful as anything ever created. These productions must have appeared to be magical, and the artists who created them may have seemed godlike to these grunting beings. Their tools were sharpened stones, animal hair, and incredibly paint that has survived the ages.

These prehistoric beings honored the animals they killed and who could kill them, and had deep respect for them. Every tribe, every nation and culture since has contributed to the art that sees. And what a fragile gamble it is, the creation of an art piece. The hand has its own intelligence and thought stops action. Nothing must interfere in the living moment. The Zen artists concentrated for hours or months upon their subject and when ready, with empty mind seized their moment of creation. To tarry even a second would invite failure. In the depths of humility and love the great Japanese master Katsushika Hokusai wrote: "From the age of six I had a mania for drawing the forms of things. By the time I was fifty I had published an infinity of designs; but all I had produced before the age of seventy is not worthy taking into account. At seventy-three I learned a little about the real structure of nature, of animals, plants, trees, birds and insects. In consequence, when I am eighty, I shall have penetrated the mystery of things; at one hundred I shall certainly have reached a marvelous stage; when I am one hundred and ten everything I do, be it a dot or a line, will be alive." As Hokusai said, he was "the old man mad about drawing."

As a child I mulled over a small section at the end of a battered old dictionary given to me by my aunt. I was intrigued by the names in alphabetical order, of their dates, and what they did in the world. I had never heard of them, but I supposed they were there because they represented achievement; they had accomplished significant things.

I was around ten, and read rather well, but my home had no such thing as an encyclopedia. I was hoping that in school I would learn about these people. But I learned nothing except George Washington never lied and Lincoln was called "honest Abe." In our music class we sang "America the Beautiful" and "We're Tenting Tonight on the Old Campgrounds." We never heard a recording of Mozart's or Bach's music.

Every day I was so bored that I could hardly keep my legs still. The teachers were dull and fat. There was nothing there to set my imagination on fire. When we drew we were given a cheap pad of paper with the Indian Chief Pontiac on the cover. Never once did the teacher care to look at our work. There were no slides of paintings, no excursions to the art museum. Doubtless I had learned something, as I still know how to do addition, but reading seemed to be my own accomplishment. And with each terrible day I waited for the bell to release me from prison. My brightest recollection was when I was nine years old and my parents on one fine day bought a piano, and I was given piano lessons. This magical instrument has been in my life ever since, even giving me the means of making a living. But well before my first piano lessons, I was enthralled with paper, crayons, pencil, ink, pens, charcoal, watercolors and tempura. Just to look at them, I tingled with pleasure. Of course these materials, even an oil set, came to me at various times and in different ways. No material was hoarded, and everything was used up in this solitary world of my own, where with my juvenile efforts I copied what I saw. I was not more than five years old when this began. Of the few things that have survived, I realize that my drawings had nothing in common with the usual children's drawings. I was patiently learning the craft of drawing. I didn't label the work good or bad, if I did not like it I tore it up. My parents had not encouraged me nor discouraged me.

Sometime later I was taken to Cleveland's Museum of Art. It's a beautiful edifice, and I vividly remember a statue outside. I was told it was by Rodin and called *The Thinker*. In 1970 it was vandalized with dynamite with irreparable damage. However, *The Thinker* even with its impairment still graces the outside of the museum. On entering the museum I found quiet and activity, and noticed that a number of people were copying paintings and drawings. Some of them used a contraption called an easel, and they worked with brushes and colors.

Here was my first awareness that for a few people this was an important activity. As I observed this concentration of whatever they were copying, I was impressed that the work looked like the originals. Later I understood that copying was an essential training for eye and

                                                     THE PAINTINGS OF DAVID DUBAL

hand. When the great Ingres was past eighty he was found at the Louvre, copying. Someone saw him and said, "You, Ingres, are still copying?" "Yes," he responded, "I am still learning." I continue to copy, though seldom for any literal sake; but before I copy a Rembrandt or Durer I study it closely and slowly, closing my eyes and going over it in my mind's eye. I like what Giacometti said, "You have to copy what you see, and at the same time you have to make a picture." Picasso felt, "Others search, I only find," and I think he meant he never stopped looking. The writer Henry Miller, who was a superb and prolific watercolorist, wrote, "Everything involves time and discipline. You must practice regularly. . . . You have to be at it every day. That is one of the reasons why a man like Picasso is so marvelous . . . . He doesn't even have to think. It's right there in his fingers. He picks up the brush, and the brush tells him what to do." At the Cleveland Museum I had my first taste of Picasso looking at his large "Blue Period" *La Vie.*

Thank goodness in every city there is an art museum. Keeping it funded is "a leap of faith." Here is civilization personified, the writer Jean Seznec wrote, "In the curve of a woman's arm in a sanguine by Watteau is the fragile epitome of civilization."

There are days when my whole body seems to involuntarily follow a call to New York's Metropolitan Museum of Art. I may stay only a quarter hour, while standing in awe of a Memling or Van Eyck. What skill and emotional power, to think Van Eyck was one of the first workers in oil paint, the medium and standard for greatness in painting.

Recently I was reading an inspiring essay, "Making Pictures" by D. H. Lawrence, who painted furiously for years. He too learnt to paint from copying pictures. He wrote "A picture lives with the life you put into it. If you put no life into it—no thrill, no concentration of delight or exaltation of visual discovery. . . . The picture must come out of the artist's inside. . . . We call it memory, but it is more than memory. It is the image as it lives in the consciousness, alive like a vision, but unknown. I believe many people have in their consciousness, living images that would give them the greatest joy to bring out. But they don't know how to go about it." Indeed, most people simply give up, not realizing that it must be a constant working or reworking. Pissarro in his letters to his son never ceases to tell him, draw, draw every day, just as you have to practice a musical instrument all the time. In Balzac's splendid short story *Gillette or The Unknown Masterpiece,* he writes, "You have caught the appearance of life but you are not expressing its fullness and the way the fullness overflows, that enigmatic quality which wanders like a cloud on the surface, in a word—that flower of life Titian and Raphael took by surprise. . . . You come to rest, you would perhaps create an excellent painting; but you grow weary too soon . . . . What is missing? Nothing. But that nothing is everything!" It may take countless attempts to achieve something of a true realization. But above all there must be a feeling of delight, and a passionate effort to bring it to life. Only God could create his Universe in a millisecond.

In my teen years I studied with two excellent artists teaching in the Cleveland school systems. Vincent Ferrara was a realistic painter who worked in oils each day. I am still intoxicated by the smell of oil paint, linseed oil, and turpentine. I closely watched Ferrara, and he gave me advice here and there but most important was his encouragement. Several of my teenage works hang in my brother's home.

In high school I was assigned some mad battleax of an art teacher, who I instinctively knew could not be worse. If I continued in her class I would have starved. But I heard that a new teacher had entered the school, and nervously I went to observe his class. I was confronted with a dynamic man of immense energy. He didn't see me in the class, but the next day I came to his room, bringing some things for him to see, and begging him with all my might to somehow get me into his class. He said it would be difficult to do. I almost screamed at him, "This is life or death." In two days I was in the class of Thompson Lehnert, and was happily with him for three years. Every Friday the class was to bring in a piece to be shown and discussed. It was the best homework I ever had.

Lehnert was a marvel of spontaneity and completely trusted his unconscious, where art lives. He knew I played the piano, and one day out of the blue he drew a caricature of me in India ink (see opposite page). It was a display of virtuosity performed in less than one minute, and I lept from the page with piano and tuxedo.

Lehnert had one main criterion for our work. Does it have "Art Quality?"—an elusive two words which mean so much.

As to my own work, I am keen on making line drawings. I have done many, frequently they stem from a life experience, or a face seen on a bus, or a dream fragment. Some are symbolic, sarcastic or humorous, with certain motifs recurring, such as flowers, people, or animals. In fact the subject matter is quite various. These "line drawings" are often compositionally complex. The line drawings always portray something of the natural world, but in a distorted view. Most of the line drawings are 11 x 14 or larger. All of them are done with pen and ink.

My paintings vary in size, from smaller 8 x 12 to many larger. I work in pastel, children's glitter, highly brilliant watercolor, acrylics, glue, colored inks, and a great deal of oil paint. Many of them are in mixed media. In the last few years I have used spray paint, and lately I paint on Styrofoam. Unlike the drawings, my paintings are often abstract and non-objective, although I have produced portraits of different types.

It is my opinion that an artist must show individuality of style. The work must be unique to the artist. If I possess such a thing, I could not be happier.

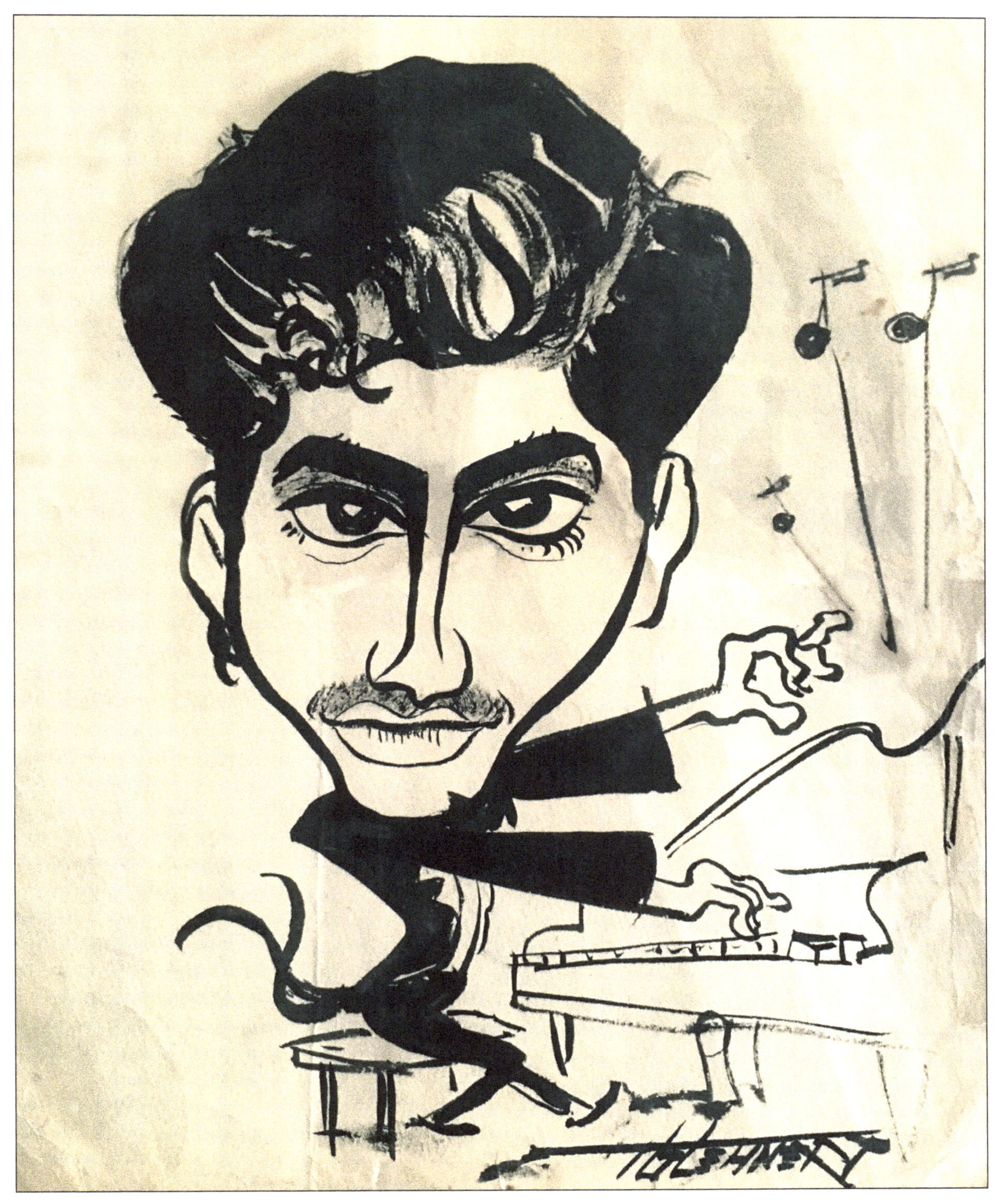

David Dubal, age sixteen.
Thompson Lehnert (1932–2020)

David Dubal: Leonardo da Vinci
(If Ever There was a Renaissance Man!)

Leonardo lived one of the greatest lives ever lived. He has been called the Lord of men. For more than half a millennium he still haunts our imaginations as to human potential.

During his lifetime, the Renaissance soared to glories undreamed of even a century earlier. Born in the village of Vinci, he was the illegitimate son of Ser Piero da Vinci, who made his living as a notary (a kind of lawyer), as did his grandfather. Leonardo's birth was inauspicious, and the event was scrawled on a page of a notary tablet by the grandfather. "1452—there was born to me a grandson, the child of Ser Piero my son. He bears the name Leonardo." His peasant mother, Caterina, was not mentioned. Soon after, Piero married a sixteen-year-old girl, who died at twenty-six. He married twice more and fathered the last of his eleven children when he was seventy-six. Not one of them had a shred of talent or distinction. But far more intriguing is Leonardo's mother, who at seventeen gave birth to a son for the ages.

In his celebrated book, *Lives of the most Eminent Painters, Sculptors, and Architects*, Giorgio Vasari called Leonardo *il divino*, and wrote, "celestial influences may shower extraordinary gifts on certain human beings, which is an effect of nature, but there is something supernatural in the accumulation in one individual of so much beauty, grace, and might." Caterina instantly vanishes from history, although it is interesting that years later in Milan, a woman, Caterina, of around sixty was Leonardo's housekeeper. When she died he paid for her funeral.

How little we know of his childhood, and one wonders when he first put pen to paper.

Vasari relates that as a boy he had wanted to paint a dragon, "and for this purpose brought to his room lizards, crickets, butterflies, grasshoppers, bats and such like animals, out of which he formed a great ugly creature." Such a painting has not survived, and the story is probably a fiction, but tells us of Leonardo the emerging naturalist and anatomist. All his life he felt deeply for animals, and at times lived with small menageries. As a youngster, he went round the market places releasing caged birds. Leonardo, who dreamed of flight, could not deprive a bird from its essence. Indeed one may call Leonardo the fountainhead of animal rights, and could not bear the cruelty to which animals were generally treated. Later, probably in the mid-1490s, he became a vegetarian, something extremely rare in his time.

Serge Bramly, in his *Leonardo: The Artist and the Man*, writes, "He asked with horror how nature could permit his creatures to live by the death of their fellows; he would not let his body become a "tomb for other animals, and an inn of the dead . . . a container of corruption. . . ." Leonardo says, "If you would be healthy, eat only when hungry, and let light fare suffice." How he must have been sickened by the typical gluttonies he saw in his princely patrons.

In 1564, the youngster moved to the fabled city of Florence, the city of the Medici, the town of Cimabue and Giotto, a place where intellect and art were honored.

Piero was well aware that his son had a gift for drawing. He had prepared contracts for the many projects of the painter and sculptor Andrea del Verrocchio, who ruled over one of the finest workshops in Florence. Piero probably asked the renowned artist to look at his son's drawings. Although Leonardo at fourteen was somewhat late in beginning an apprenticeship; however, Verrocchio was impressed and accepted him. Piero would pay for his teachings, food, and lodging. It did not take long for Leonardo to realize his good fortune, and for the next years he stayed close to his master.

Verrocchio was himself a true man of the Renaissance, and opened the doors for his pupil to geometry, anatomy, perspective, mathematics, goldsmithing, the experimenting in and making paint, and indeed much more, including music. Leonardo had a clear, sweet voice, devoting much energy to his lute, and was an outstanding improviser. He avidly studied Plato and Aristotle and the exciting new writings of Alberti. His contact with Verrocchio was the central event of his youth, and it is curious that in Leonardo's thousands of pages of writing, his master is never mentioned. The workshop was a hotbed of activity and the young man met the great and the near great such as Perugino, Botticelli, and Lorenzo di Credi, and a maze of other talented men.

Sadly, Verrocchio's life was shadowed by tragedy. When fourteen, being with friends, for fun they began throwing stones at one another. Verrocchio hit a boy on the forehead, a blow that killed him. When sculpting his *David* at Florence's Bargello, he refused to portray a slingshot.

As an artist, Verrocchio seldom receives his due, but often he touched genius. The art historian Bernard Berenson, writing to Isabella Stewart Gardner, called him, "only less great than Leonardo," and Berenson's admiration for Leonardo was unbounded.

As a draughtsman, Paul J. Sachs calls Verrocchio's *Head of a Woman* at Christ Church, Oxford, "one of the boldest most inspiring masterpieces of fifteenth-century draughtsmanship."

An important moment for Leonardo came in 1473. Verrocchio assigned his pupil with painting the left angel holding Christ's garment in his painting *The Baptism of Christ.* Verrocchio was so moved that he never painted again. The story is not true, but Walter Pater found "the angel as a space of light." Leonardo's painterly skill was of a new order. After the "Baptism of Christ" he was voted into the prestigious Guild of St. Luke.

Around this time he came to the notice of influential Florentines, who admired his brilliant conversation and musical gifts. He was slender and handsome, wearing garments of his own design. He appeared as an apparition, and was surrounded by young men fascinated by his many gifts and personal magnetism.

The thought that Leonardo may have been homosexual has been repugnant to many of his biographers building a legendary Leonardo, the all-encompassing "Renaissance Man." In 1476, he was charged with sodomy but quickly exonerated. His Victorian biographers could not abide such a possibility, claiming he was in love with various women, including, of course, Mona Lisa.

However, there is no evidence that Leonardo ever formed any relationship with a woman, even in friendship. There were two important friendships in his life, one of which was Giocamo Salai, a willful, wild, youngster who from age ten lived with Leonardo for thirty years until the end of the artist's life. Salai's parents apparently had no problem with the arrangement. The other valuable relationship was with a fifteen-year-old youth whom Leonardo met in 1507. Francesco Melzi was dazzlingly handsome, an excellent painter, and remained a consolation to Leonardo—he too living with him until his death.

Leonardo's sexuality was doubtless complex. He was far from asexual, but polymorphously erotic. His every pore open to erotic energy, which he furiously translated into drawings of nature, often depicting uncontrolled forces.

As for sexual congress itself, he wrote, "The act of procreation and everything connected with it is so disgusting that the human race would soon die out if there were no pretty faces and sensual dispositions."

Of his religious beliefs, the creator of the "Last Supper" wrote of the religious hierarchy, "They produce many words, receive much wealth, and promise paradise . . . who trade

Leonardo.
11 x 14. Pen and ink.
1982.

THE PAINTINGS OF DAVID DUBAL

in tricks and simulated miracles, duping the foolish multitudes; and if nobody unmasked their subterfuge, they would impose them on everyone." It was the Age of the Inquisition, as Marguerite Yourcenar wrote, "to dissemble secret and dangerous truths, just as the reverse script of Leonardo da Vinci helped preserve him from the scaffold."

Around 1478, the young artist, now independent, painted the *Madonna and Child*, now at the Hermitage in St. Petersburg. In 1480 he painted the twisted body of his *Saint Jerome*, housed at the Vatican, a tortured, anguished painting, left unfinished. Perhaps he felt he had solved the difficult spatial problems between Jerome in relation to the angry lying lion.

Another unfinished picture is the huge 246 cm x 243 cm (97 in x 96 in) *Adoration of the Magi* from 1482 which adorns the Uffizi at Florence. Here are a variety of Leonardo's characteristic facial types, as well as his original vision of landscape, so different from other painters of the Quattrocento. The eye seems to travel upward, following the dark tree, yet somehow through his marvelous sense of space brings the eyes to gaze on the whole composition at once.

From 1483—1486 he completed his famous *Virgin of the Rocks*, now at the Louvre. By this time Leonardo possessed the most all-encompassing painterly technique ever honed.

Of the *Virgin of the Rocks,* Berenson exclaims, "No one has succeeded in conveying by means of light and shade a more penetrating feeling of mystery and awe than he in his 'Virgin of the Rock.' Add to this a feeling for beauty and significance that have scarcely ever been approached. . . . Leonardo is the one artist of whom it may be said with perfect literalness— nothing that he touched but turned into a thing of eternal beauty."

Florence and the Mediceans had dried up for Leonardo, and we find Leonardo by 1483 in Milan at the luxurious court of Duke Ludovico Sforza. Under Ludovico, Leonardo engineered many instruments of war, and as Leonardo wrote to the Duke, "In time of peace, I believe myself able to vie successfully with any in the designing of public and private buildings, and in conducting water from one place to another. . . . I can carve sculpture out of marble, bronze, or clay, and also in painting, I can do as well as any man. . . ." As Kenneth Clark writes, "at the Court of Ludovico there were ingenious men in plenty, doctors, scientists, tacticians, mathematicians, military men, engineers, men of fact and experience, who could feed Leonardo's insatiable craving for information."

The Duke viewed Leonardo as the chief glory of his court, and Leonardo would stay in Milan until Ludovico was defeated by the French, going into exile in 1502.

We must thank Ludovico for *The Last* Supper, begun in 1495. Many painters have used the subject but Leonardo's is the last word on the perennial dinner. Although much damaged and cleaned time and again, the tragic mural retains something of its original magic, especially with the expert restoration completed in 1999 by Pinin Brambilla Barcilon. Leonardo worked on it in fits and starts, at times sitting for hours contemplating his mighty construction on its scaffolding, only to leave after painting a stroke or two. From piety to curiosity, many a Milanese wandered into the refectory of the Dominican Church of Santa Maria delle Grazie to watch its progress. In each generation since its completion, countless spectators have wept. It has become the central painting of Christianity. Lord Clark declared, "It seems no longer to be the work of Man but of Nature."

Leonardo's gifts travelled in all directions. Indeed his subject matter concerned all of the world's phenomena, but it was as a painter that he was his original self. Painting, he felt, possessed the divine, and thought the great painter was nearest to the mind of God.

His painted conceptions would seldom attain the perfection that only he could have imagined. It is absurd to criticize him on the grounds that he did not complete many works or to say he was undisciplined. No artist has ever been more keenly aware of the living moment, and his creative potency was beyond anyone in history. He lived in uncharted territory. He wrote, "The greater the sensibility, the greater is the suffering."

Leonardo's portraits are magnificent. His *Portrait of a Musician* in the Ambrosiana in Milan, created around 1485, may be the portrait least damaged by the ravages of time. More renowned is the exquisite *Portrait of Cecila Gallerani*, mistress of Ludovico, painted in the mid-1480s, now housed at the National Museum in Cracow, and the only Leonardo in Central Europe. Often called Lady with an Ermine (though Leonardo gave no titles to his picture), the work was celebrated from its first viewing. Again, it is damaged, but much is retained, and Lord Clark is at his best in describing it. "The hand shows an understanding of anatomical structure and a power of particularization which none of Leonardo's pupils possessed. But most convincing of all is the beast. The modelling of its head is a miracle; we can feel the structure of its skull, the quality of the skin, the lie of the fur. No one but Leonardo could have conveyed its stoatish character, sleek, predatory, alert, yet with a kind of heraldic dignity."

I have long loved *Cecilia Gallerani*, holding an ermine, the animal being one of Ludovico's emblems. I remember some years ago being in Cracow giving some Chopin lectures. I was excited to look at the fabled painting, but to my chagrin was told the museum had closed for the day. I beseeched the guard to no avail. "I must see it, please!" I cried. Miraculously, a very old man silently came to me: "Be very quiet. I will go with you to where she hangs." I thanked him with all my heart. Looking at her, I was staggered by her radiance. In half an hour, which seemed like a minute, the man returned and gently took me away. I was sad that in the same room were paintings still missing—stolen by the Nazis—"waiting for their return."

In April 1500 Leonardo returned to Florence for five productive years, spending time as military engineer to Caesar Borgia, who was fond of him, and Leonardo actually being with him on his terrible attack on Urbino, where he encountered Niccolò Machiavelli, who became a close friend. At this time he made the famed red chalk drawing of *Three Angles of Caesar Borgia*. During those years Leonardo was deeply involved with geometry and taught himself Latin.

In Florence in 1503, he began the world's most loved portrait of either man or woman, the *Mona Lisa*. For more than five hundred years she remains the epitome of loveliness, and if time has taken from her some of her luster, she still enthralls the world. It was a face that Leonardo

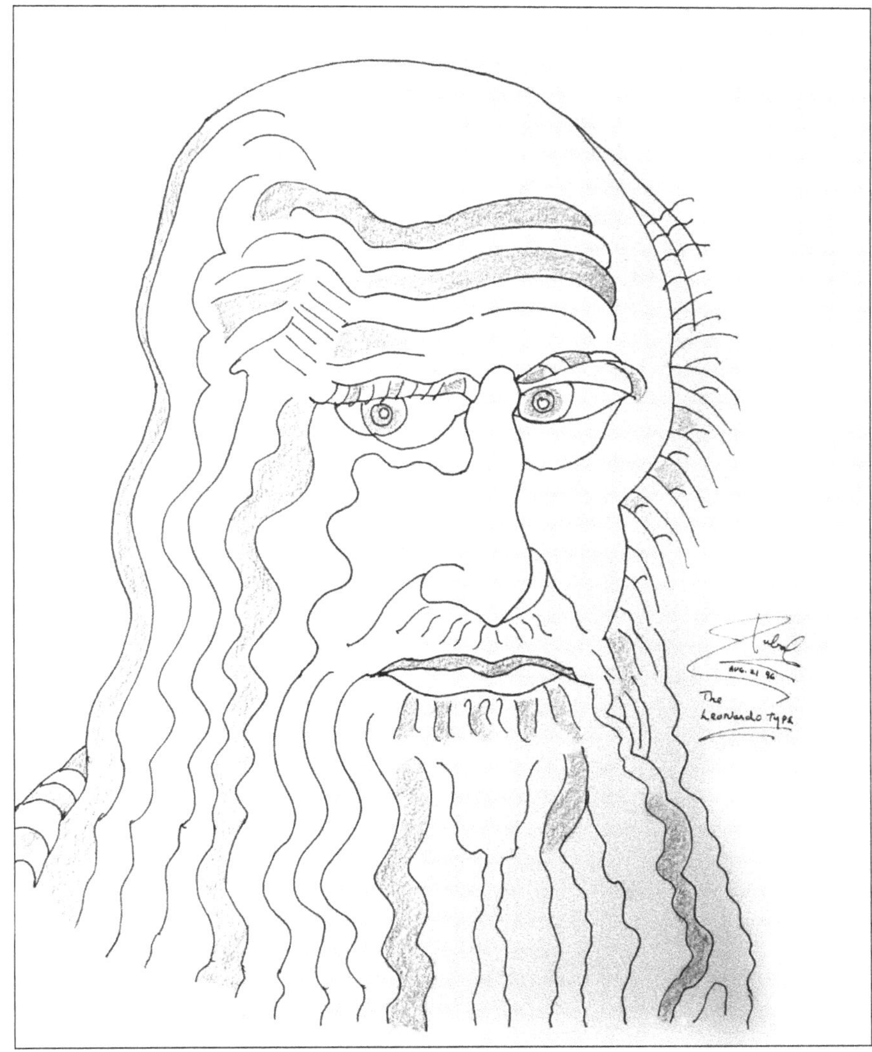

The Leonardo Type.
11 x 14. Pen and ink and
blue crayon on paper.
1996.

loved. As Clark exclaims, "How else can one account for the fact that while he was refusing commissions from popes, kings, and princesses, he spent his utmost skill and, as we are told, three years in painting the second wife of an obscure Florentine citizen?" Walter Pater thought, "By what strange affinities has the dream and the person grown up thus apart and yet so closely together?" When Leonardo began the painting she was twenty-four. Writers have poured lyric rhapsodies over her, Walter Pater's celebrated piece being one of the keystones of his writings.

The nineteenth-century Romantics were obsessed with Lisa. Her mysterious smile becoming for Taine, "licentious, Epicurean, deliciously tender, ardent, sad." For Théophile Gautier she "haunts one's memory like a symphonic theme," seemingly referring to Berlioz' *idée fixe* of his *Symphonie Fantastique*. Gautier continues, "Beneath the form *expressed*, one feels a thought which is vague, infinite, inexpressible, like a musical idea. One is moved, troubled, images already pass before one's eyes, voices whose note seems like a familiar whisper, languorous secrets in one's ears; repressed desire, hopes which change to despair stir painfully in the shadow shot with sunbeams, and you discover that your melancholy arises from the fact La Gioconda (her married surname) three hundred years ago greeted your avowal of love with this mocking smile, which she retains even today on her lips."

Let me continue with D'Annunzio, writing, "Diffused over her face was the dark pallor which I adore. . . . Upon her mouth was the glorious, cruel smile which the divine Leonardo pursued in his paintings. This smile was in sad contrast with the sweetness of the long eyes, and gave a superhuman charm to the beauty of the heads of women which the great da Vinci loved. The mouth was a dolorous flower. . . ."

Here is the very acme of the paroxysms of the Romantic writers. However, as Mario Praz, in his book *The Romantic Agony* writes, "the essence of Romanticism consequently comes to consist in that which cannot be described."

Walter Pater, whose essay on Leonardo was read by every esthete of the third quarter of the nineteenth-century, made *Lisa* even more enigmatic, by calling it a face of doubtful sex—"the unfathomable smile, always with a touch of something sinister." Mario Pomilio says, "The image is such that catalyzes the gaze of the observer, provoking mystical and sensual feelings; we can say everything and the opposite of everything about it." When Rodin called Leonardo a mystic, perhaps he was thinking of the *Mona Lisa*.

Freud, great explorer of the psyche, wrote, "It was quite possible that Leonardo was fascinated by the smile of Mona Lisa because it had awakened something in him which had slumbered in his soul for a long time, in all probability an old memory."

Leonardo would probably not be amused at Lisa's endless literary effusions, and he would be appalled to see billboards, tee shirts, ashtrays and the like, or Duchamp giving her a mustache. But nothing disturbs her mass appeal. She speaks eloquently to so many people in so many differing ways. At the Louvre, crowds can hardly restrain their excitement standing patiently for their five-second glance. All talk stops as the observer grows closer to the glassed image, the captivating power of "mere" paint here epitomized.

In 1963, when the *Mona Lisa* was loaned to the Metropolitan Museum and to Japan, as well, she was treated with the precious care that no royal potentate ever achieved. John Canaday, in his book, *Late Gothic to Renaissance Painters*, reports: "People lined up by the thousands and had to be marched four abreast past it, with a pause of a few seconds to contemplate it from a distance, as if exposure to its radiant powers could culturally or spiritually be beneficial, much in the way that touching a holy relic is supposed to be healing. Indeed, it is painting's holy grail, and public acclaim, poor condition and crackled as it is, it remains a masterpiece of oil painting, and psychological penetration. . . . The haze between the woman and the observer, like an invisible curtain . . . is created by Leonardo's *sfumato*. This effect, named after the Italian word for *smoke,* was so astonishing to Leonardo's contemporaries that it seemed beyond

　　　　THE PAINTINGS OF DAVID DUBAL

technical explanation." Leonardo's *sfumato* was attempted in thousands of paintings. Raphael made drawings of the *Lisa* and absorbed much from it in his magical portraits.

In the far distant future if there be a celestial art museum for all the universe's creatures to view, *Mona Lisa* will still be the most cherished of all portraits. The novelist Sherwood Anderson wrote, "Occasionally I cry out with pain. My woman is made up of all the women of the world. She is no longer young nor is she old. She is beautiful." She is *The Mona Lisa.*

In our age of the photograph it may be difficult to realize what the portrait meant to an ever-growing self-awareness. Owning a fine portrait was a treasured possession. How desperately did the beautiful Isabella d'Este want an oil portrait from the searching hand of Leonardo, repeatedly pestering him. She did get a portrait, but the noble woman wanted an oil and was not content with his magnificent profile drawing of her. The French King Louis XII exclaimed, "Perhaps I shall cause him also to make my own portrait."

If Leonardo's paintings completely crumble with unmerciful time, we still have his drawings. He drew in all media—silverpoint and other metals, pen and ink wash, black chalk, and was a pioneer of red chalk.

Here is Leonardo delving into the world's vast subject matter from the skull to the hands, from the entrails of plant life, to horses in motion.

Agnes Mongan wrote of the study for *Horse and Rider*, "Surely, no words could possibly give the effect of movement of the horse and rider coming forward with a powerful easy

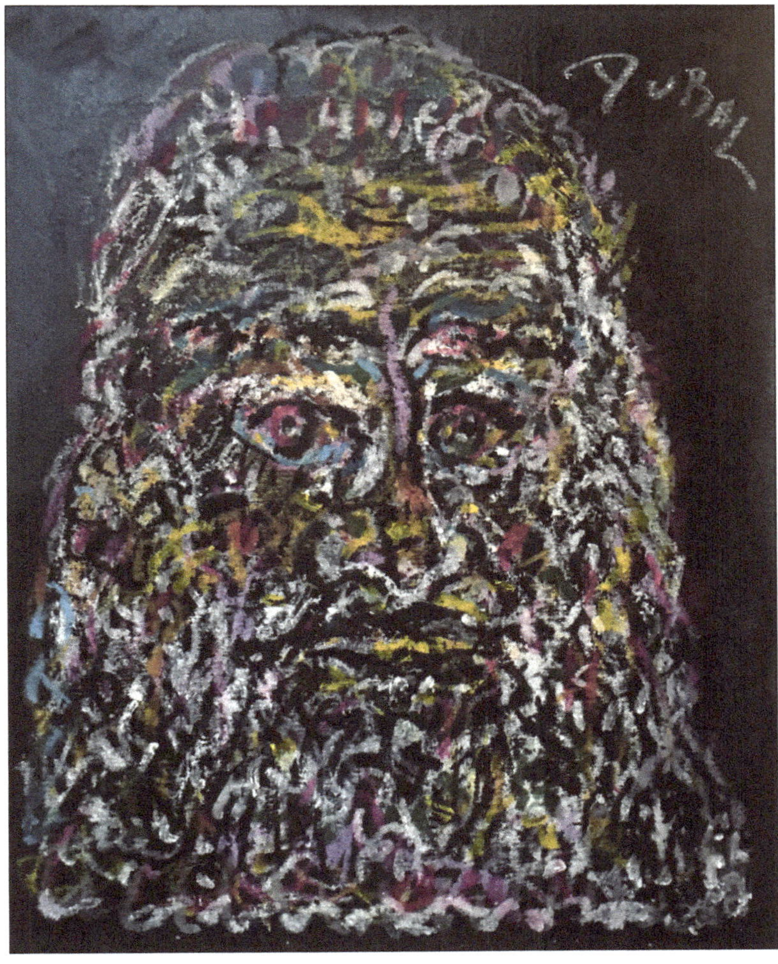

Portrait of Leonardo after His Self-Portrait.
16 x 24. Grease paint on canvas. 2019.

rhythm out of the background. With his acute instantaneous vision, Leonardo has seen the rider with his head up and with it lowered and has revealed both." He may have seen deeper and more acutely than any single person ever has.

As a draughtsman Leonardo gives us the art of seeing as no one before or after him. He records in his notebooks, "O wretched mortals, open your eyes."

Delacroix, that fabulous virtuoso draughtsman, wrote in his celebrated journal, "In Leonardo's drawings above all, the touch is not seen, the sentiment alone reaches the mind. I still remember the time, not long ago, when I harassed myself endlessly for not being able to reach that dexterity in execution."

In my case, many times have I attempted to copy *Head of a Young Woman*, of which Sachs says, "It is not an overstatement to speak of the drawing as one of the most beautiful in the world."

Unlike the great German Albrecht Durer, Leonardo left no self-portrait as a young man. But his 1512 self-portrait in red chalk (at right) gives us a clairvoyant wizard seven years before his death. Here he is turned inward; there is wisdom and perhaps a hint of cynicism; but the compassion in the eyes are saying, "Perhaps, I have seen all." And one feels the tragic sense of life, the limits of one lifetime.

By 1513 we find Leonardo in Rome. Imagine! Raphael, Michelangelo, and Leonardo each working at the Vatican, along with the great architect Bramante. Have ever there been such towering geniuses steps away from one another? Leonardo lived at the Belvedere with his loyal Salai and Melzi; however, he was uneasy being with his great colleagues, and he disliked the frenetic pace of the many artists and artisans, and the petty politics. He was used to being slow and deliberate, and while at the Vatican he was enmeshed in his studies of hydrodynamics and geology rather than painting.

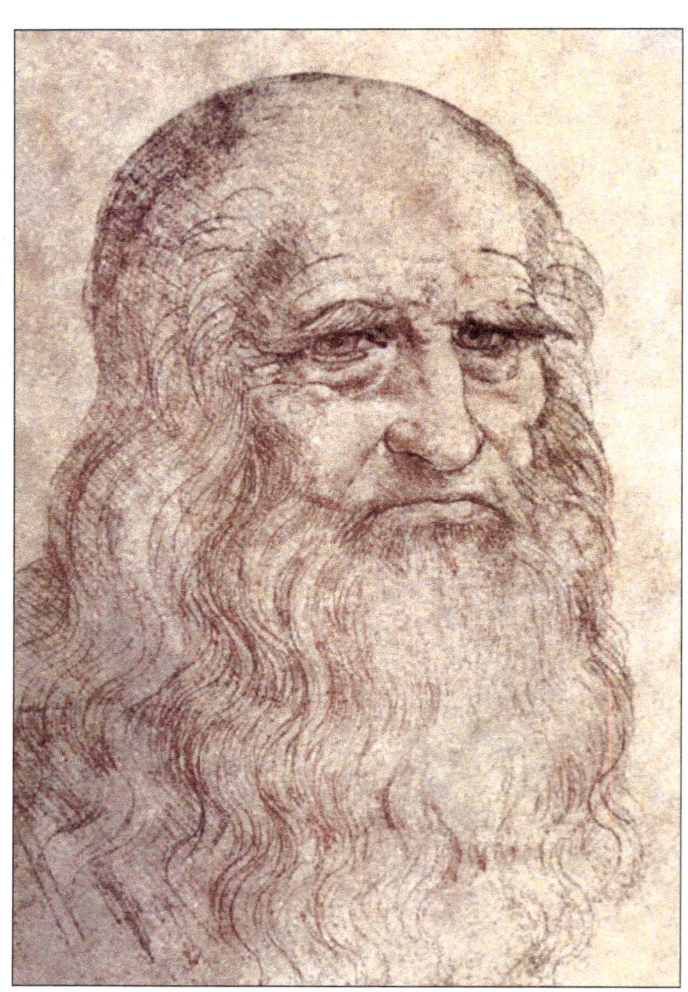

Leonardo's 1512 self-portrait in red chalk.

THE PAINTINGS OF DAVID DUBAL

Leo X, a Medeci Pope, had been installed in 1513, and was piqued at Leonardo's lack of productivity. The Pontiff snarled, "Here is a man, alas, who will never do anything, since he is thinking of the completion of his painting before he has started."

Leonardo left over five-thousand pages of notes in his tiny script in mirror writing. They are one of the treasures of the human mind with their diagrams and sketches. The critic Thomas Craven in *Men of Art* writes, "The illustrations to the notebooks afford us a beautiful proof of the difference between artistic drawing and photography. Here we have sketches of scientific apparatus, interiors of gun foundries, canon, hydraulic engines, the skull, muscle, bone, fossils, leaves, trees, and cloud formations, all of which are a joy to behold. None but Leonardo could have made these drawings. They are separated from photographs by a gulf as wide as that which separates the poetry of Shelly from the tabulated reports of the New York Stock exchange. Did he, as a scientist, merely attempt to represent and describe with cold-blooded accuracy the object before him? Obviously not. The artistic impulse, co-existent and predominant, incited him to reconstruct his materials, to add himself to them, to make infinitesimal alterations of contour, to introduce light and shade and subtle variations of natural appearances for the sake of harmony. Thus a dead skull or a cogwheel becomes a living organism—a creature of Leonardo's brain, a dynamic part of the world remade."

Of the notebooks, Berenson is ecstatic, "They are a revelation of a mind so vast, so varied, so masterful that I feel as if trying to keep pace with the stars in their endless courses. The singular thing is that on top of everything else Leonardo had the greatest literary gifts. His words are chiseled, and when at his best, his phrase is polished as you will never again find it in Italian. . . . He has such exquisite perceptions, and such moral depth. There was a man!"

Early in 2003, the Metropolitan Museum held an historic exhibit of Leonardo's drawing, one-hundred-eighteen in number. In the next few weeks, something like 400,000 people lined up to see the exhibit, standing for hours. The rooms were uncomfortably packed, but the determination to see the works was palpable as was the excitement. There was an overriding sense of reverence, and a remarkable silence. . Berenson once wrote, "His art is life communicating . . . . His personality is life-enhancing . . . . And all that he demanded of life was the chance to be useful! Surely such a man brings the gladdest of all tidings—the wonderful possibilities of the human family, of whose chances we all partake."

Because of Leonardo's glamour and prestige, the artist had become elevated beyond a mere servant, artisan, or craftsman. The high Renaissance had become interested in artists as special beings; their foibles, habits, and eccentricities were noted. Although artists still had to bow and scrape to princes and prelates, without him Michelangelo's grumpy irritability and impossible habits would not have been tolerated, nor Raphael's love affairs gossiped about.

In less than two years, Leonardo left the Vatican. He was exhausted and his eyesight failing. Life had always come to him, and his concluding chapter was indeed fortunate. The French King François I, became his adoring protector. He had long coveted the *Mona Lisa*, which

Leonardo had never parted with. The warrior-king invited him to come to his Castle of Cloux at Amboise; the king expected nothing of him except the pleasure of his company, and to learn from his gentle, melodious, voice.

And so it was that Leonardo left Italy behind forever in 1516. With him were Melzi and Salai. The king gave him an ample income, a splendid residence, with a chapel, gardens, meadows, and streams. It was said that the king had constructed an underground tunnel connecting his house with the royal palace.

At sixty-seven, he made his will, leaving Melzi the mighty mass of his writings. Supposedly the young king entered Leonardo's bedroom in his last moments, the artist dying in his arms. The story is a fiction, but the scene was delightfully romanticized by Ingres in an 1818 oil painting.

Leonardo did die at the Castle of Cloux, on May 2, 1519.

He had once written "Just as a well-filled day brings blessed sleep, a well-employed life brings a blessed death."

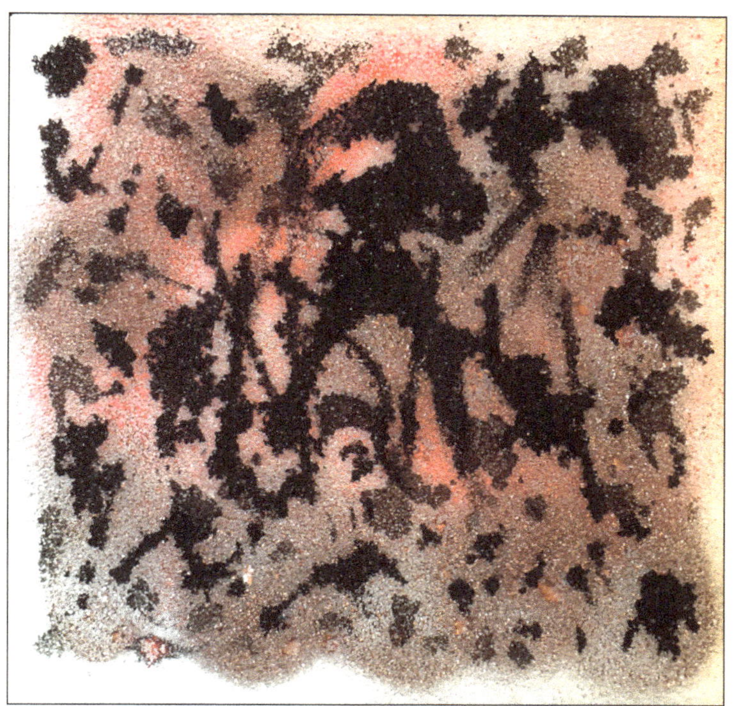

Lost Soul Changed.
11½ x 11½. Black ink, spray paint,
on Styrofoam. 2018.

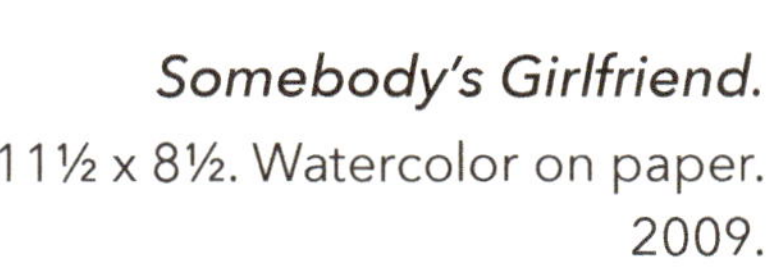

Somebody's Girlfriend.
11½ x 8½. Watercolor on paper.
2009.

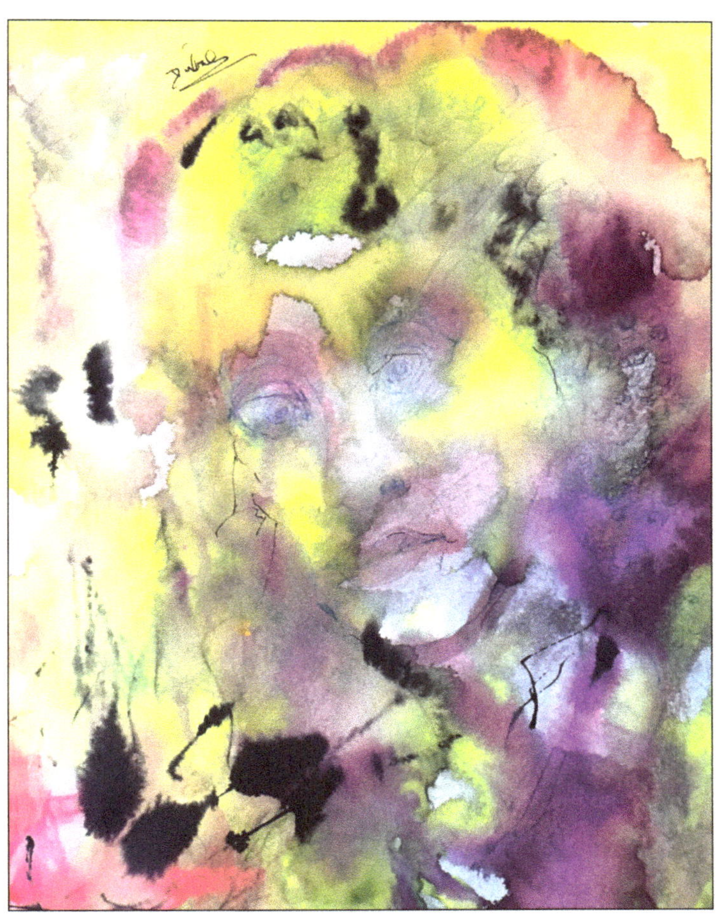

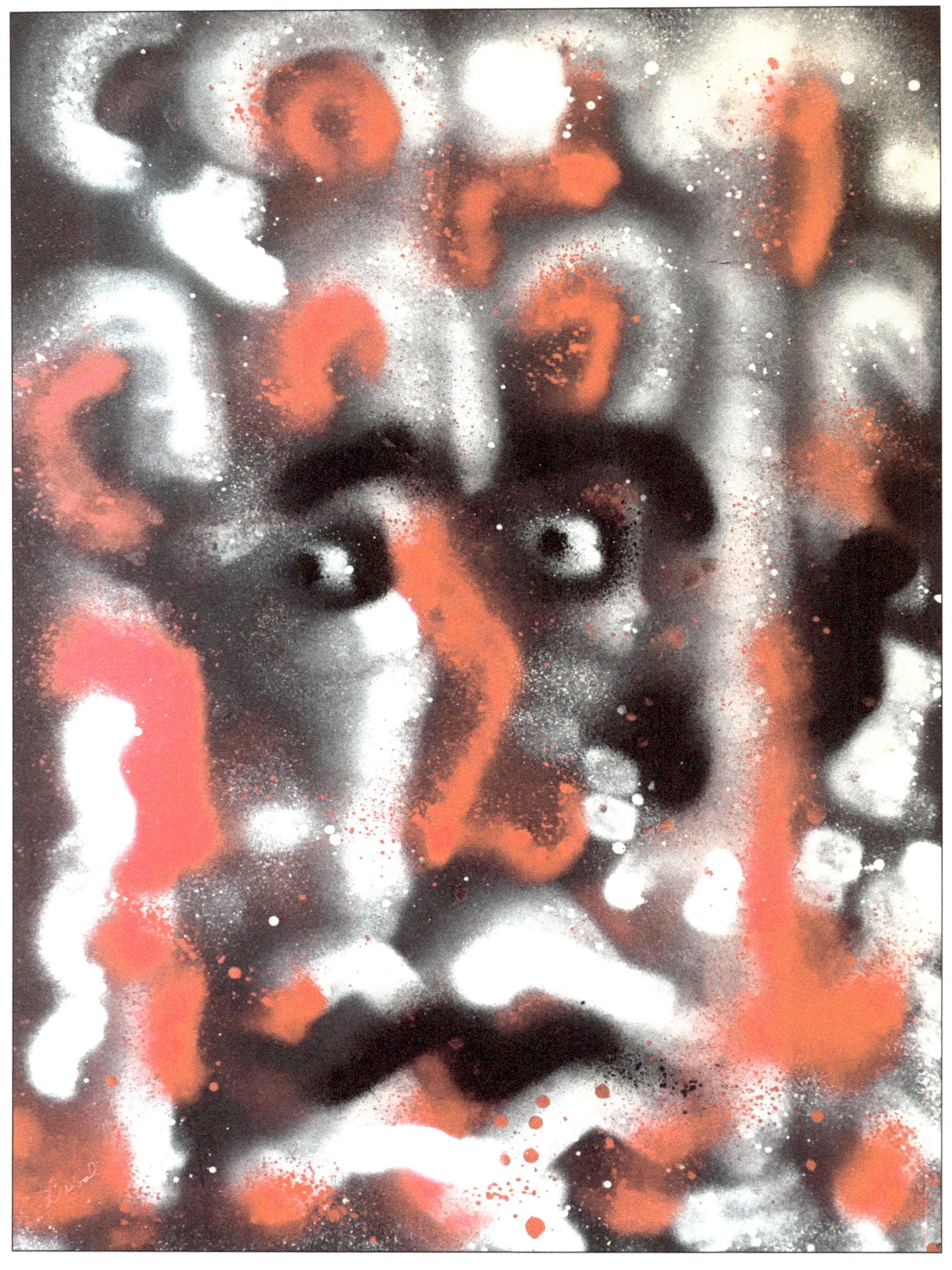

Truly Suspicious.
30 x 20. Spray paint on black board. 2013.

THE PAINTINGS OF DAVID DUBAL

Floating Entities.
11½ x 11½. Ink, spray paint on
Styrofoam. 2018.

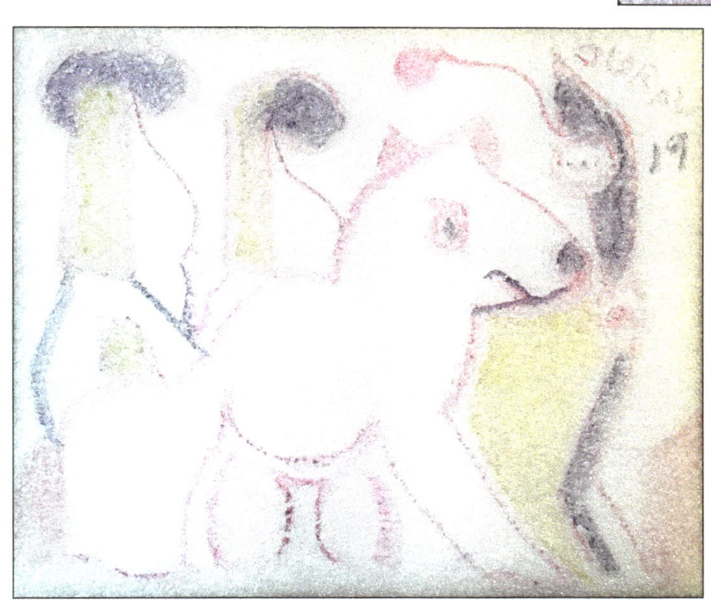

Cute Animal with Musicians.
8 x 8. Mixed media on Styrofoam.
2019.

A Hidden Head.
11½ x 11½. Spray paint on Styrofoam.

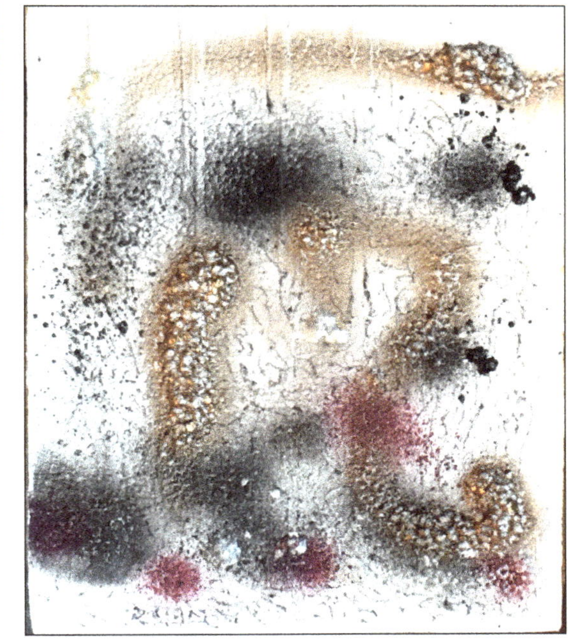

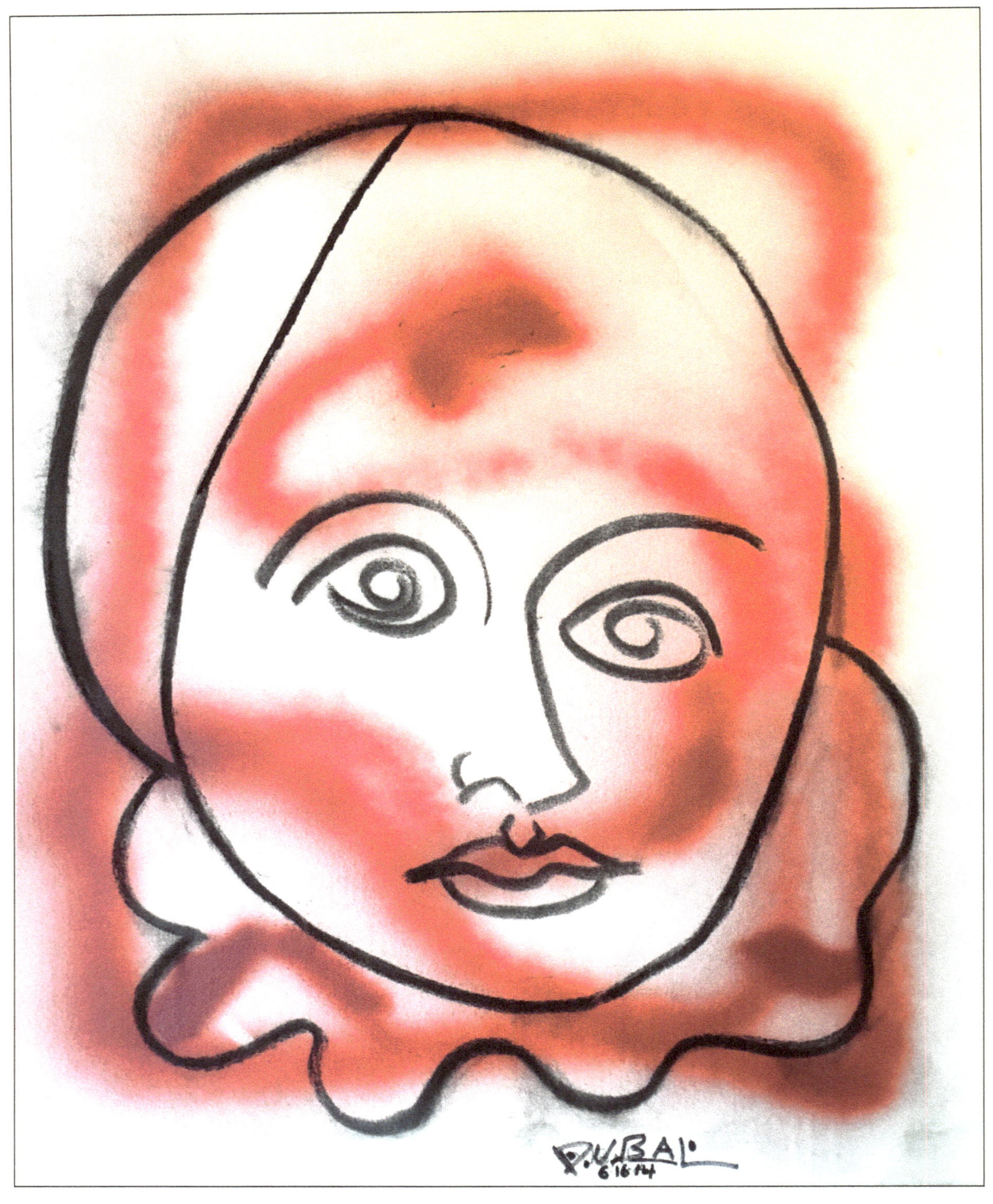

Young Woman with Ruff and Cap.
30 x 24. Red spray paint and charcoal on canvas. 2014.

 THE PAINTINGS OF DAVID DUBAL

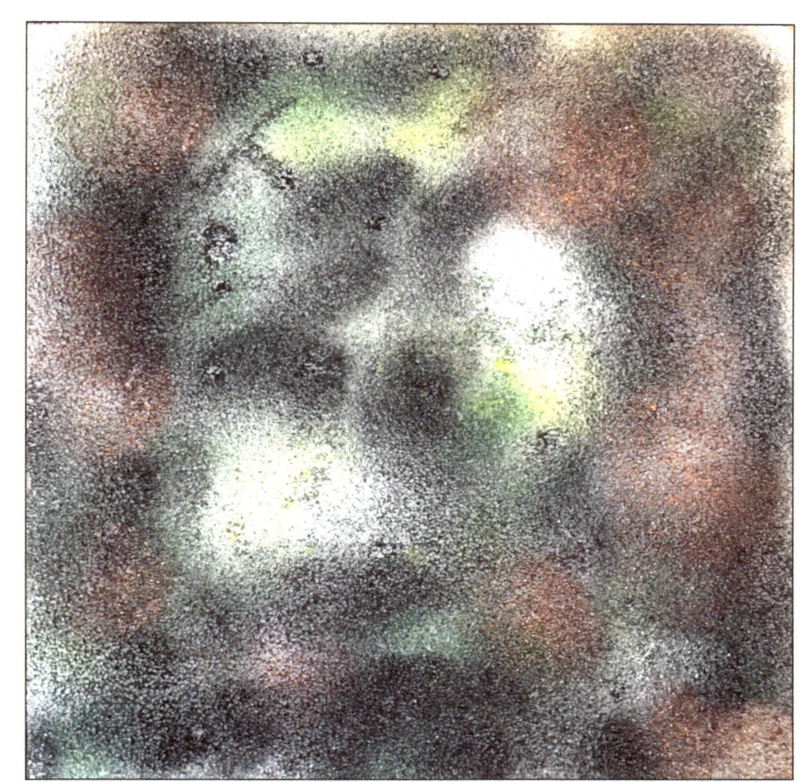

Hamlet.
11½ x 11½. Spray paint on
Styrofoam. 2018.

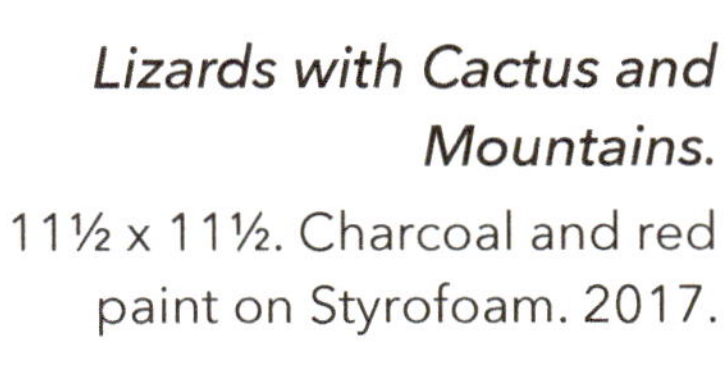

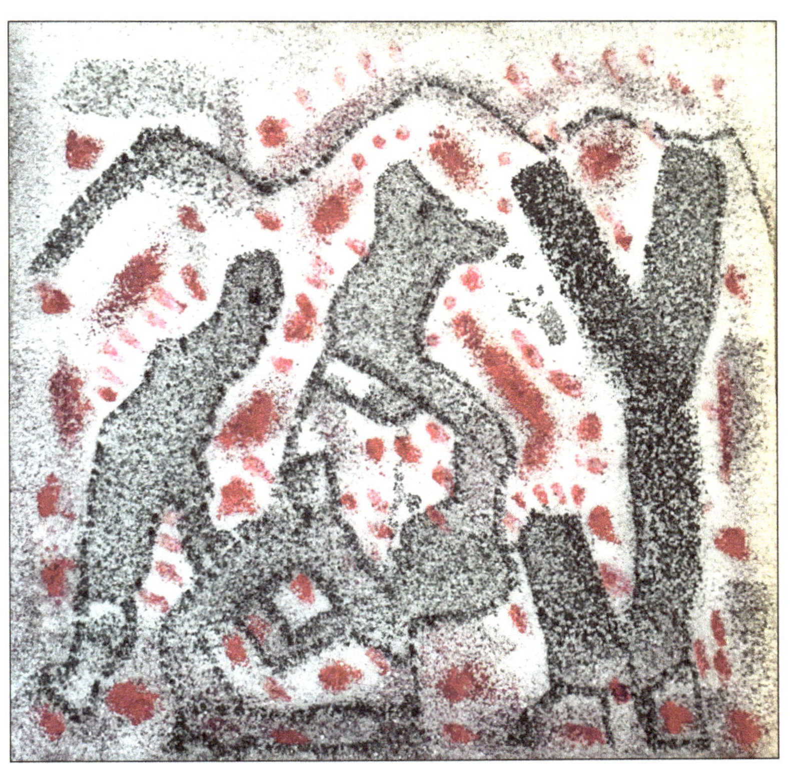

*Lizards with Cactus and
Mountains.*
11½ x 11½. Charcoal and red
paint on Styrofoam. 2017.

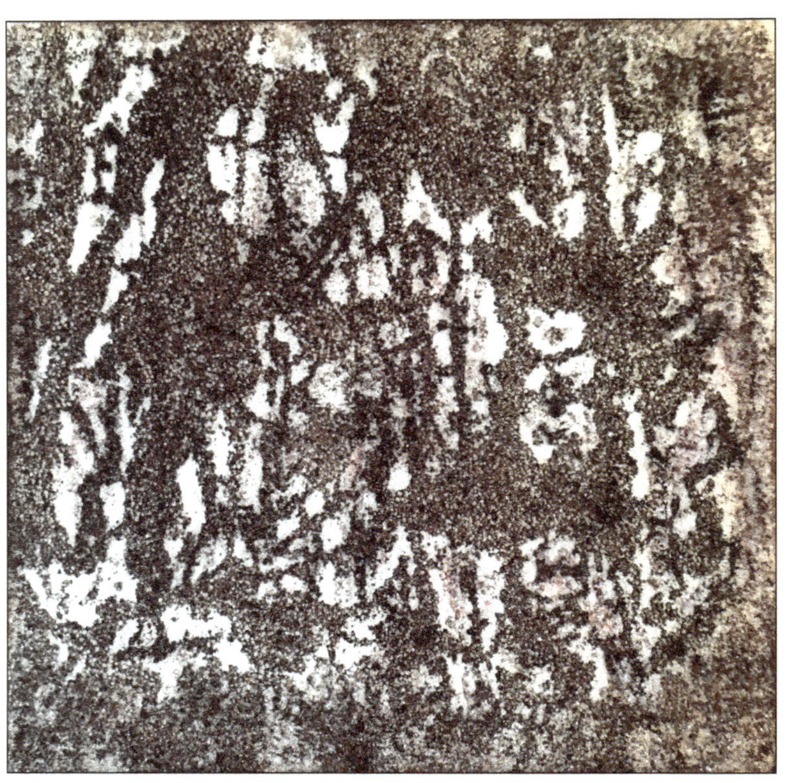

Forest Murmurs.
11½ x 11½. Spray paint on Styrofoam. 2018.

Landscape in Blue.
11½ x 11½. Blue ink on Styrofoam. 2018.

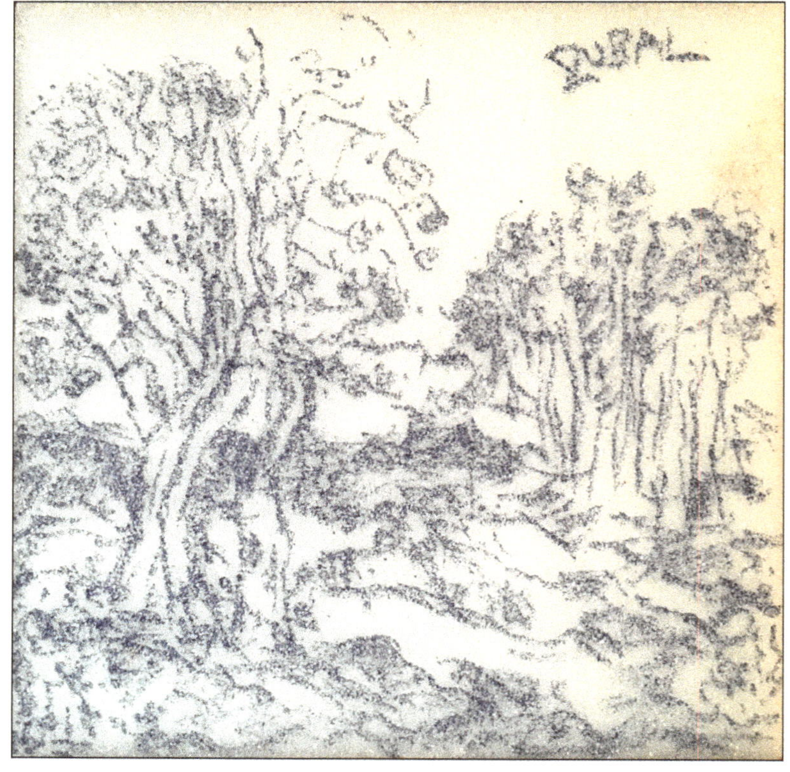

THE PAINTINGS OF DAVID DUBAL

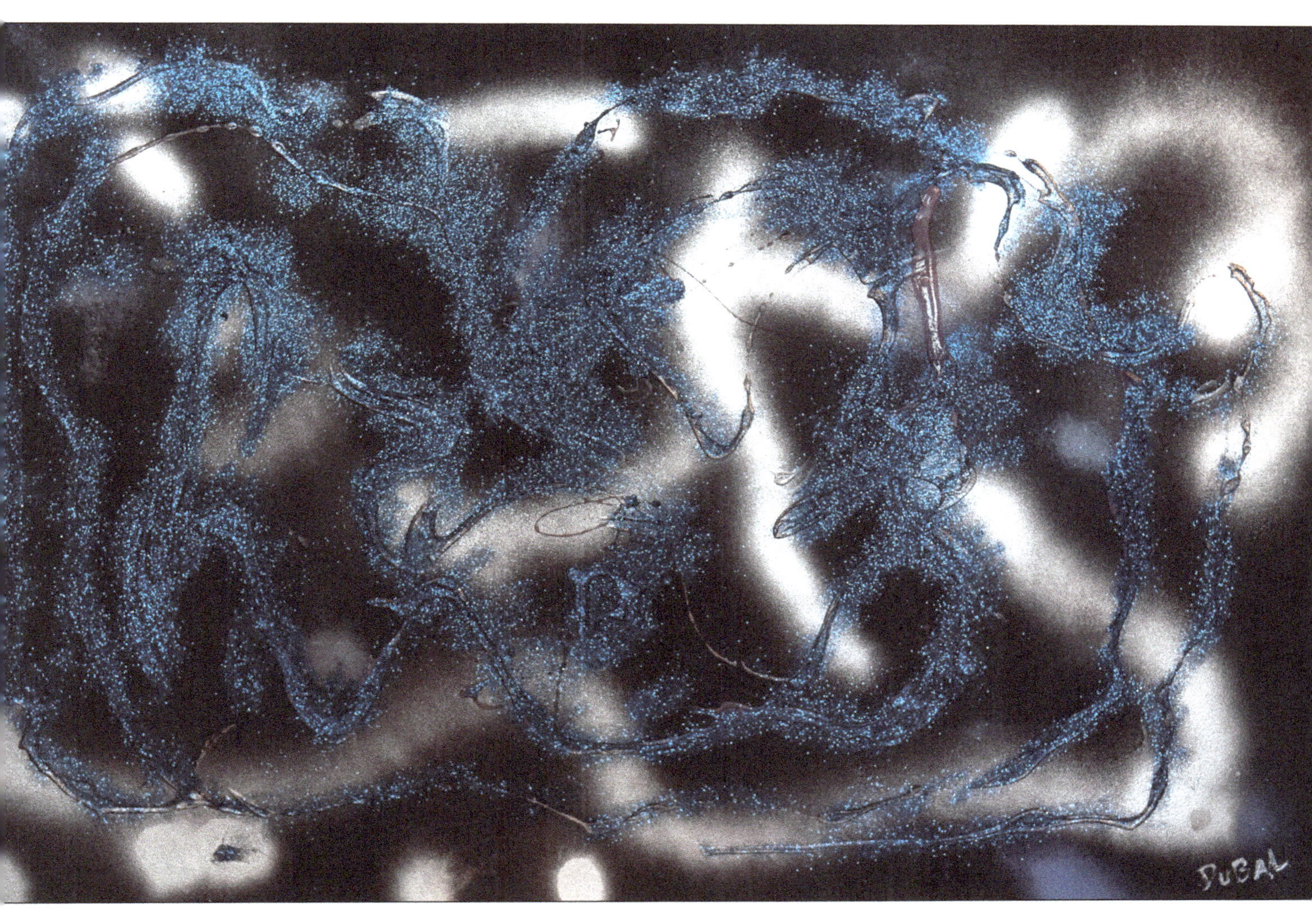

Alternative Universe.
20 x 30. White paint, glue, and blue paint on black board. 2014.

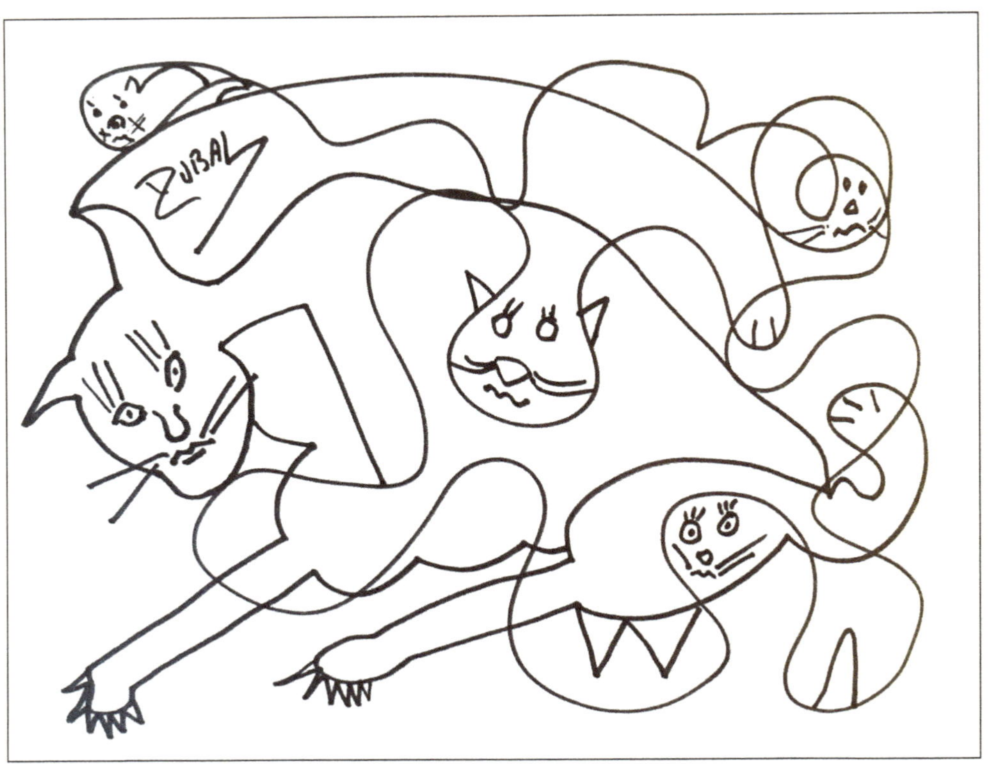

Cats Hold Their Own.
11 x 14. Pen and ink on paper.
2020.

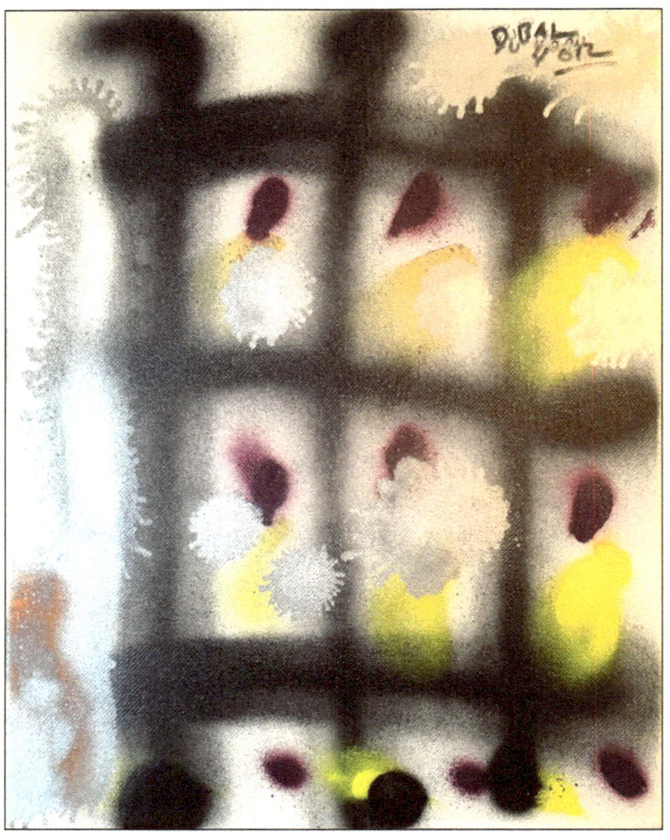

Who Is Outside?
14 x 11. Spray paint on canvas.
2012.

THE PAINTINGS OF DAVID DUBAL

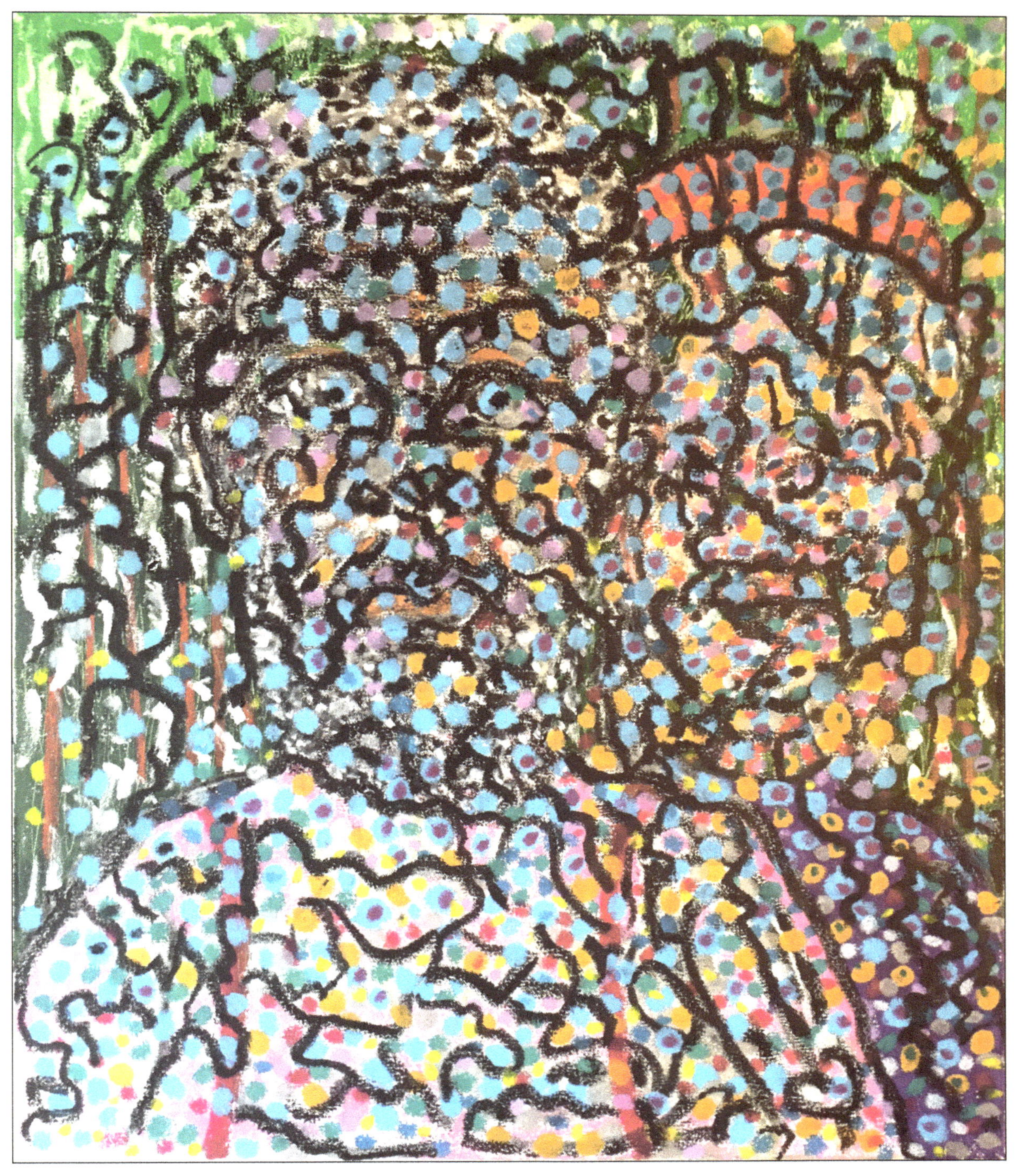

Father and Daughter.
30 x 24. Paint on canvas. 2019.

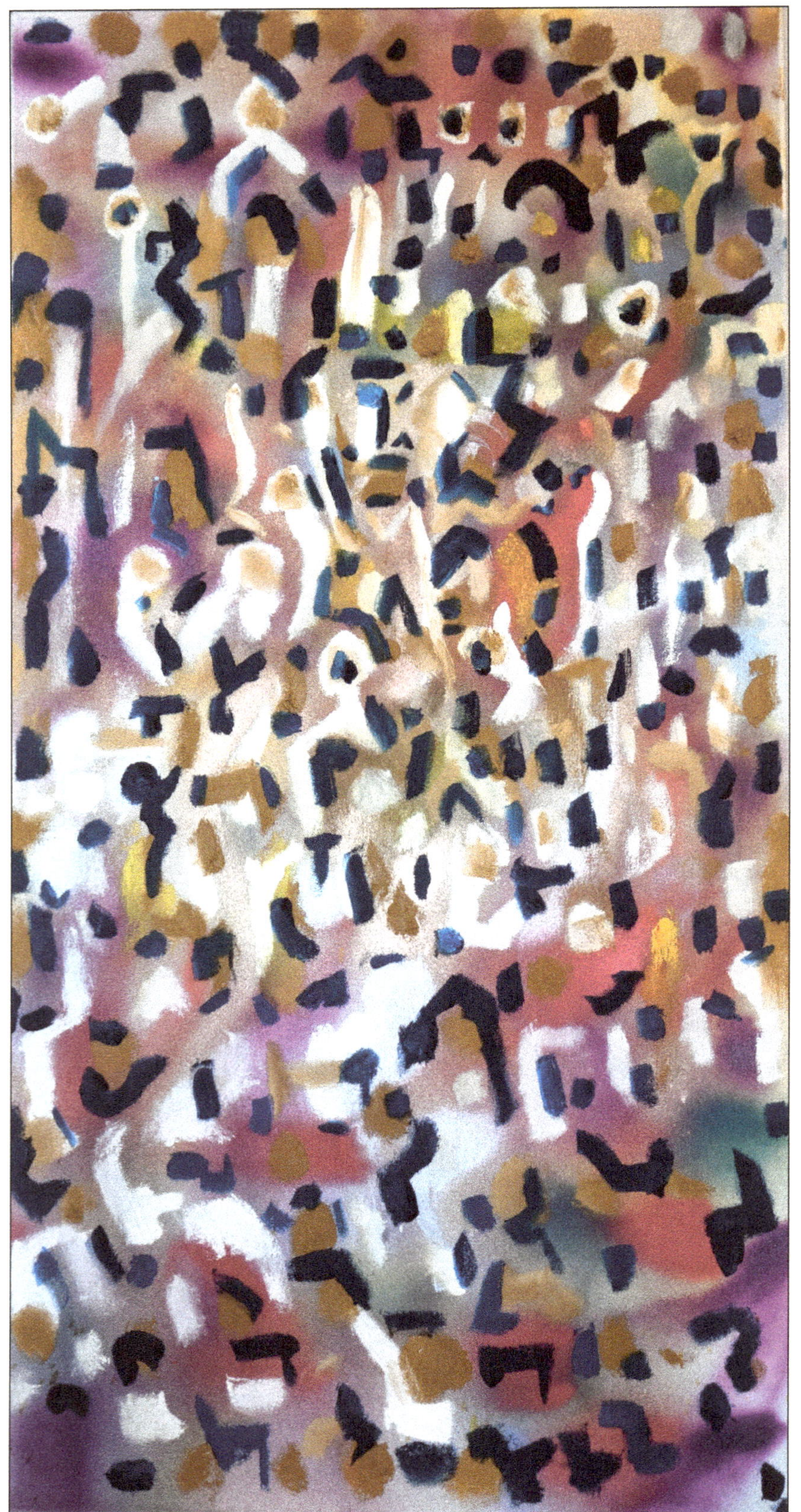

A Surprise.
46 x 24. Oil on Canvas.
2013.

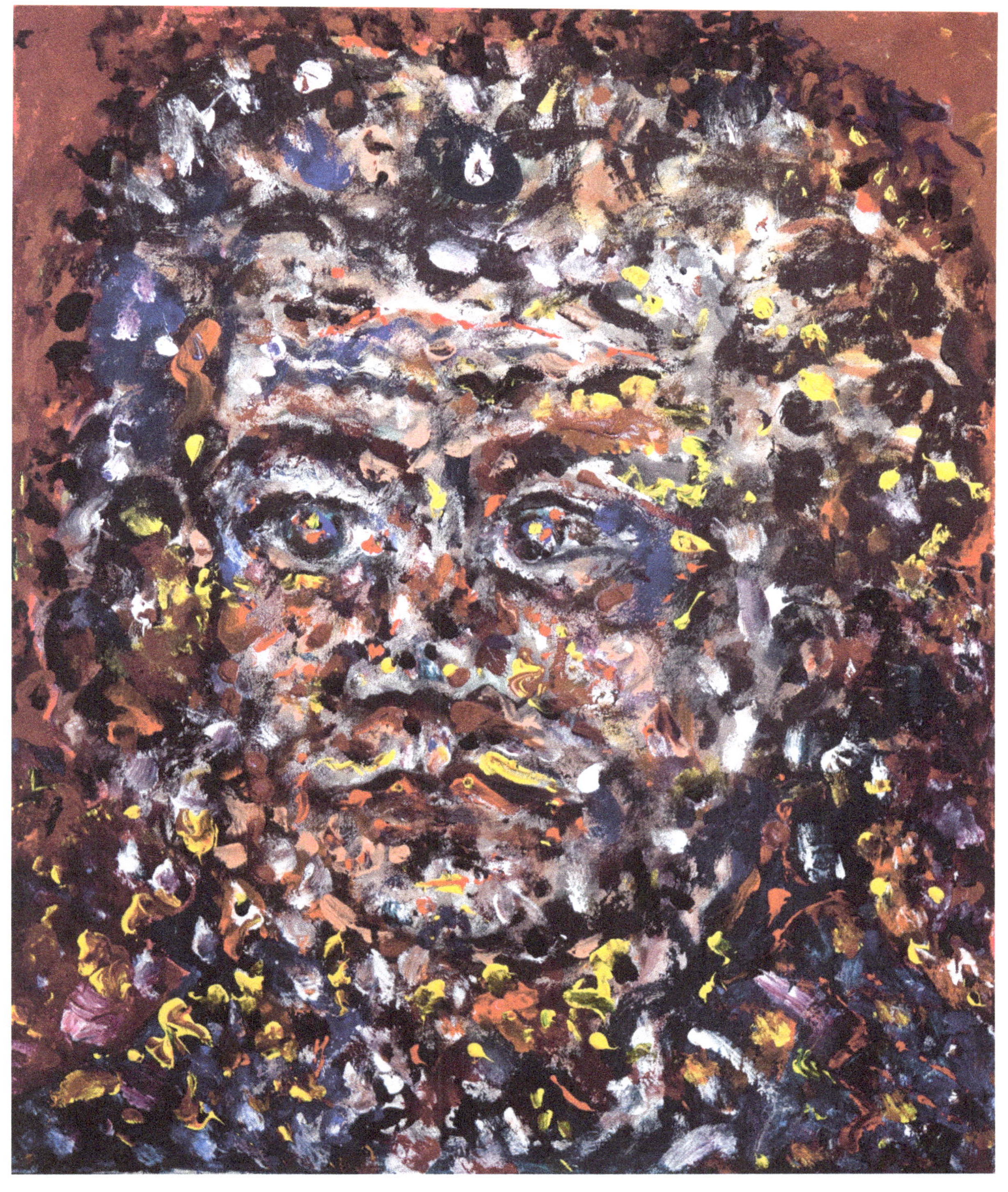

The Agony of Deafness.
24 x 20. Oil on canvas. 2002.

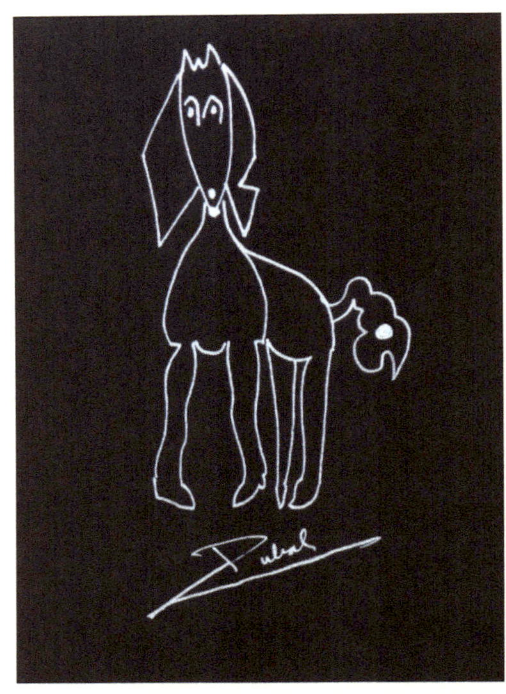

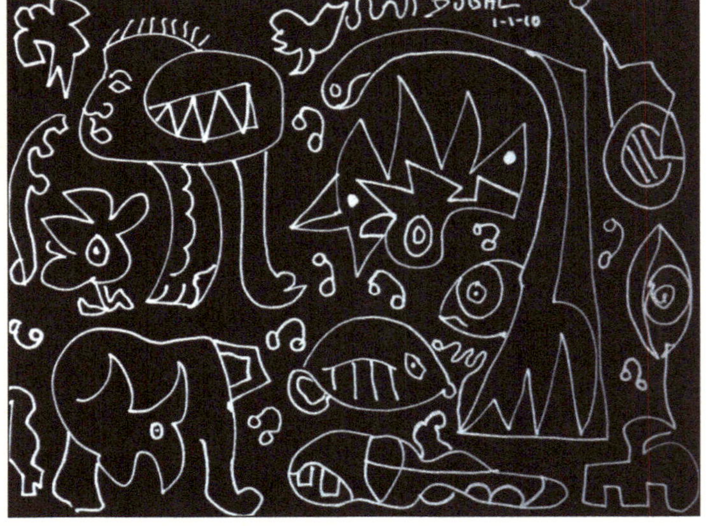

The Gelding.
10 x 8. Silver ink on black board. 2009.

Crazy World.
10 x 8. Silver ink on black board.
2009.

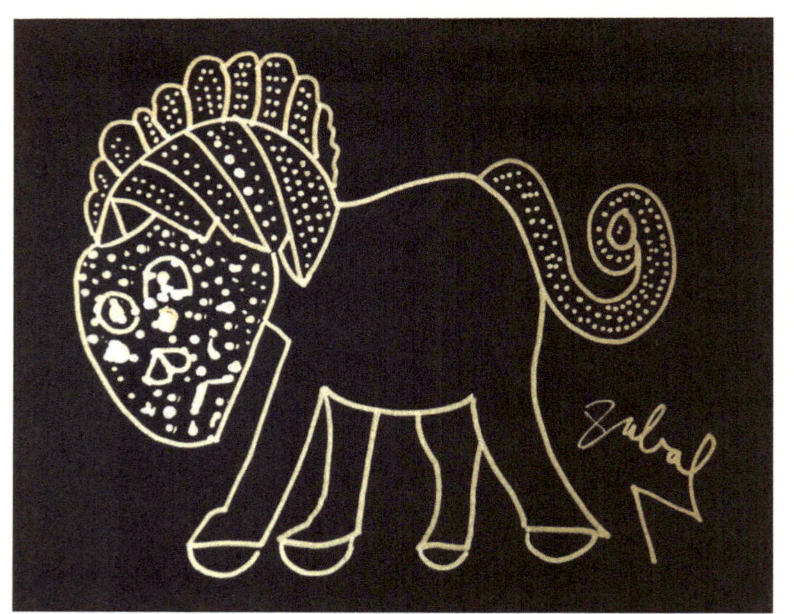

Bejeweled Dog.
8 x 10. Silver ink on black
board. 2010.

THE PAINTINGS OF DAVID DUBAL

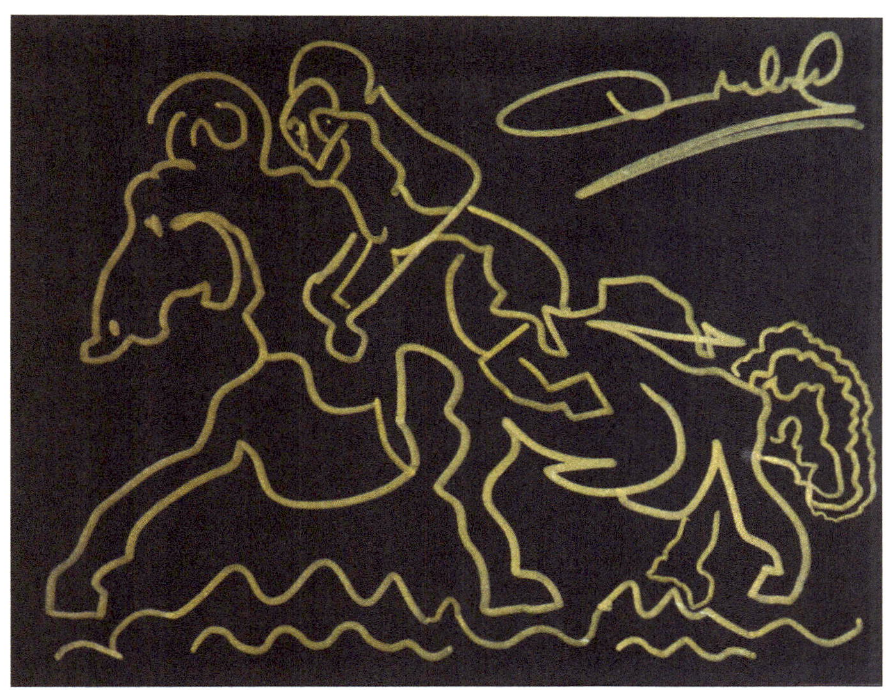

Valiant Rider.
8 x 10. Silver ink on
black board. 2010.

Don't Shake My Hand,
The Angel Said.
11 x 14. Blank ink on
paper. 1996.

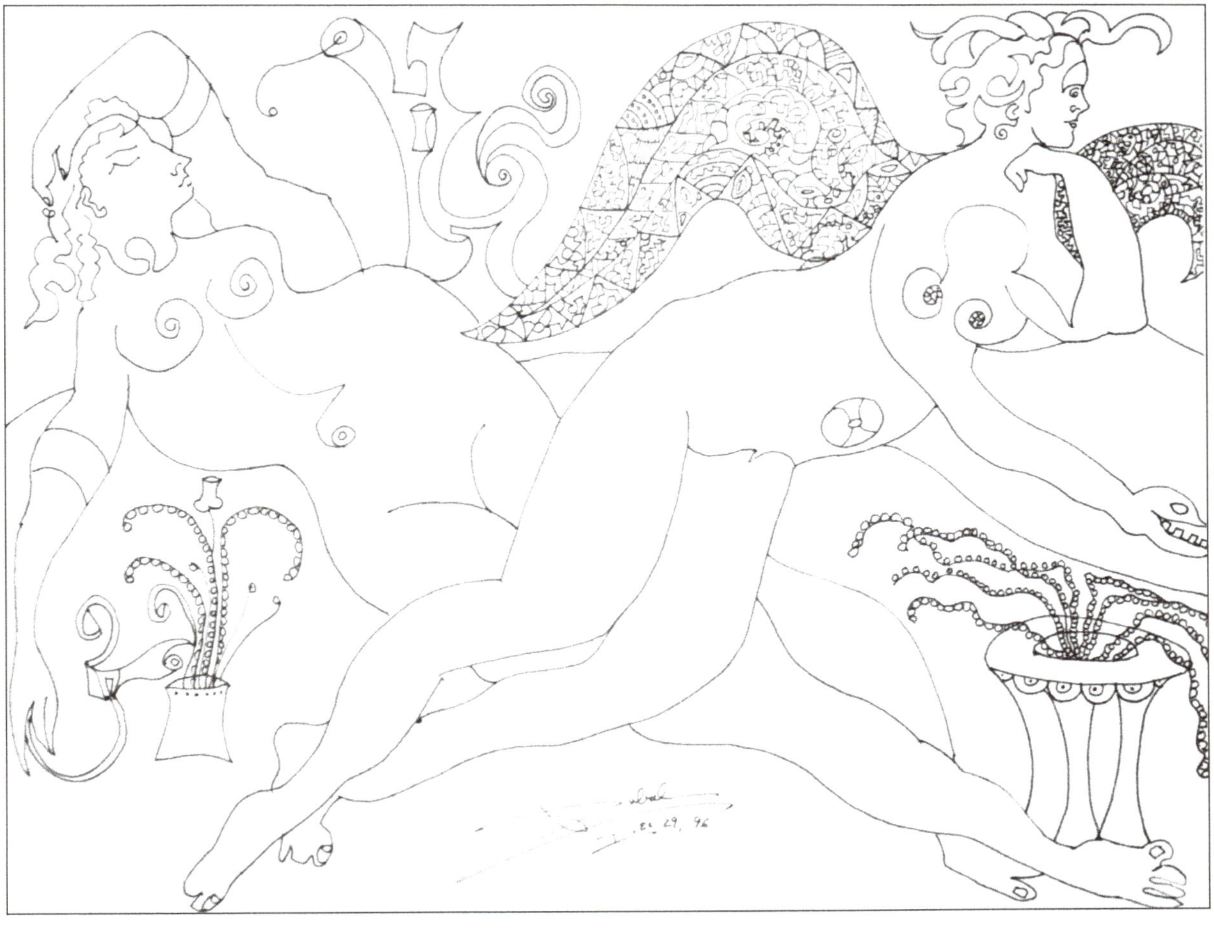

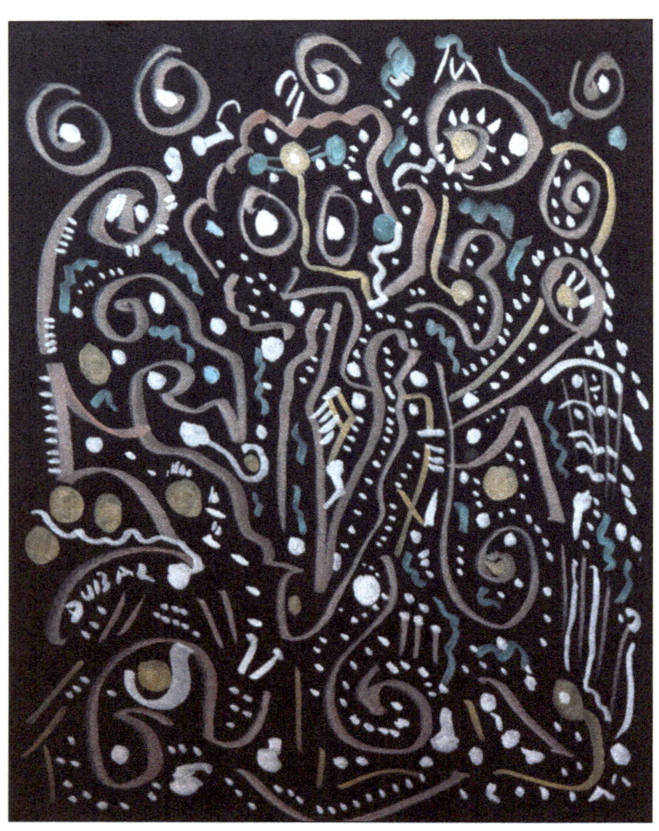

The Jingle Machine.
20 x 16. Colored inks on
black board. 2011.

The Hothouse Salon.
11 x 14. Ink on paper.
2012.

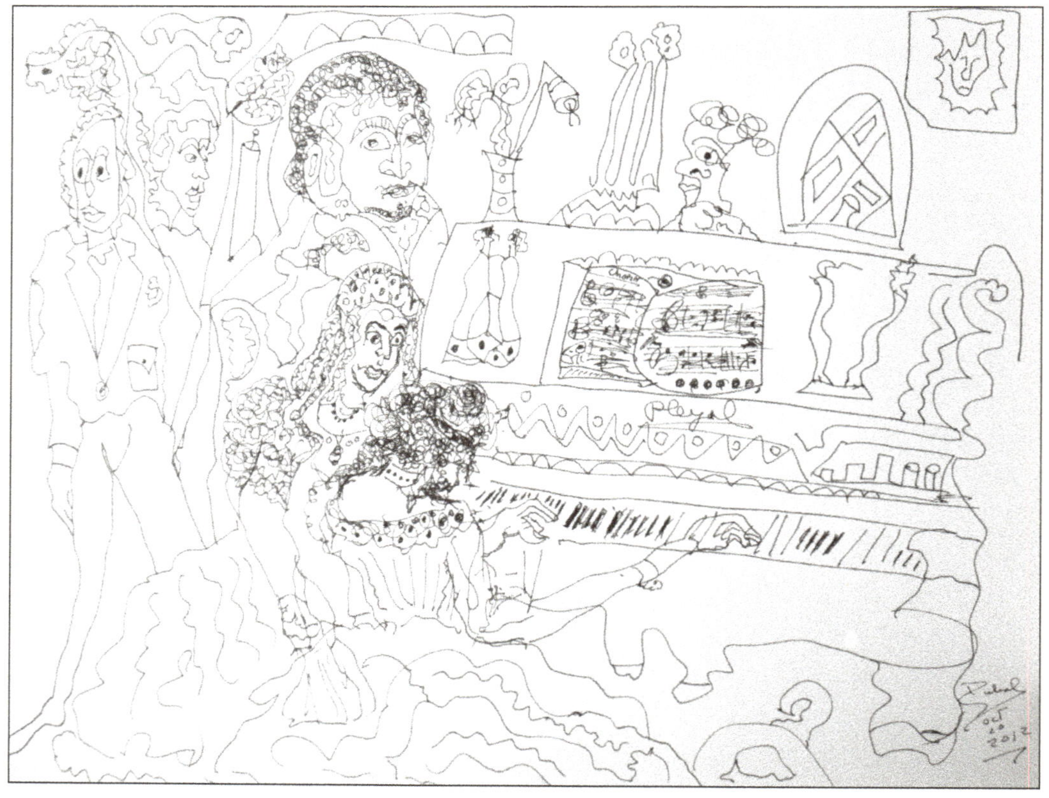

THE PAINTINGS OF DAVID DUBAL

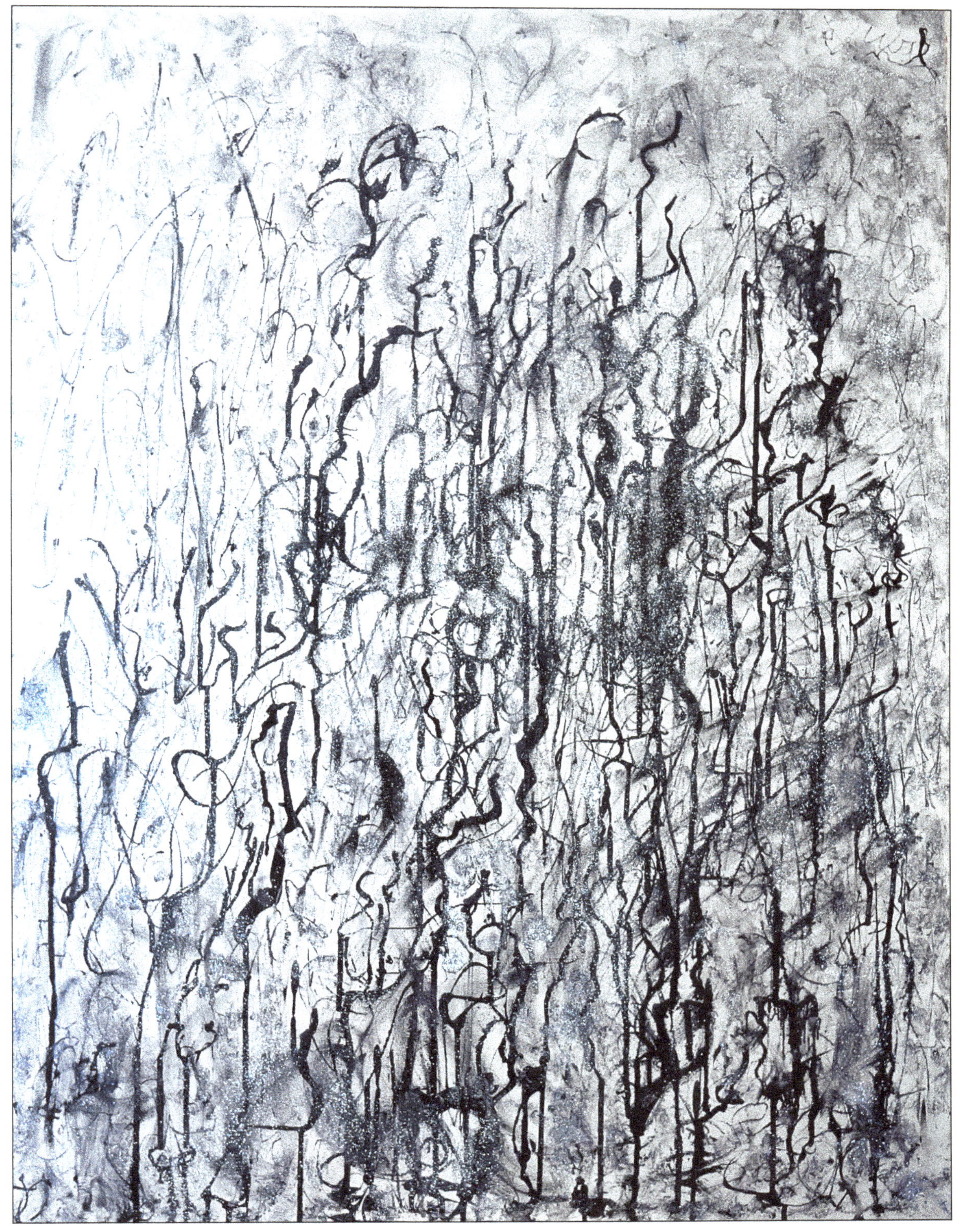

The Debut.
37½ x 30. Colored inks on canvas. 2013.

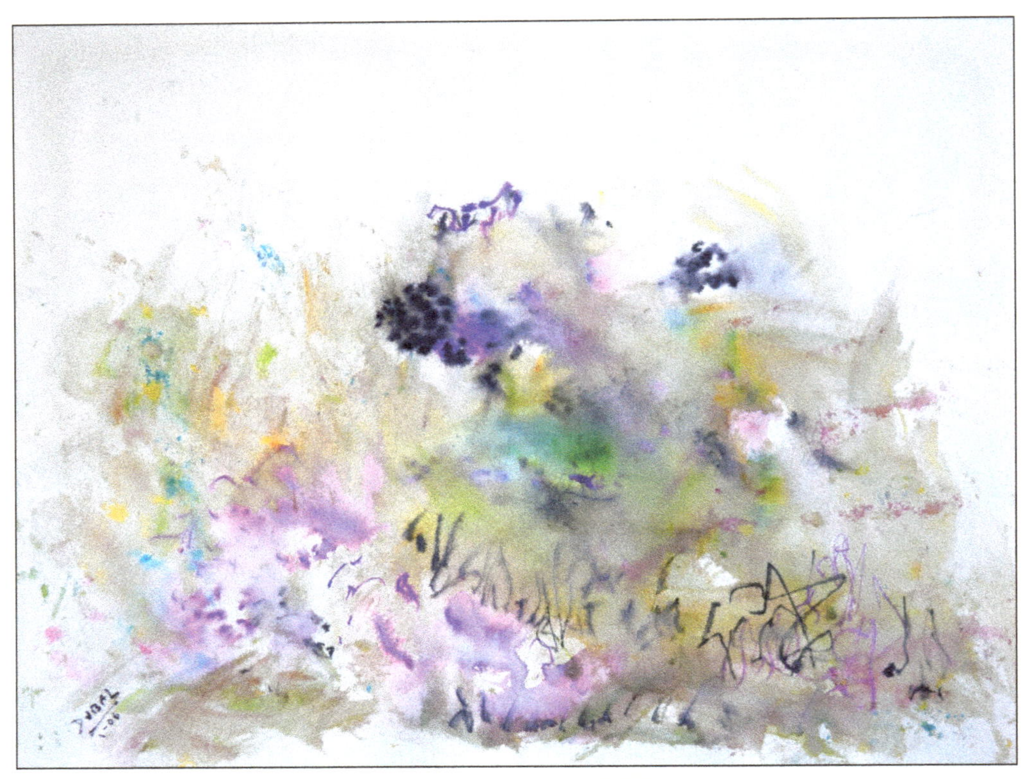

Eau de parfum.
11 x 14. Watercolor on paper.
2004.

Cleopatra's Best.
18 x 12. Oil on canvas board.
2000.

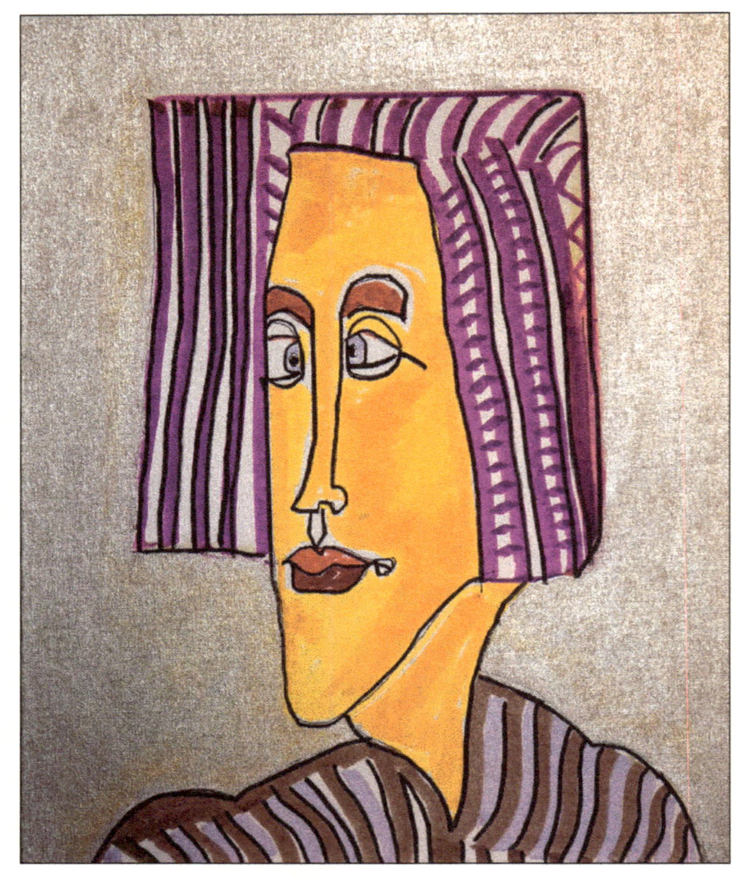

THE PAINTINGS OF DAVID DUBAL

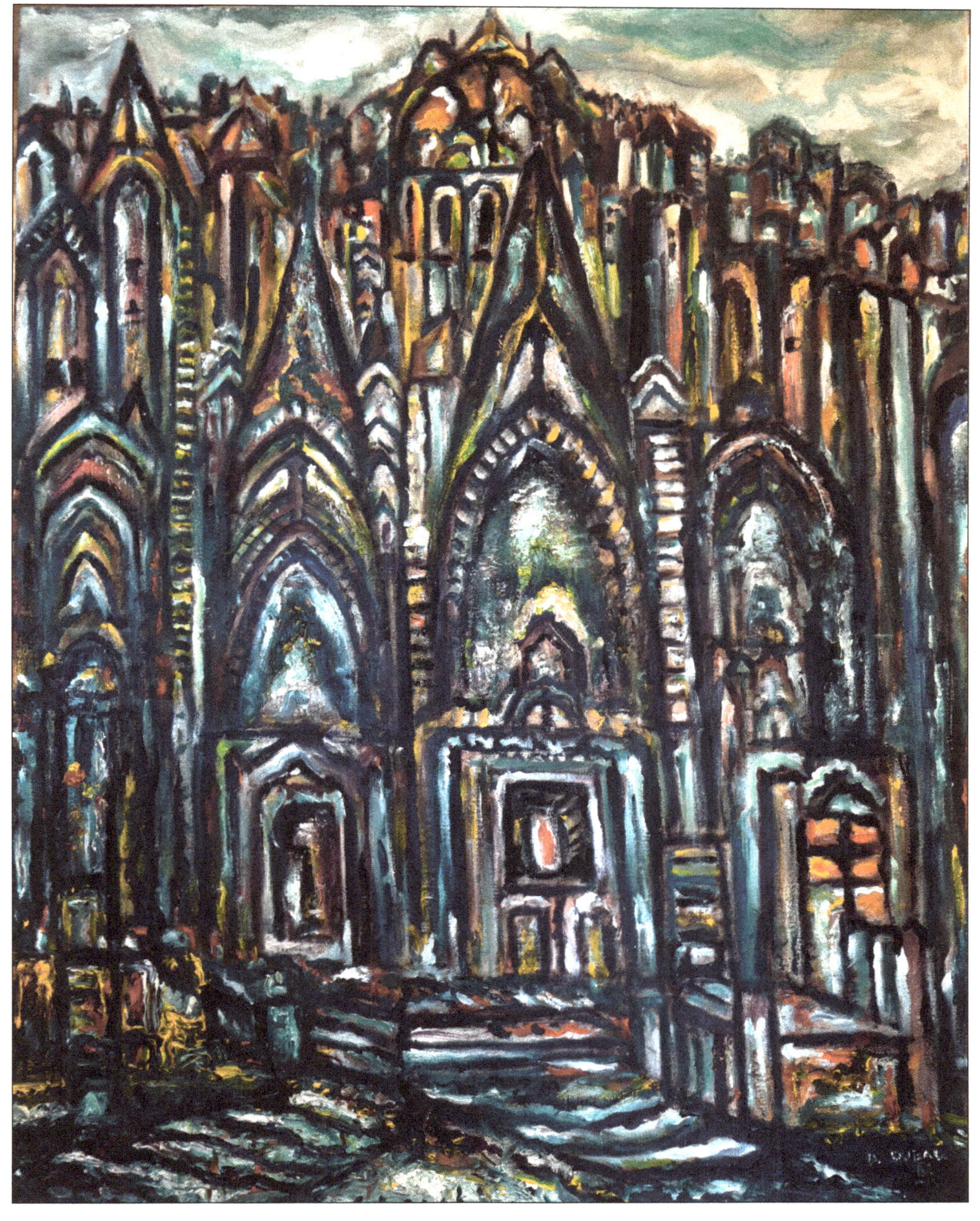

My Cathedral.
44 x 34. Oil on canvas. 1991.

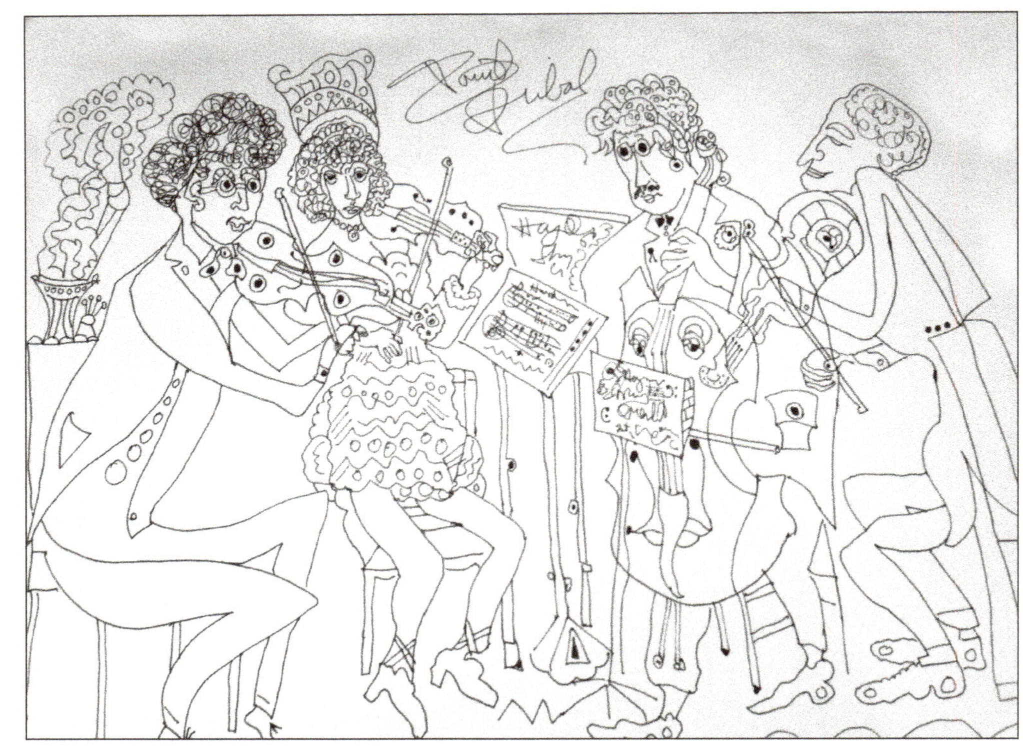

Haydn String Quartet. 12 x 17. Pen and ink on paper. 2014.

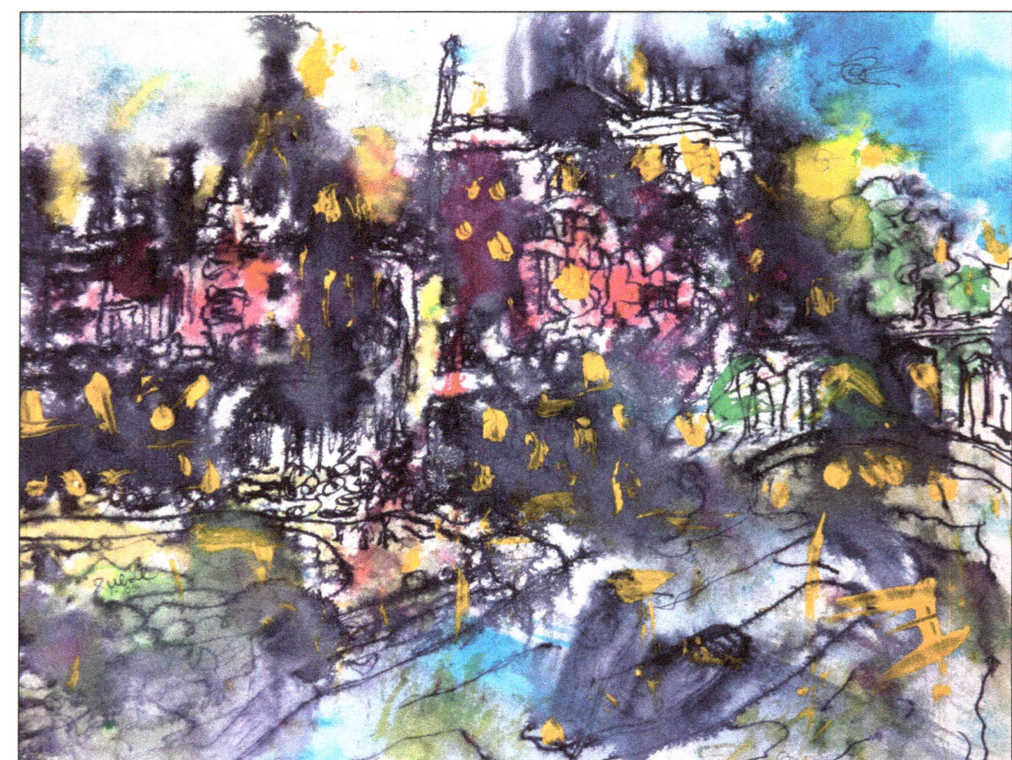

Metropolitan Scene. 11 x 14. Watercolor and paper. 2007.

THE PAINTINGS OF DAVID DUBAL

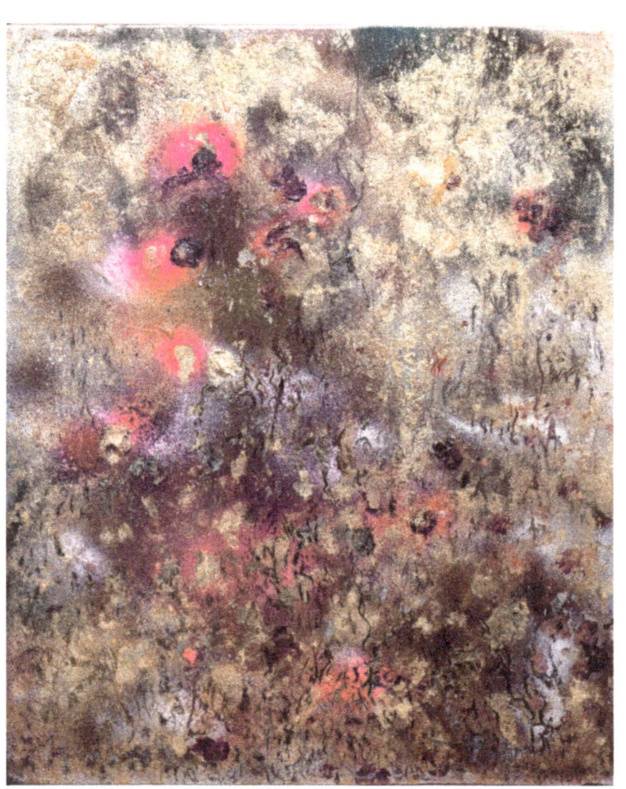

Golden Harvest.
18 x 14. Oil on canvas.
2017.

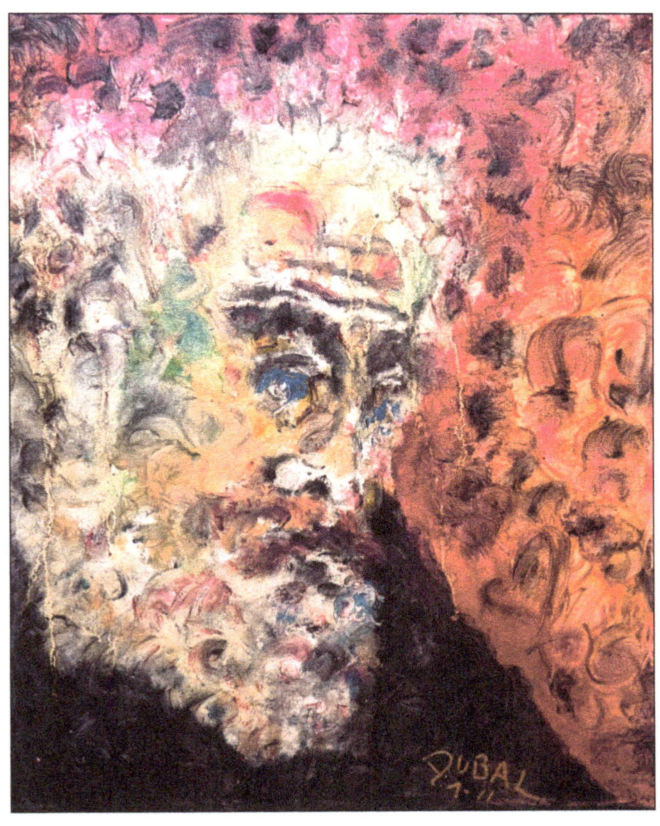

An Old Guy.
18 x 16. Oil on canvas.
2011.

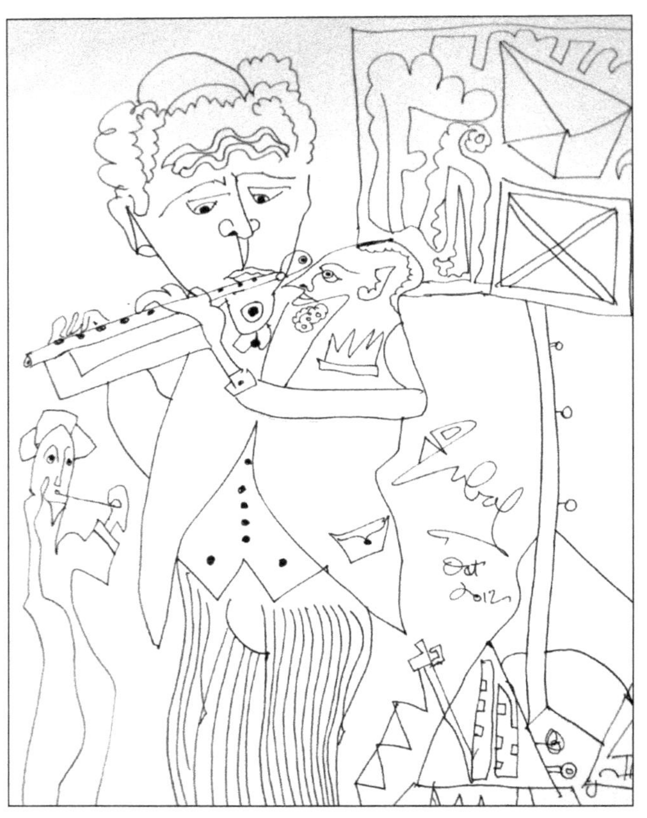

Flutist with Helper.
11 x 14. Pen and ink on paper.
2012.

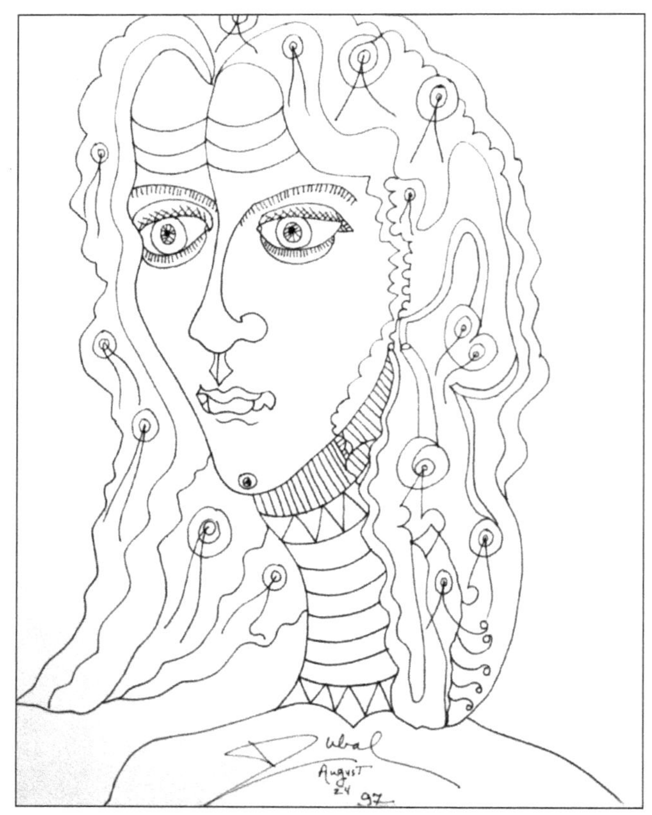

Goddess of Daffodils.
11 x 14. Pen and ink on paper.
1997.

THE PAINTINGS OF DAVID DUBAL

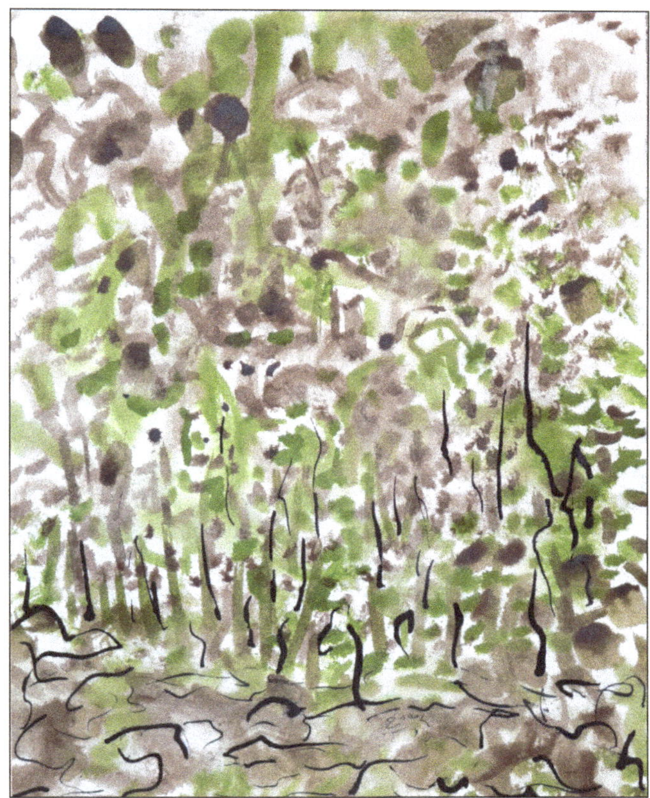

Leaves in June.
14 x 11. Watercolor. 2005.

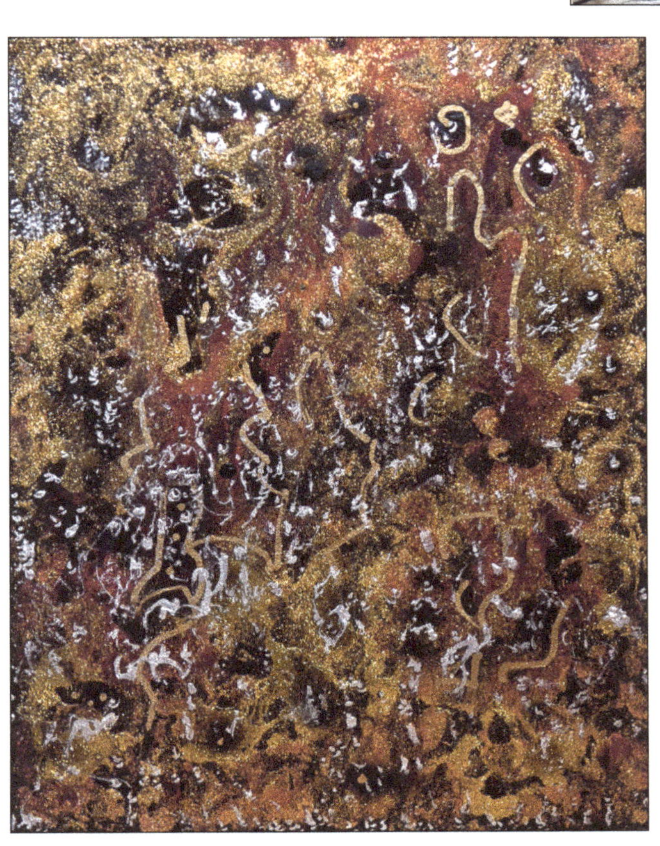

Layering on Gold.
14 x 11. Mixed media on canvas.
2016.

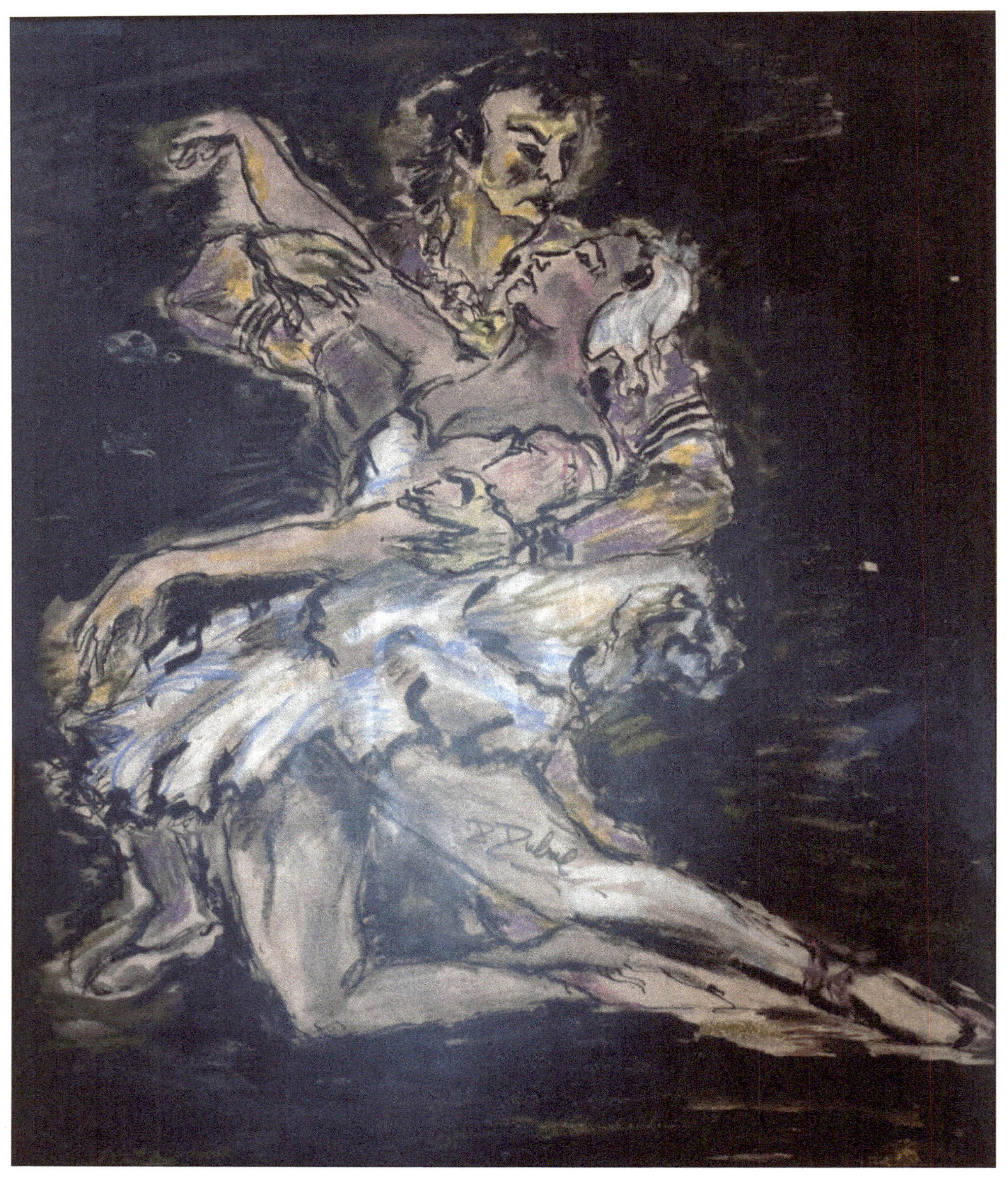

Love and Death.
16 x 12. Pastel on canvas. 1993.

     THE PAINTINGS OF DAVID DUBAL

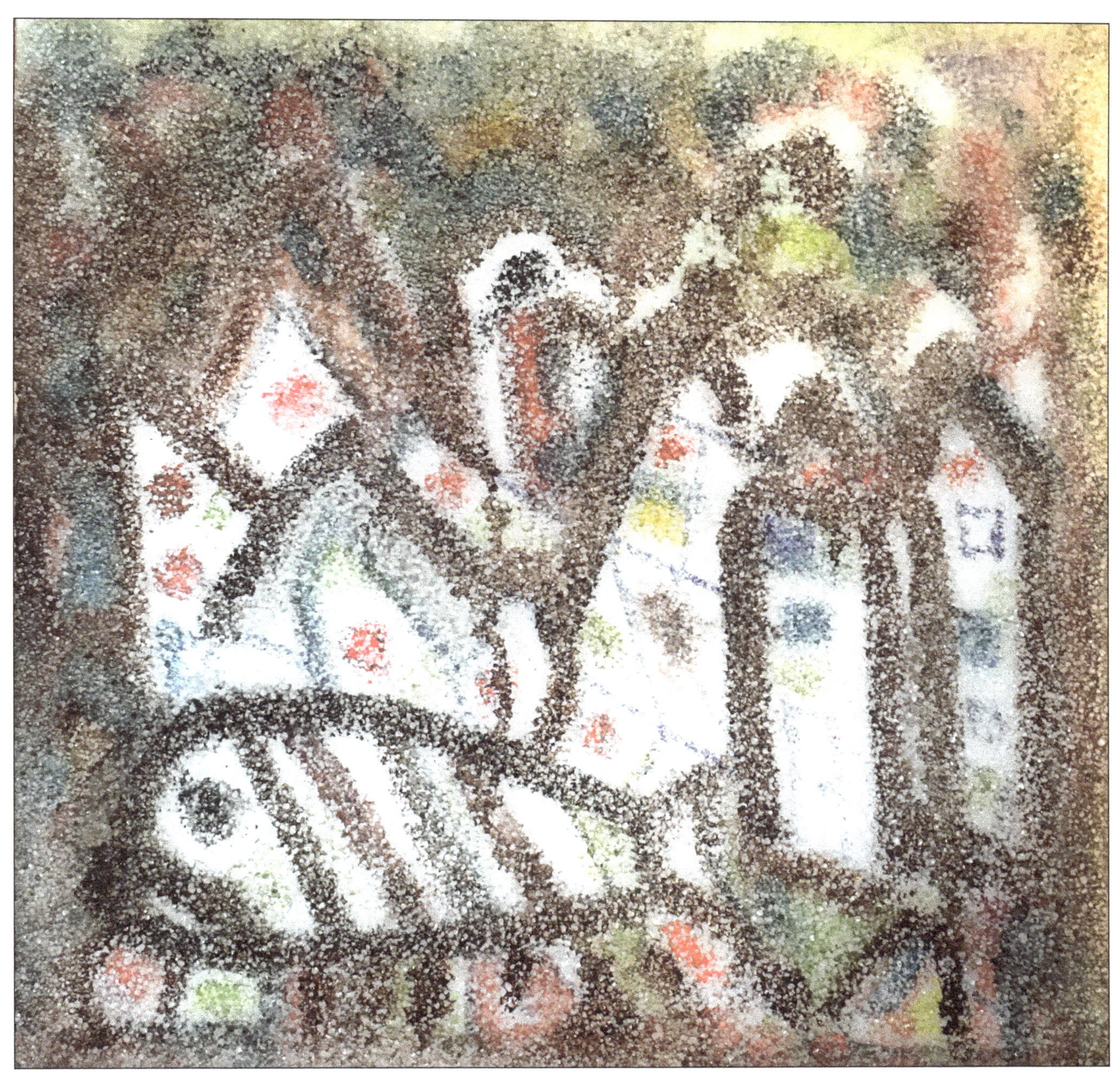

Fishing Village at Night.
11½ x 11½. Watercolor on Styrofoam. 2019.

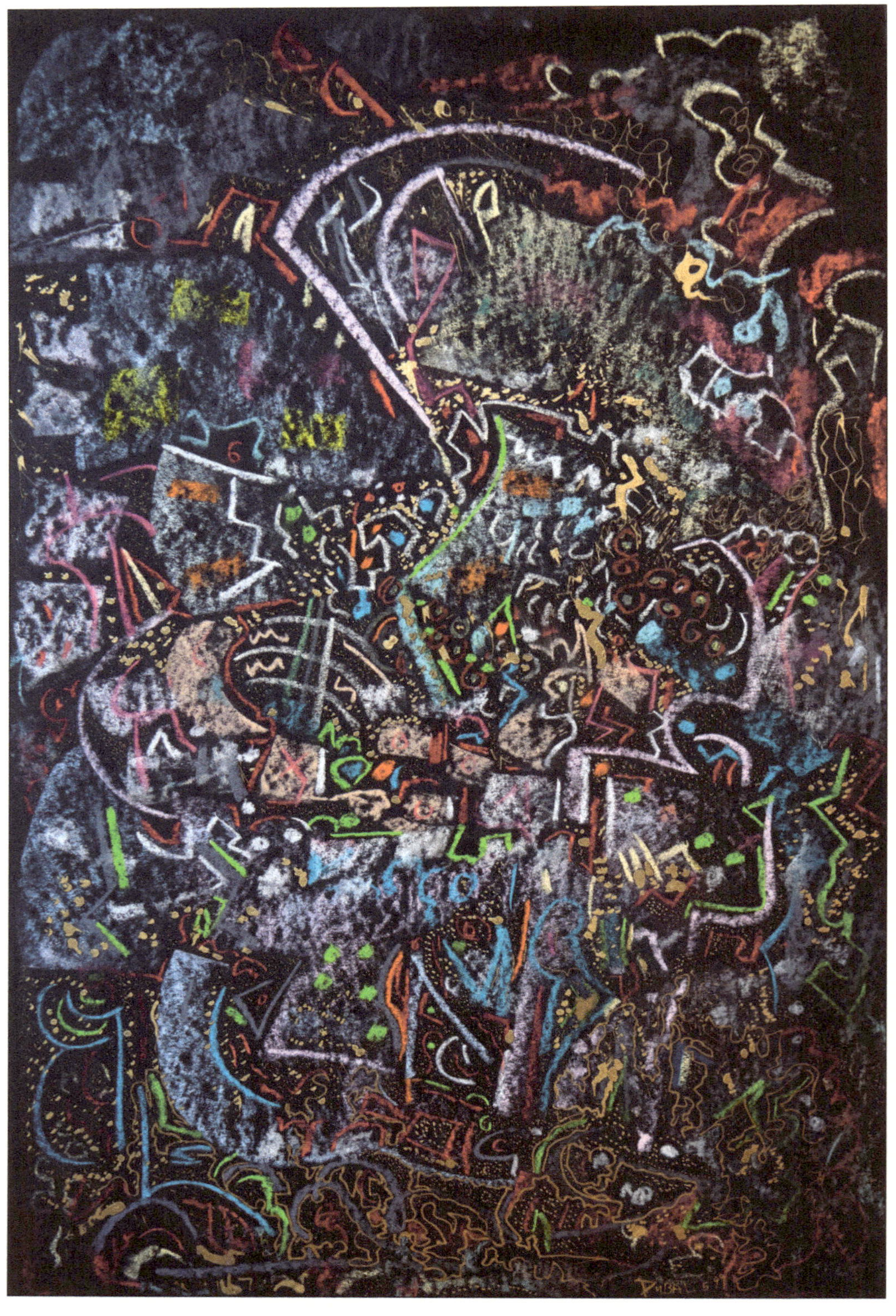

The Chinese Peacock.
30 x 30. Pastel on black board. 1999.

THE PAINTINGS OF DAVID DUBAL

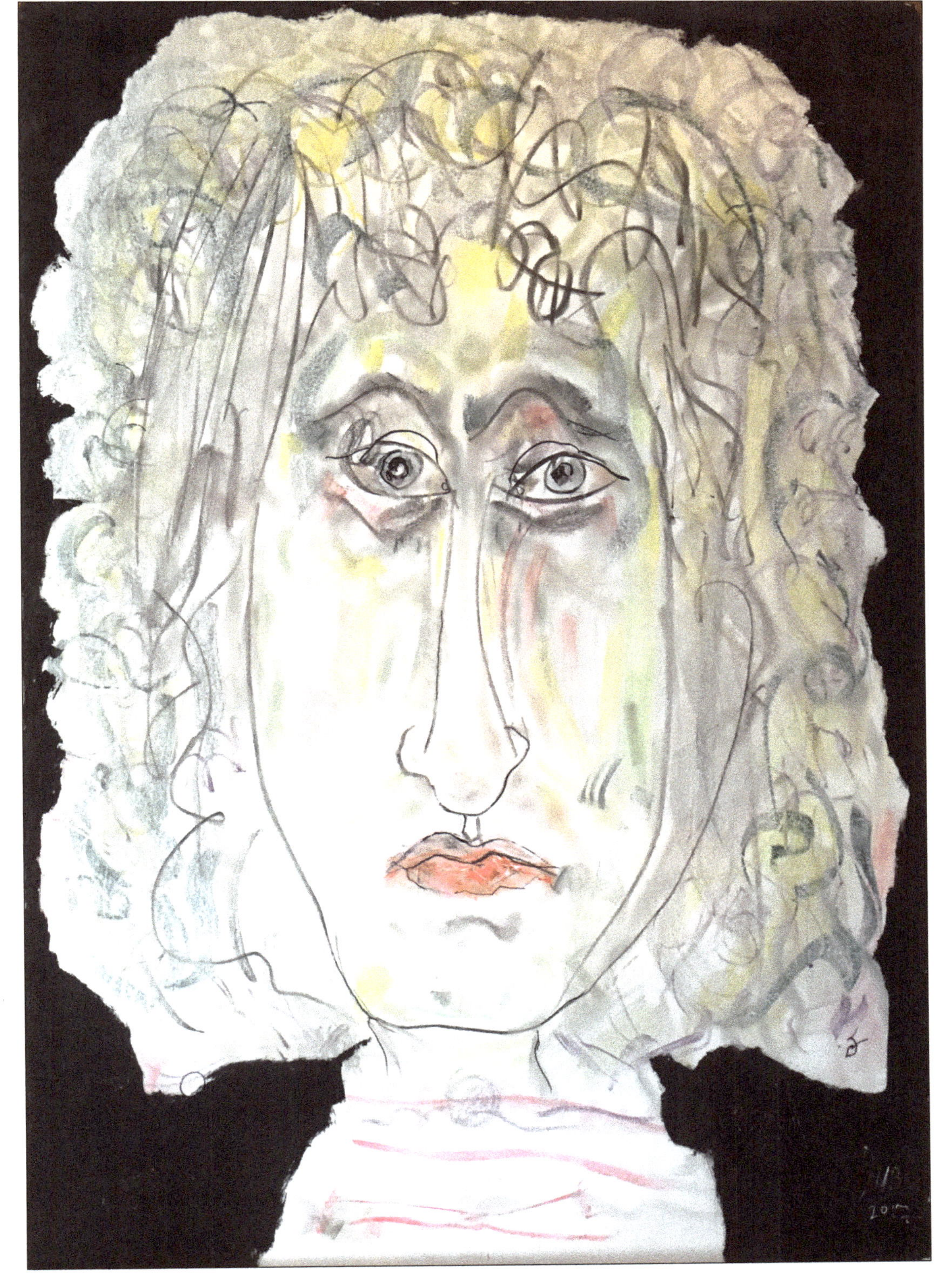

Fatal Attraction.
35 x 24. Mixed media on board. 2008.

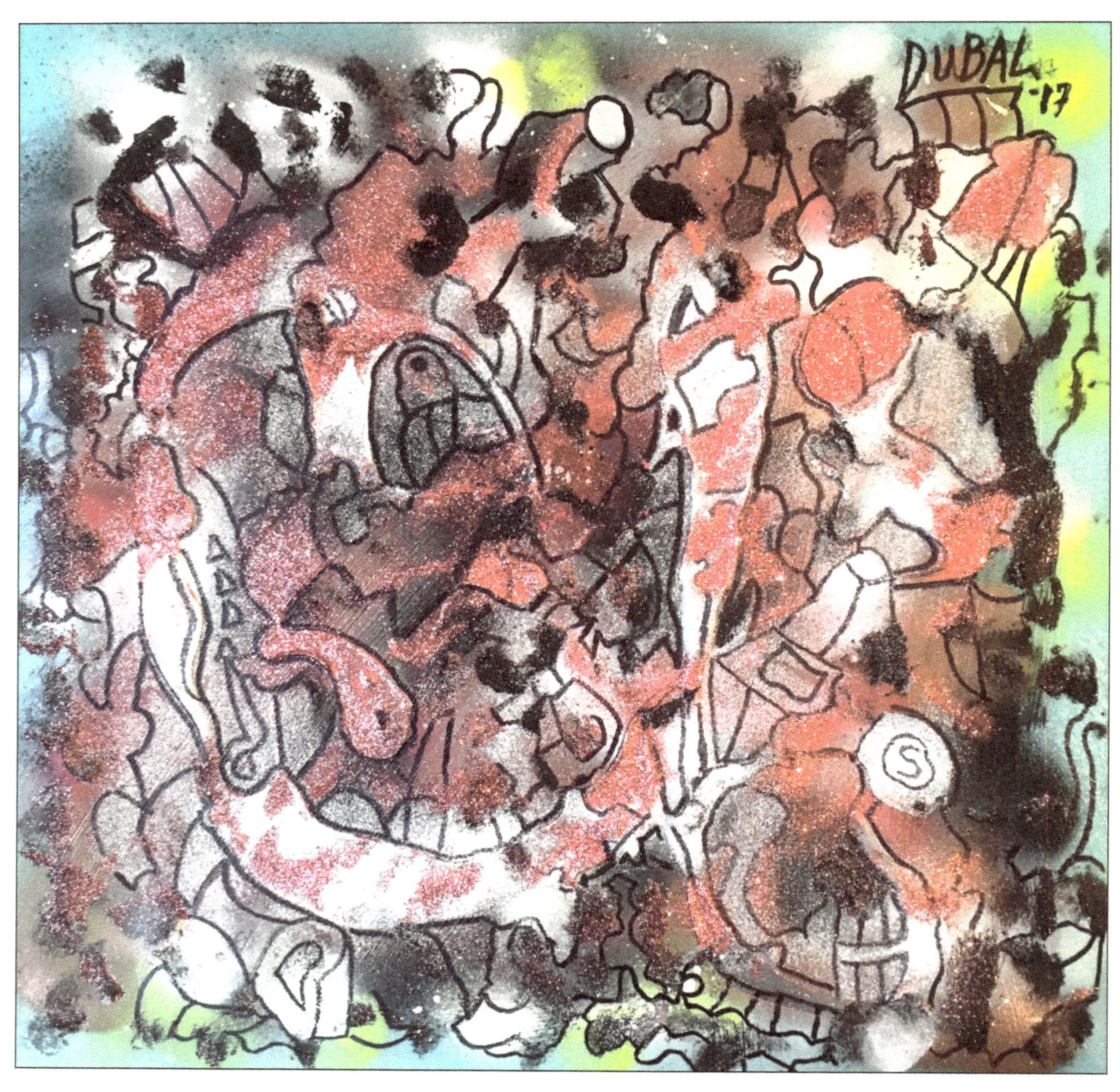

A Hot Party.
15 x 15. Mixed media on canvas. 2017.

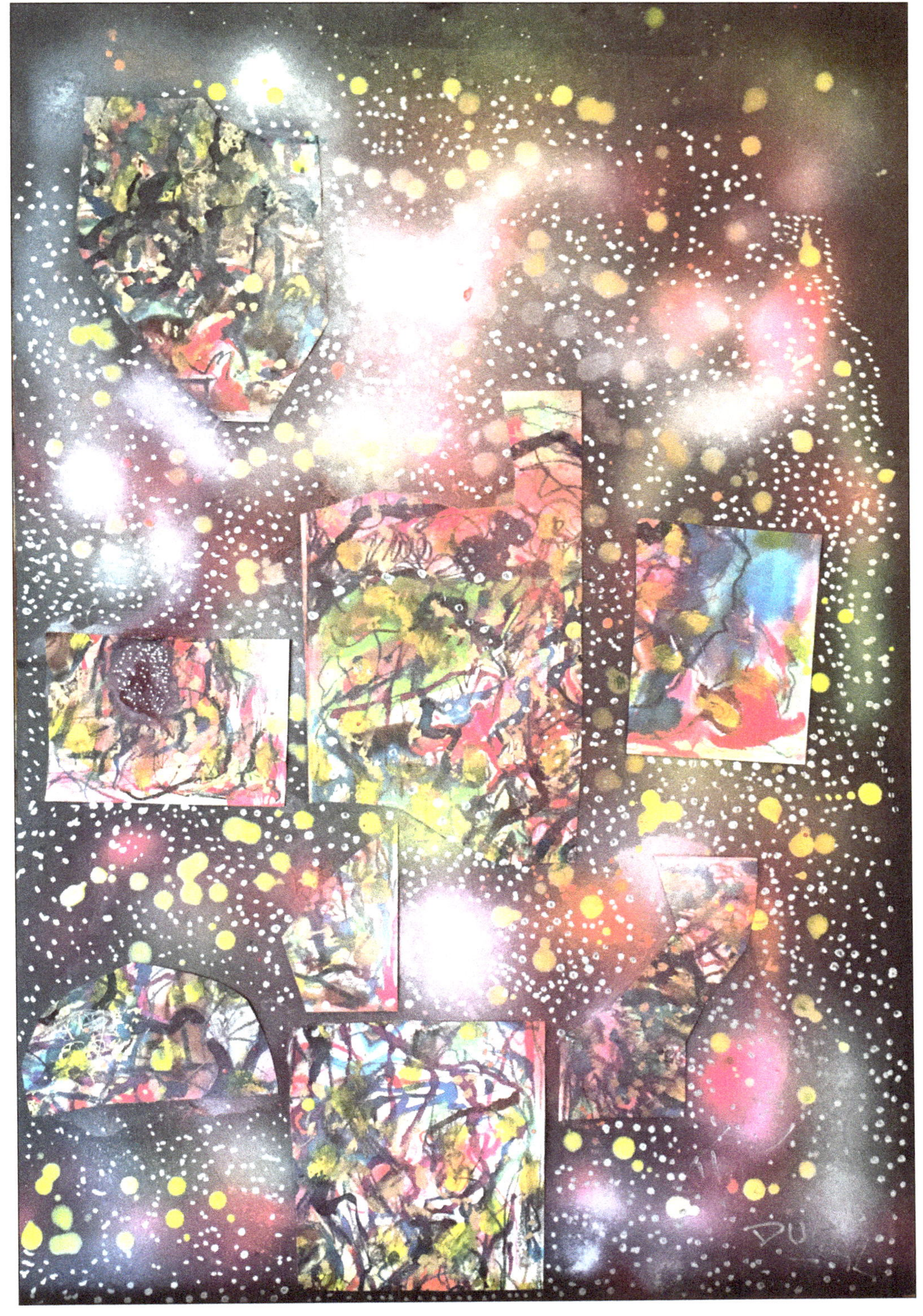

The Ghost Prophet.
30 x 20. Mixed media on black board. 2002.

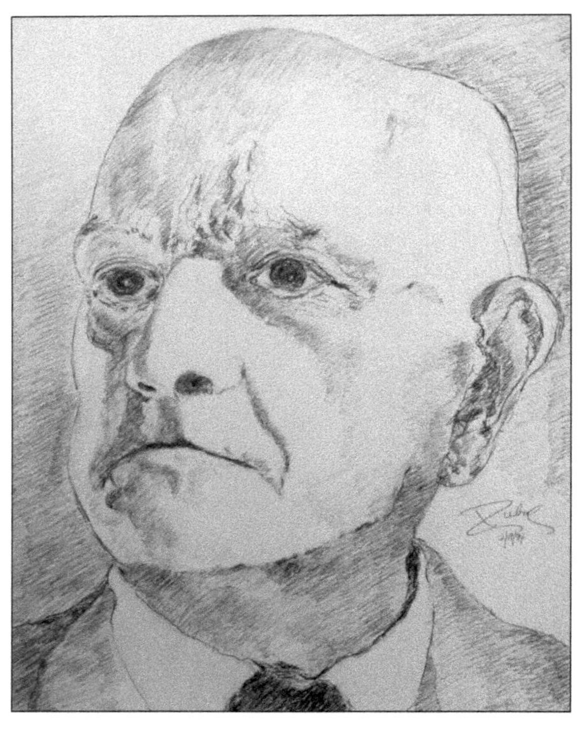

Jean Sibelius.
11 x 14. Pen and ink on paper. 1999.

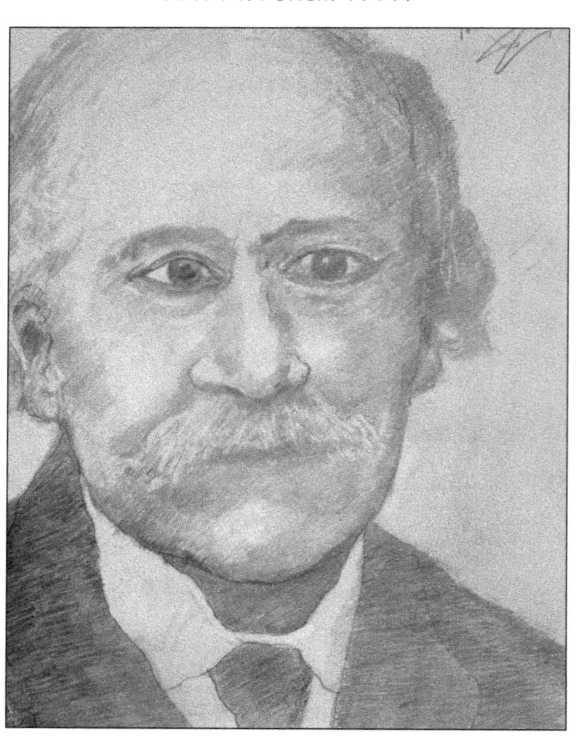

Hugo Wolf.
11 x 14. Pen and ink on paper. 2000.

Georges Bizet.
11 x 14. Pencil. 1999.

Jules Massenet.
11 x 14. Pencil. 1999.

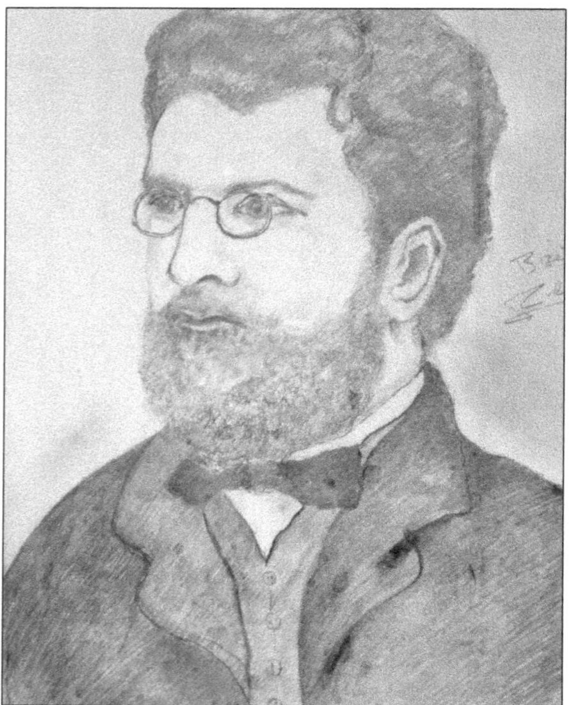

THE PAINTINGS OF DAVID DUBAL

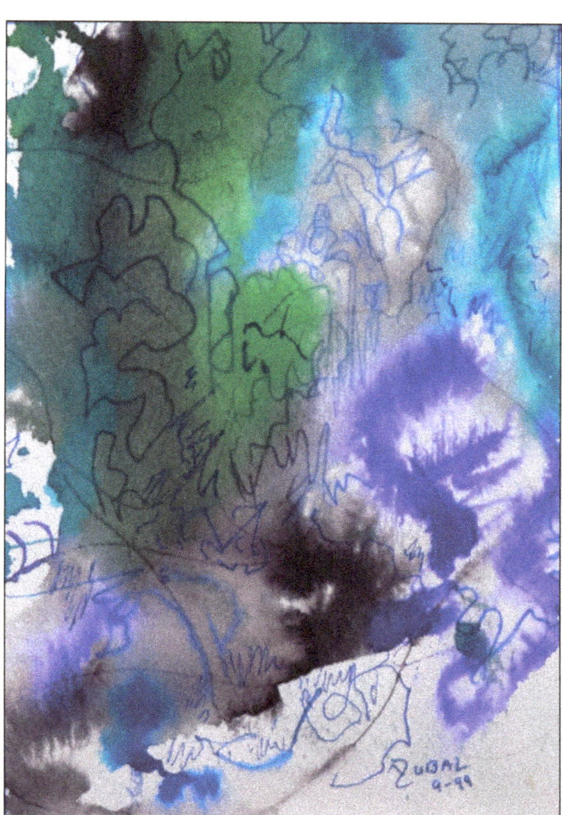

A Brilliant View.
8 x 5. Watercolor on paper.
1997.

Map of Venus.
8 x 5. Watercolor on paper.
1998.

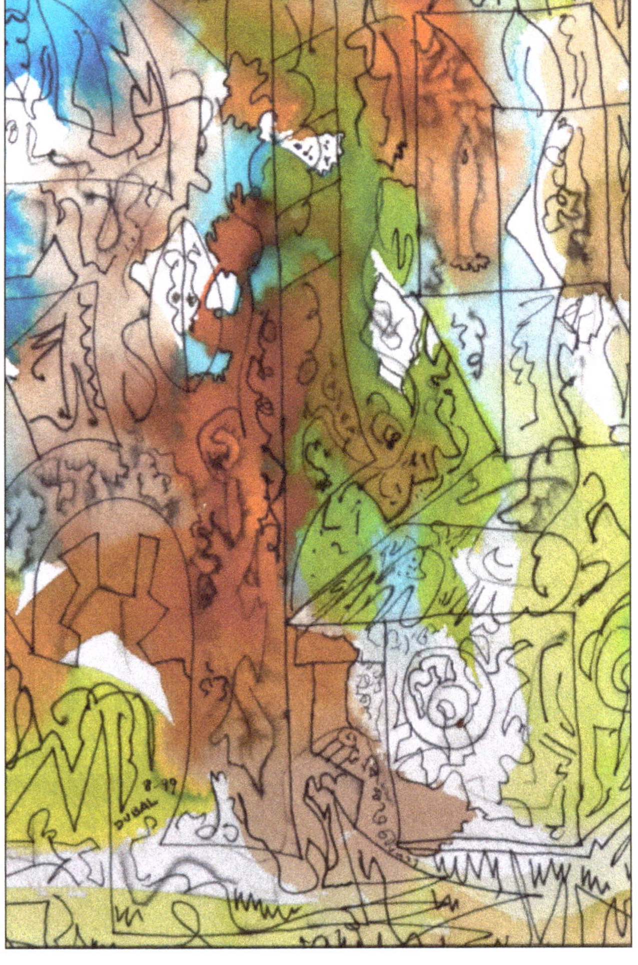

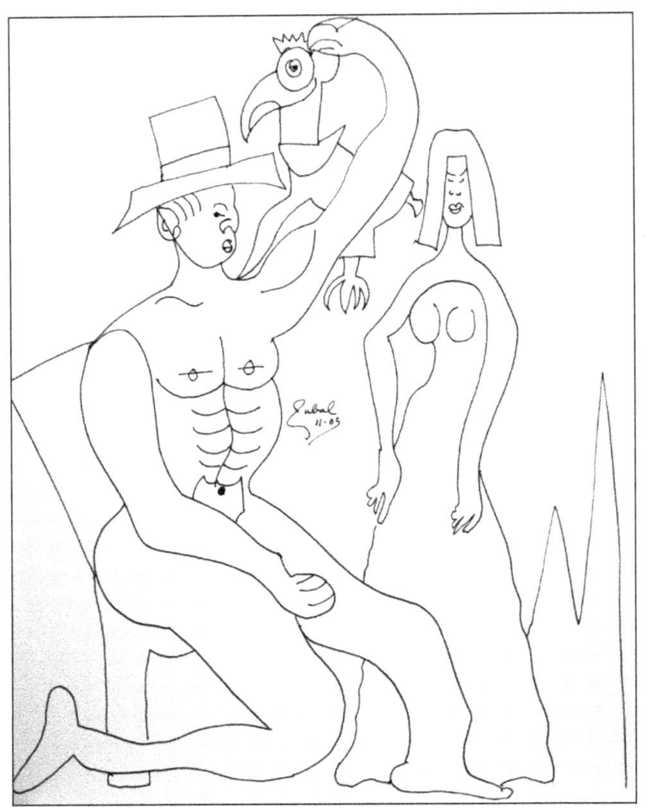

Man, Women, and Bird.
11 x 14. Pen and ink.
2005.

What a Girl!.
11 x 14. Pen and ink.
1997.

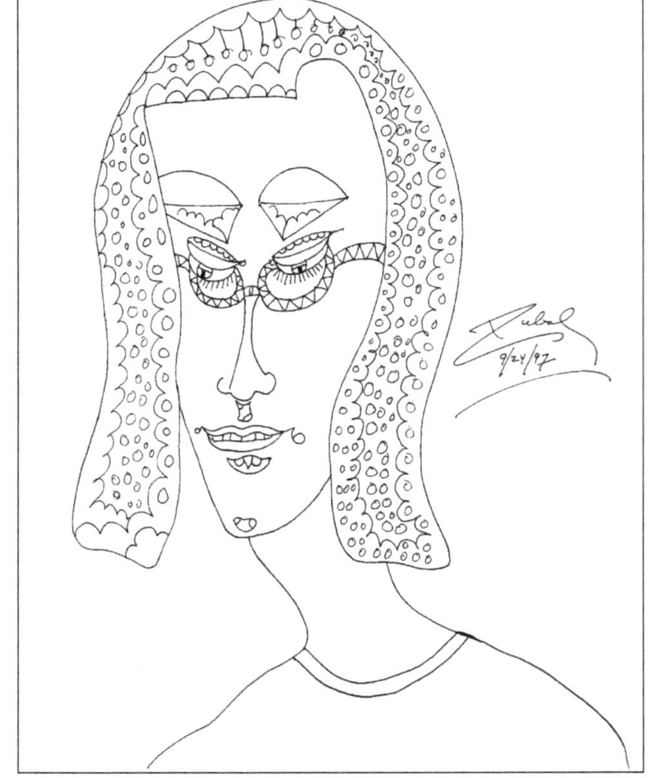

THE PAINTINGS OF DAVID DUBAL

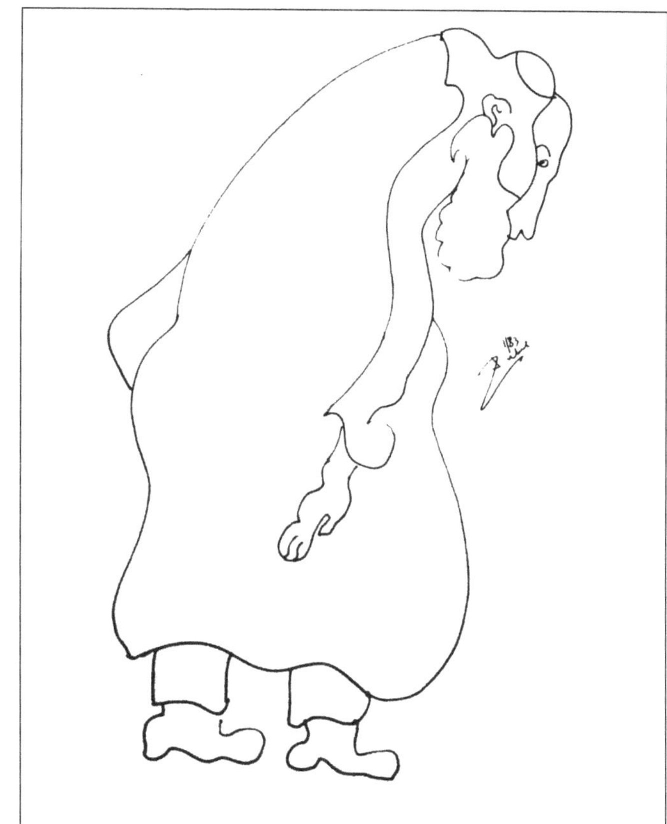

The Old Codger.
8 x 10. Pen and ink on paper.
1983.

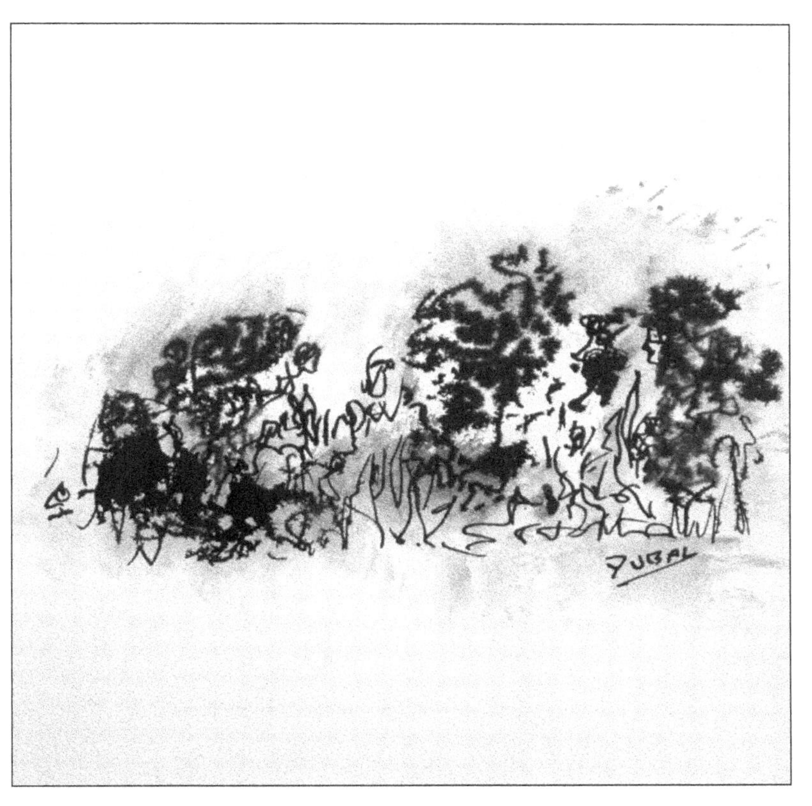

Trees to Look at.
12 x 12. Black ink and wash.
2001.

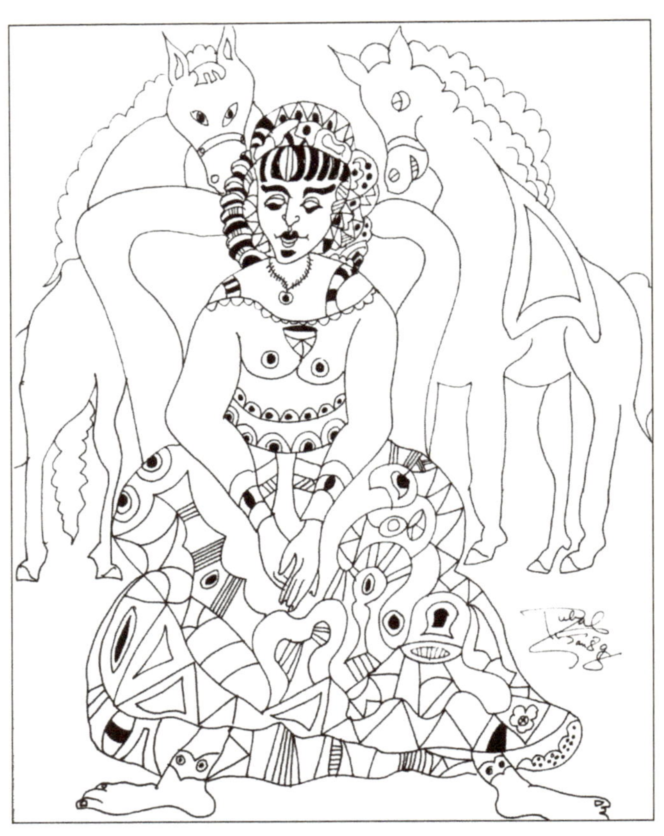

Dancer with Horses.
11 x 14. Pen and ink on paper. 1998.

Crystal Colors.
8 x 10. Watercolor. 1999.

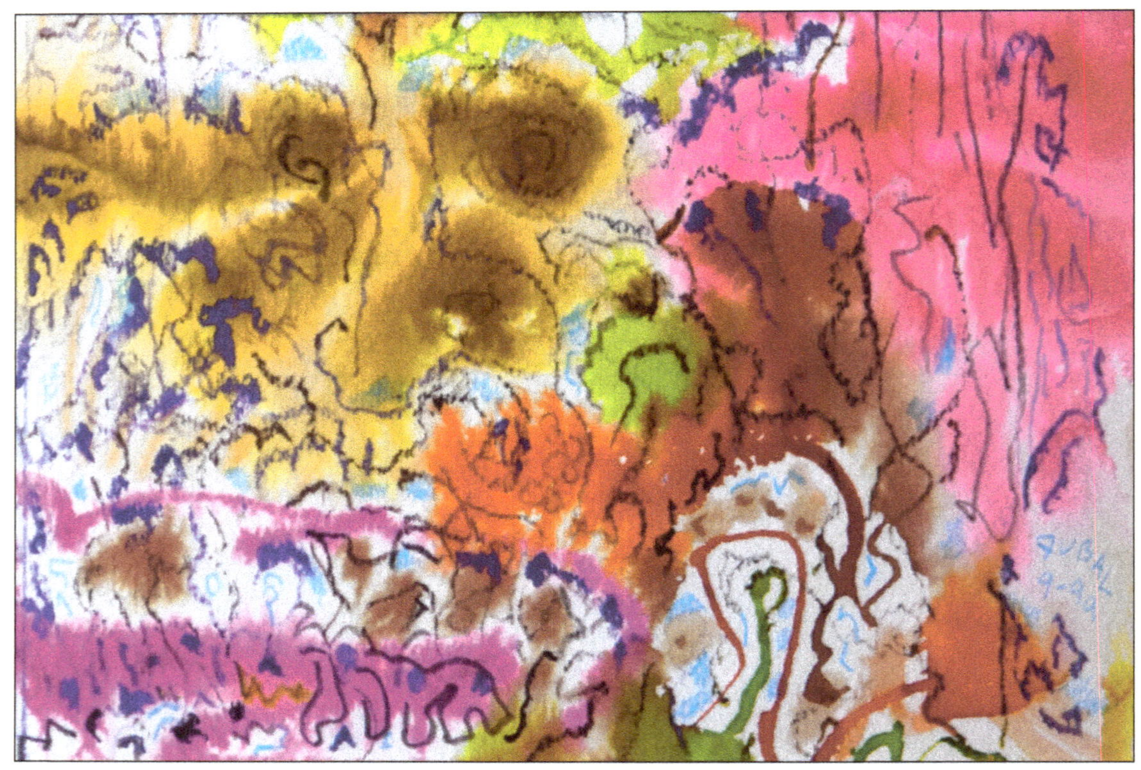

THE PAINTINGS OF DAVID DUBAL

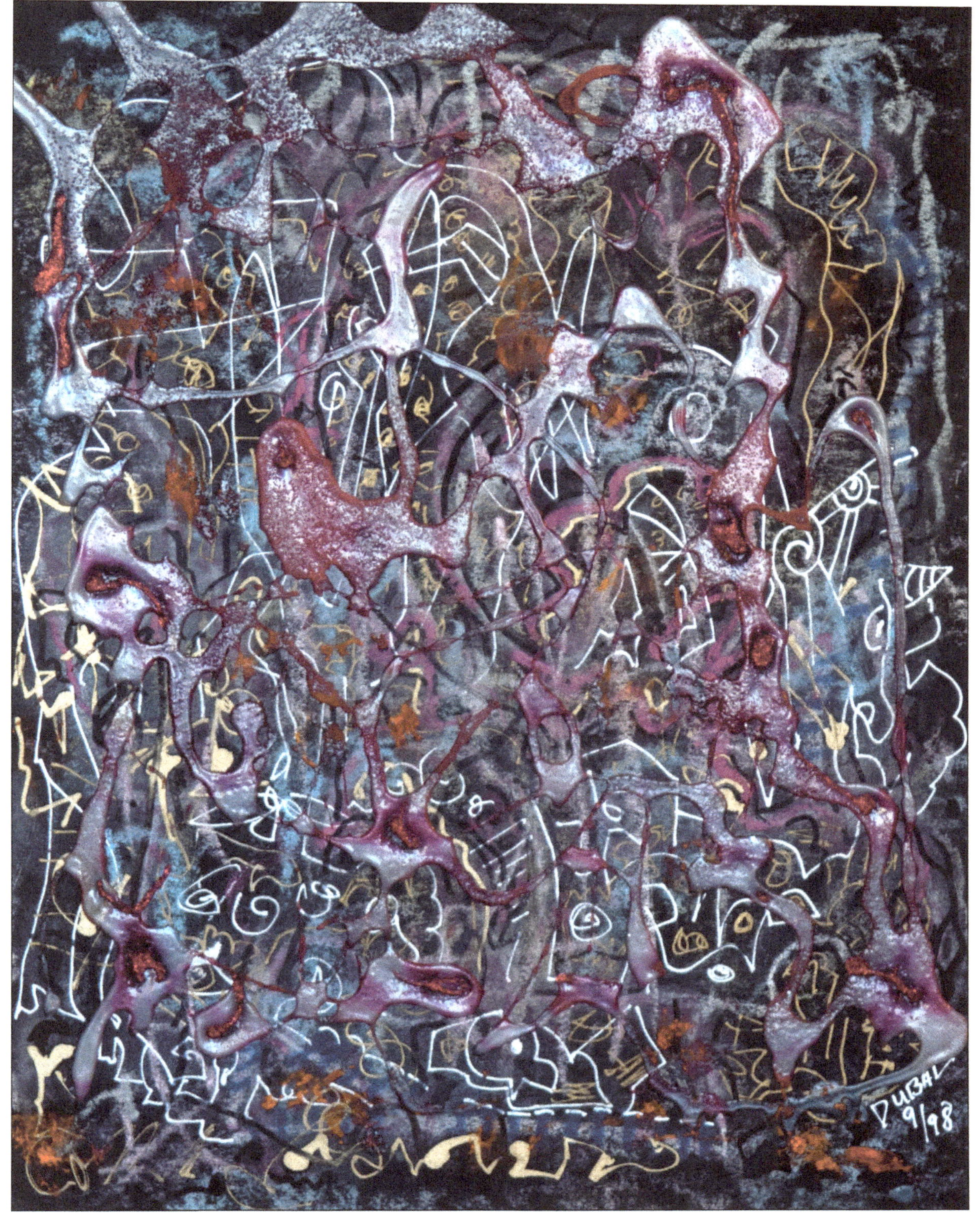

Glue Jungle.
15 x 12. Mixed media. 1998.

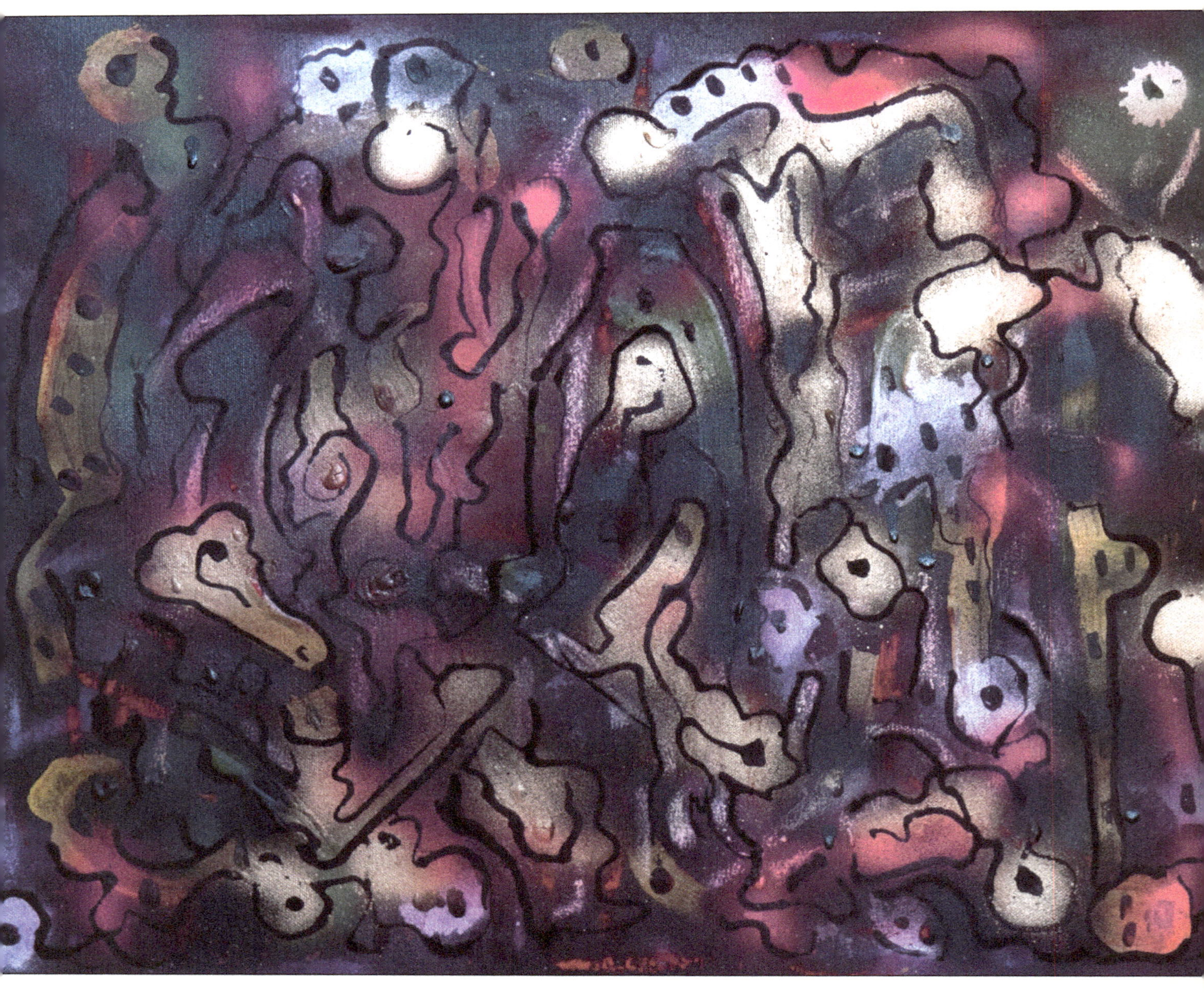

Night Sounds.
16 x 20. Spray paint on canvas. 2016.

          THE PAINTINGS OF DAVID DUBAL

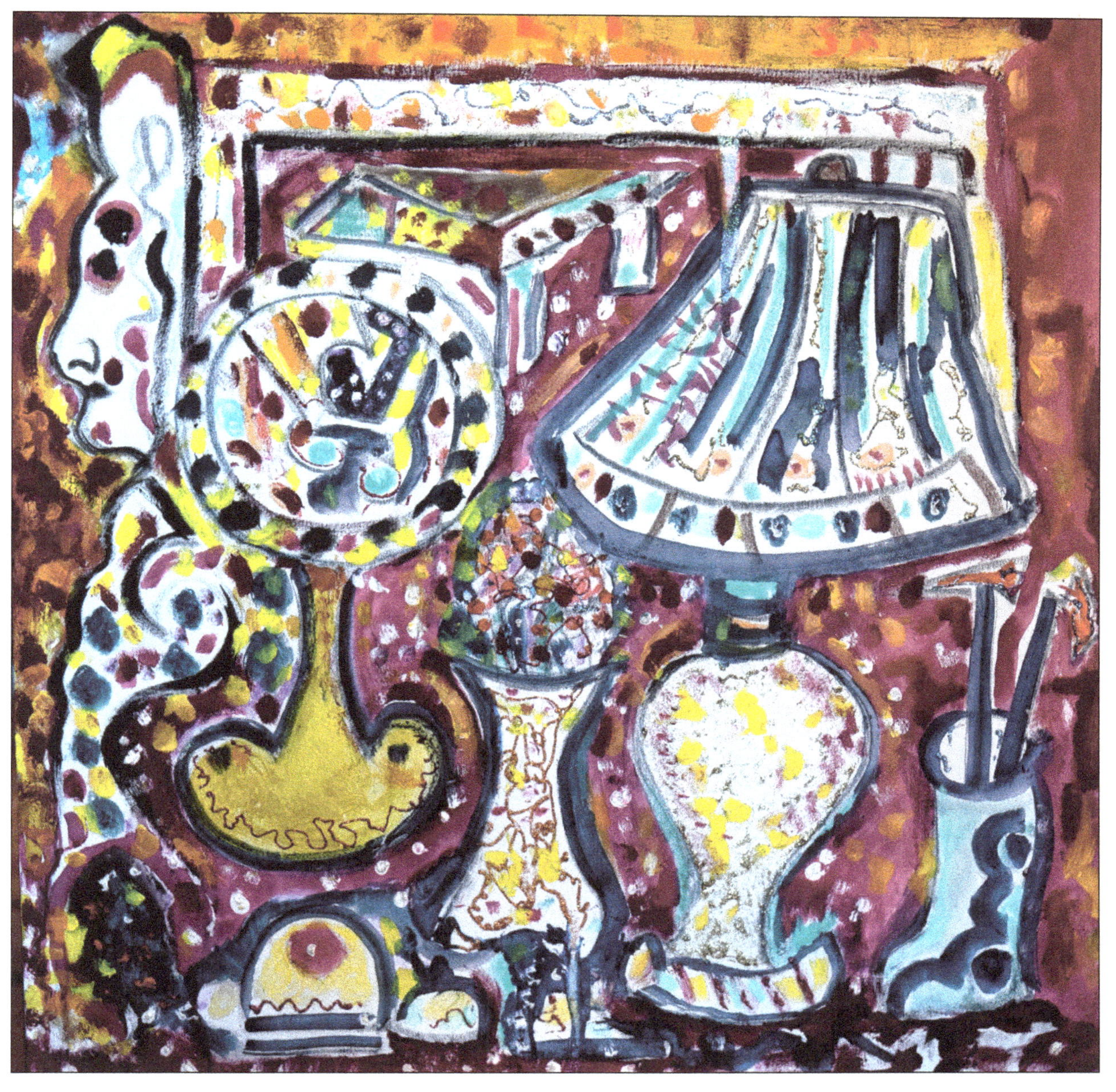

My Desk.
30 x 30. Oil on canvas. 2011.

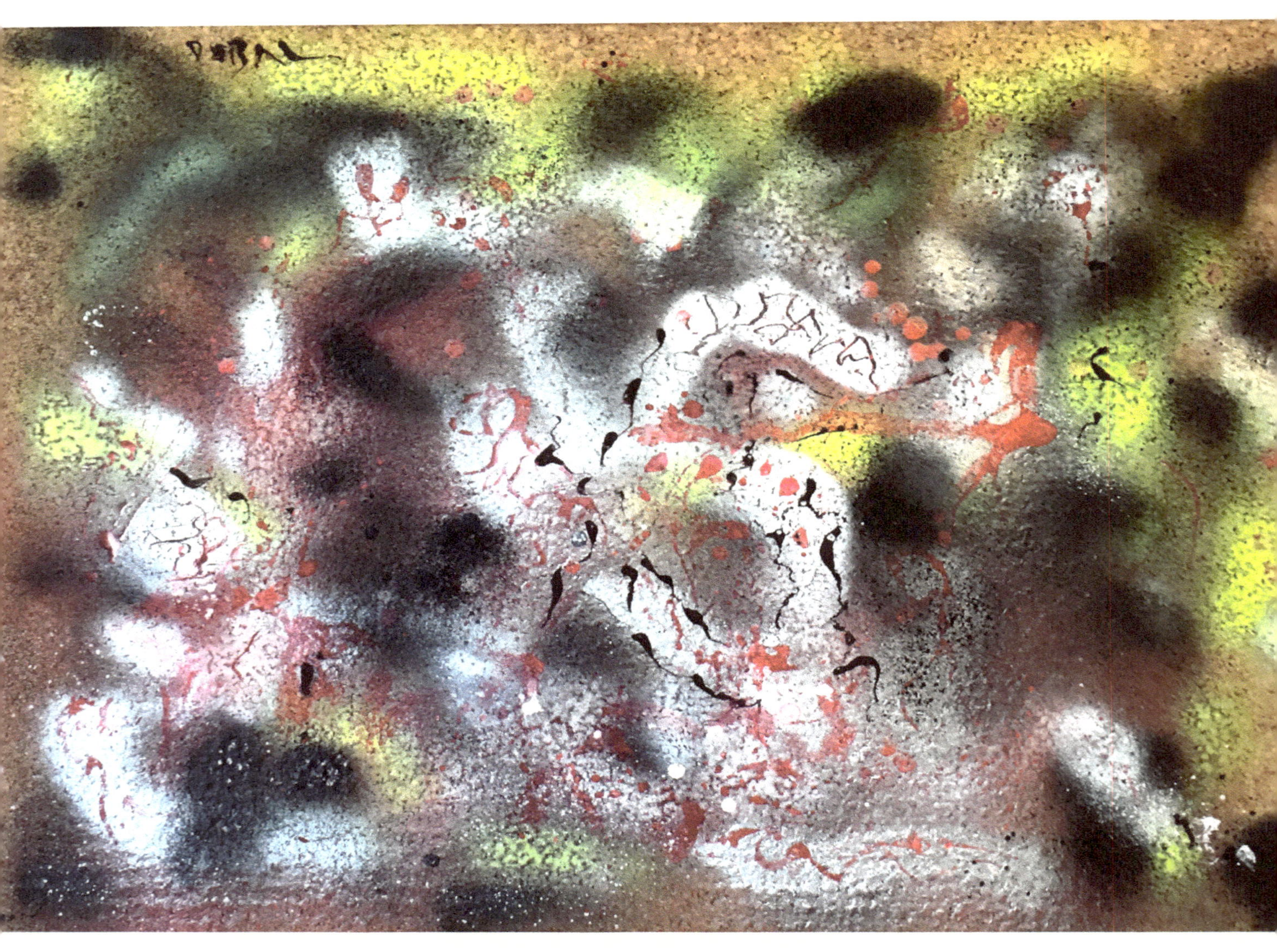

The Internal.
16 x 23. Spray paint on board. 2017.

     THE PAINTINGS OF DAVID DUBAL

The Night Zebra.
8 x 10. Silver ink on black board. 2009.

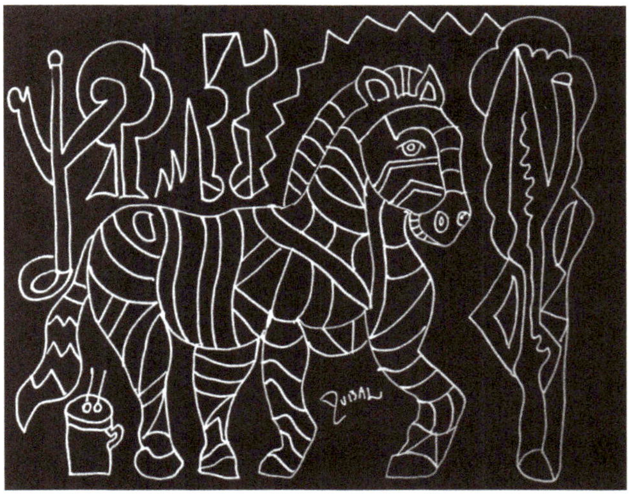

Cool Dream.
8 x 10. Silver ink on black board. 2009.

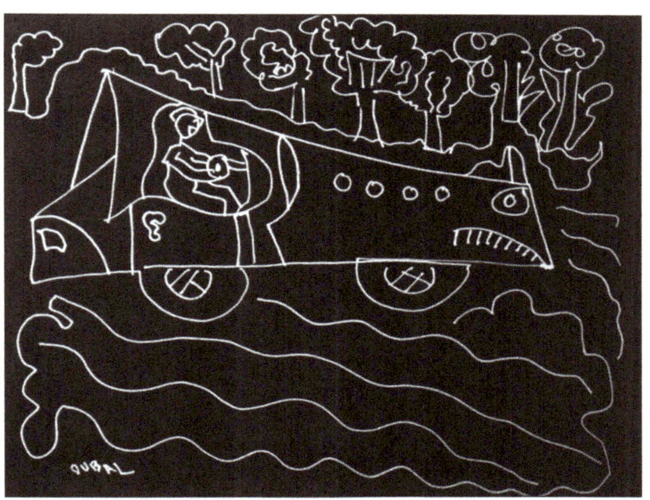

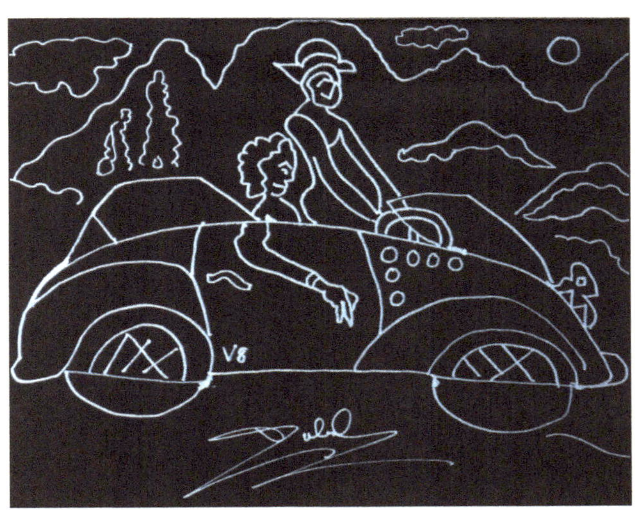

Two Joy Riders, with Mountains and Moon.
8 x 10. Silver ink on black board. 2009.

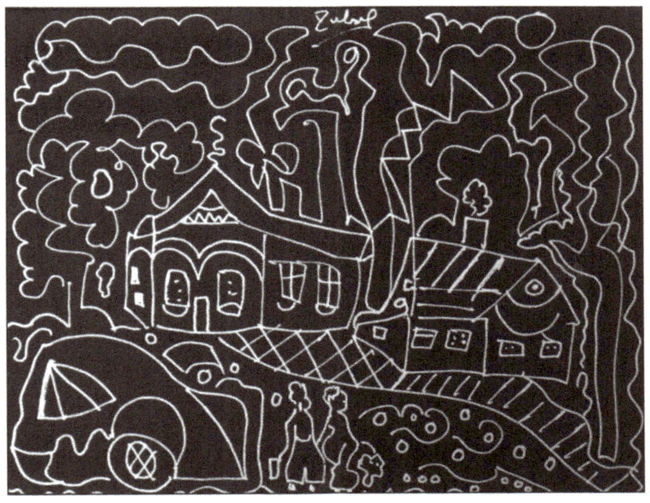

Two People with Fun Auto.
8 x 10. Silver ink on black board. 2009.

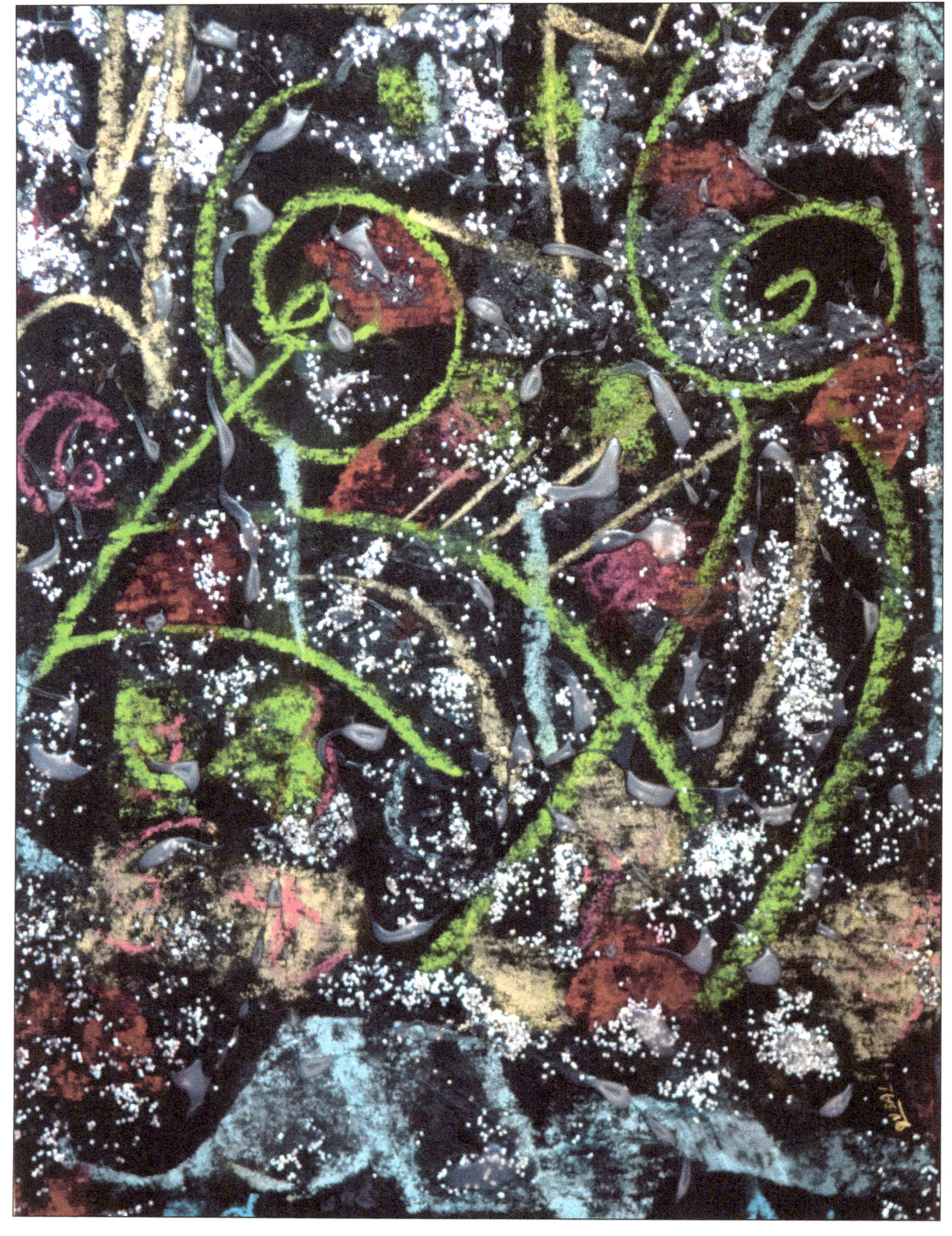

Plangent.
22 x 14. Mixed media. 2010.

THE PAINTINGS OF DAVID DUBAL

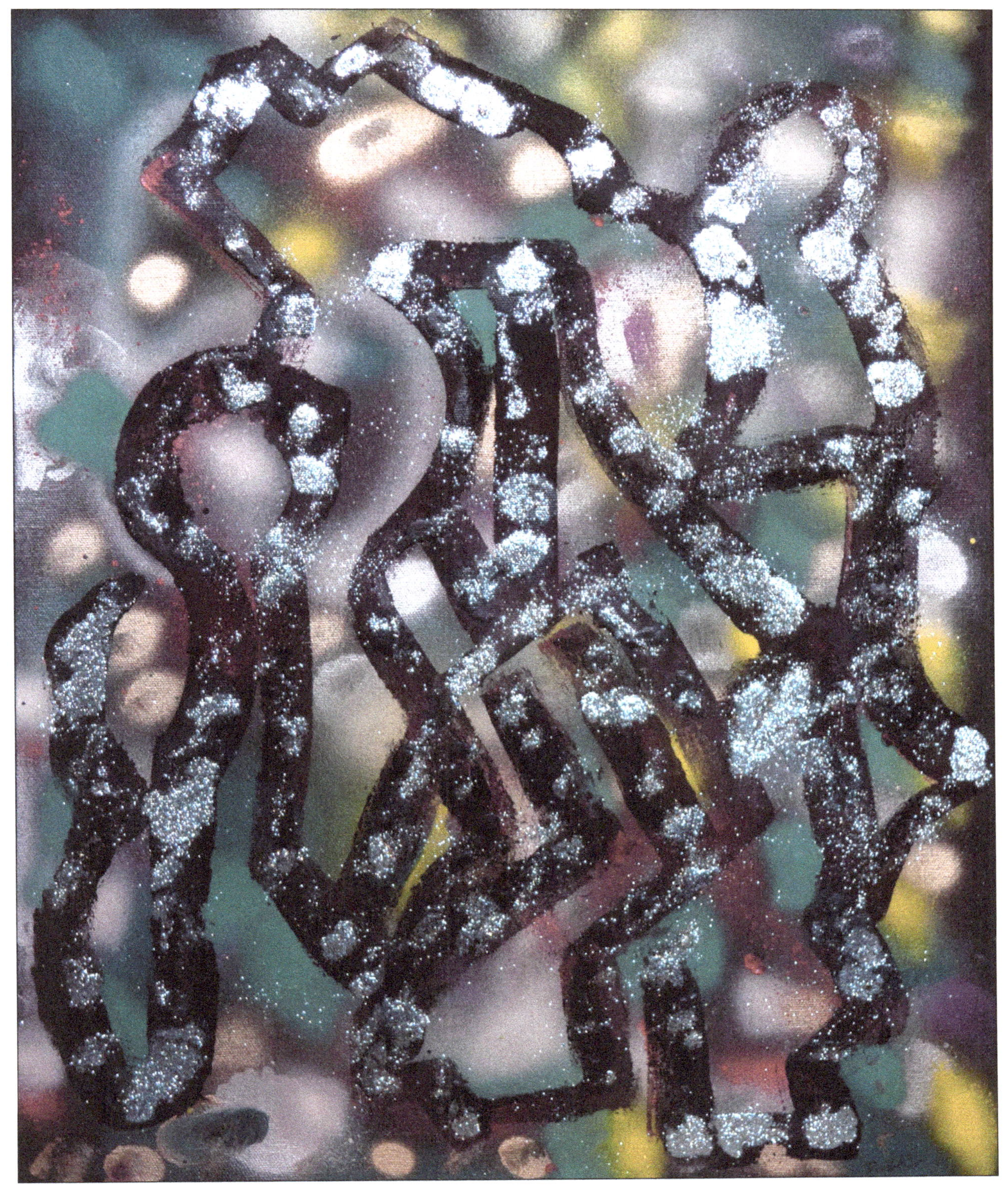

The Black Dancers.
20 x 15. Spray paint. 2012.

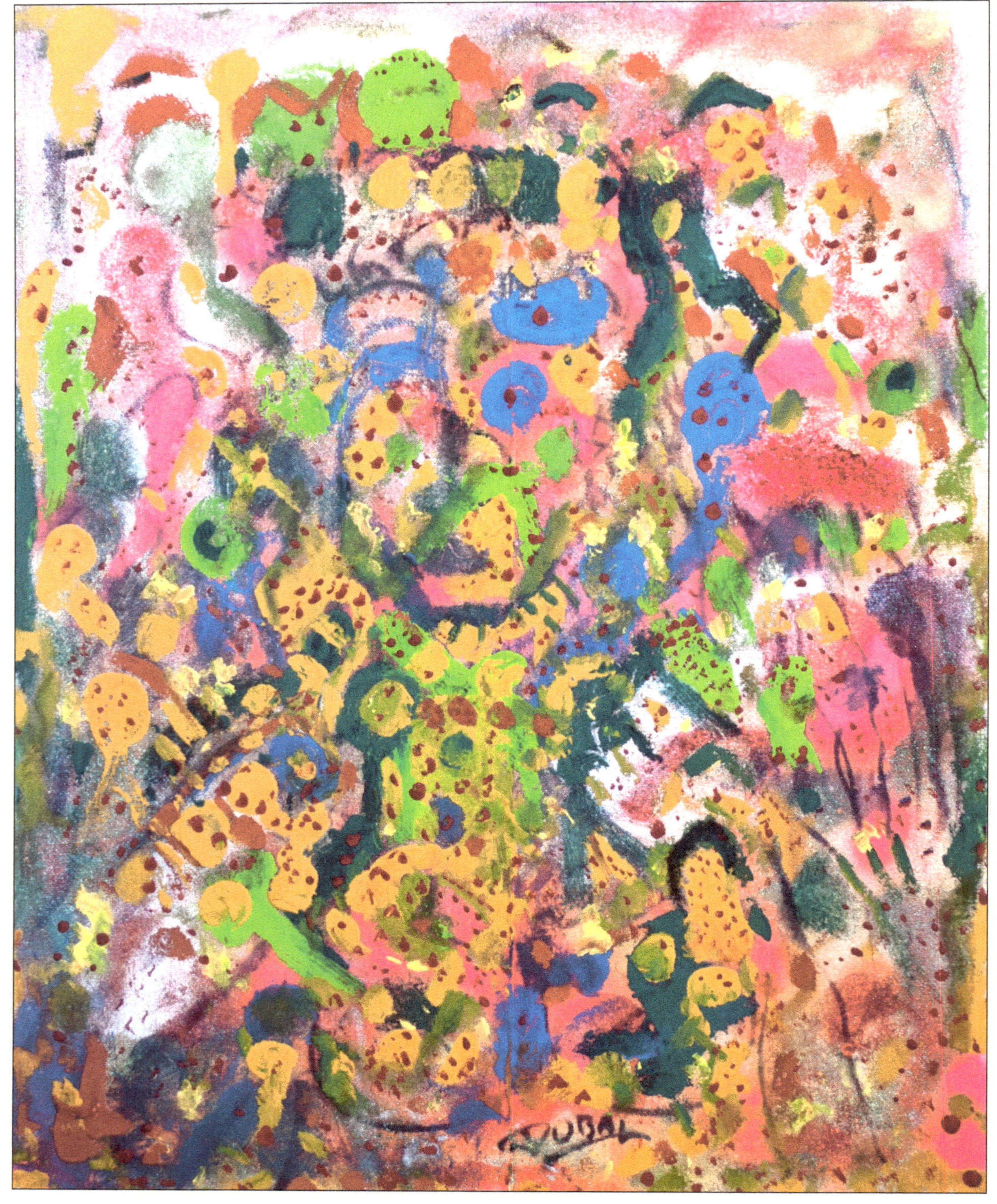

Oriental Potentate.
10½ x 14. Watercolor on canvas board. 1997.

 THE PAINTINGS OF DAVID DUBAL

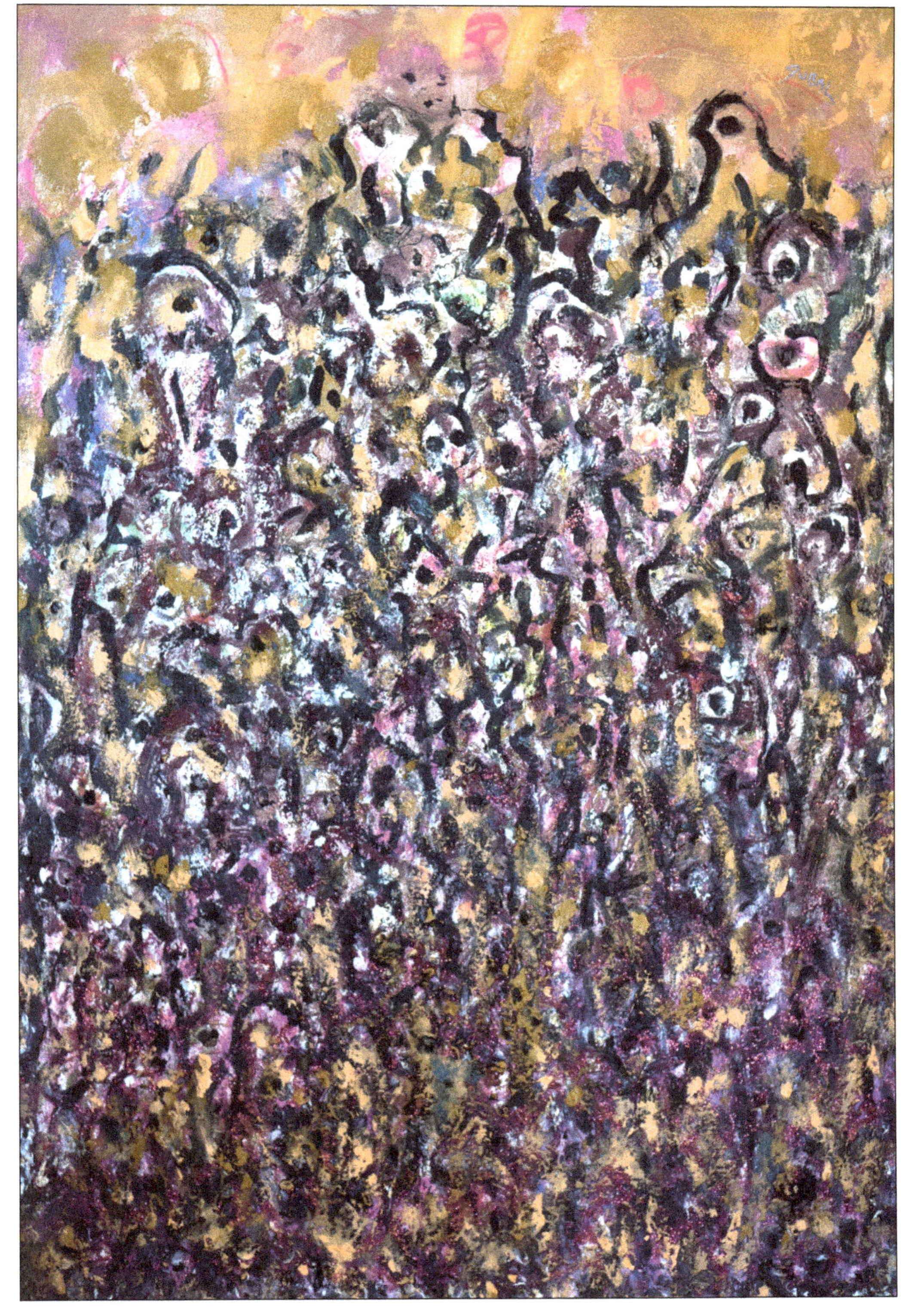

Maze.
11 x 17. Oil on canvas. 1999.

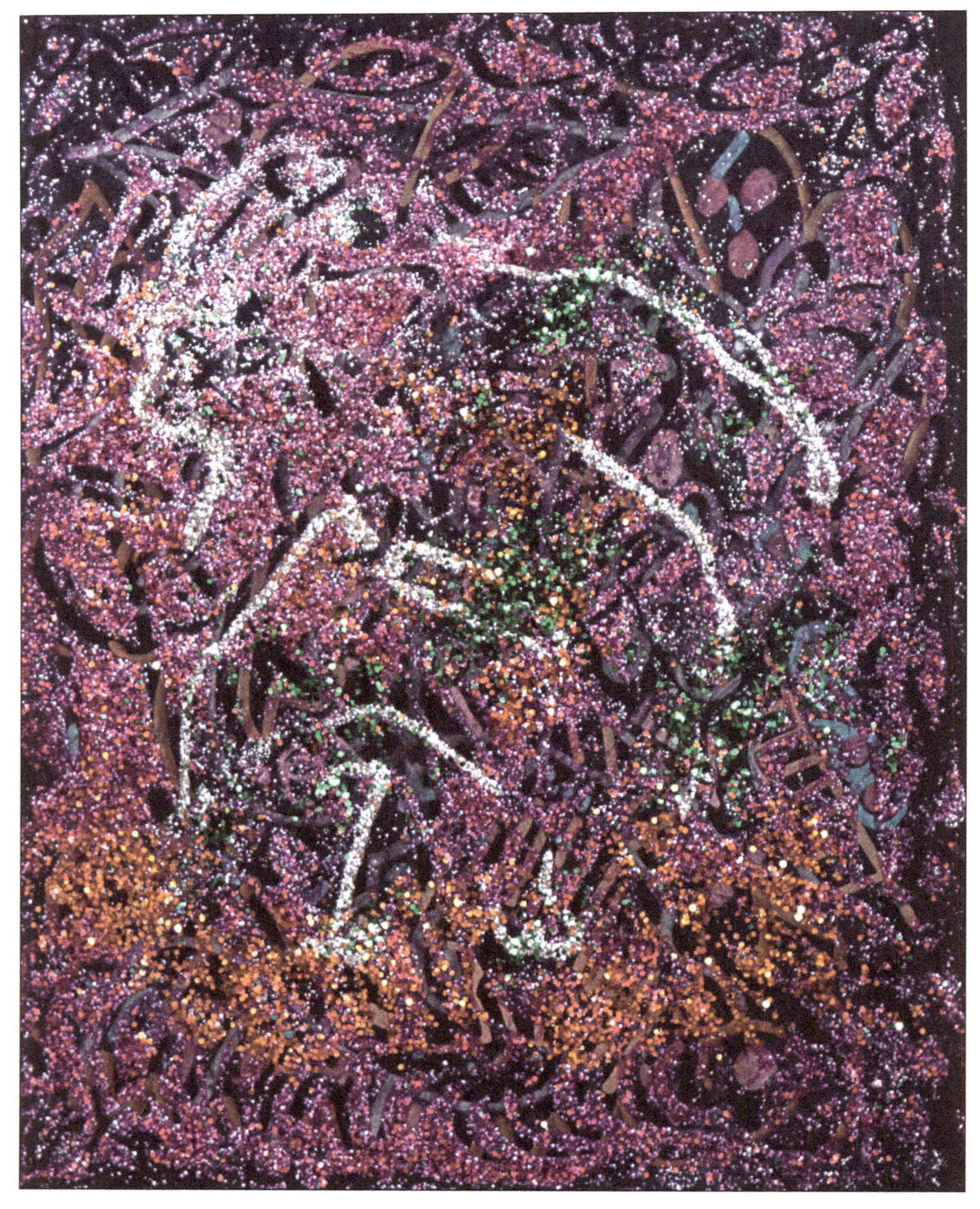

Aires.
11 x 14. Mixed Media. 2014.

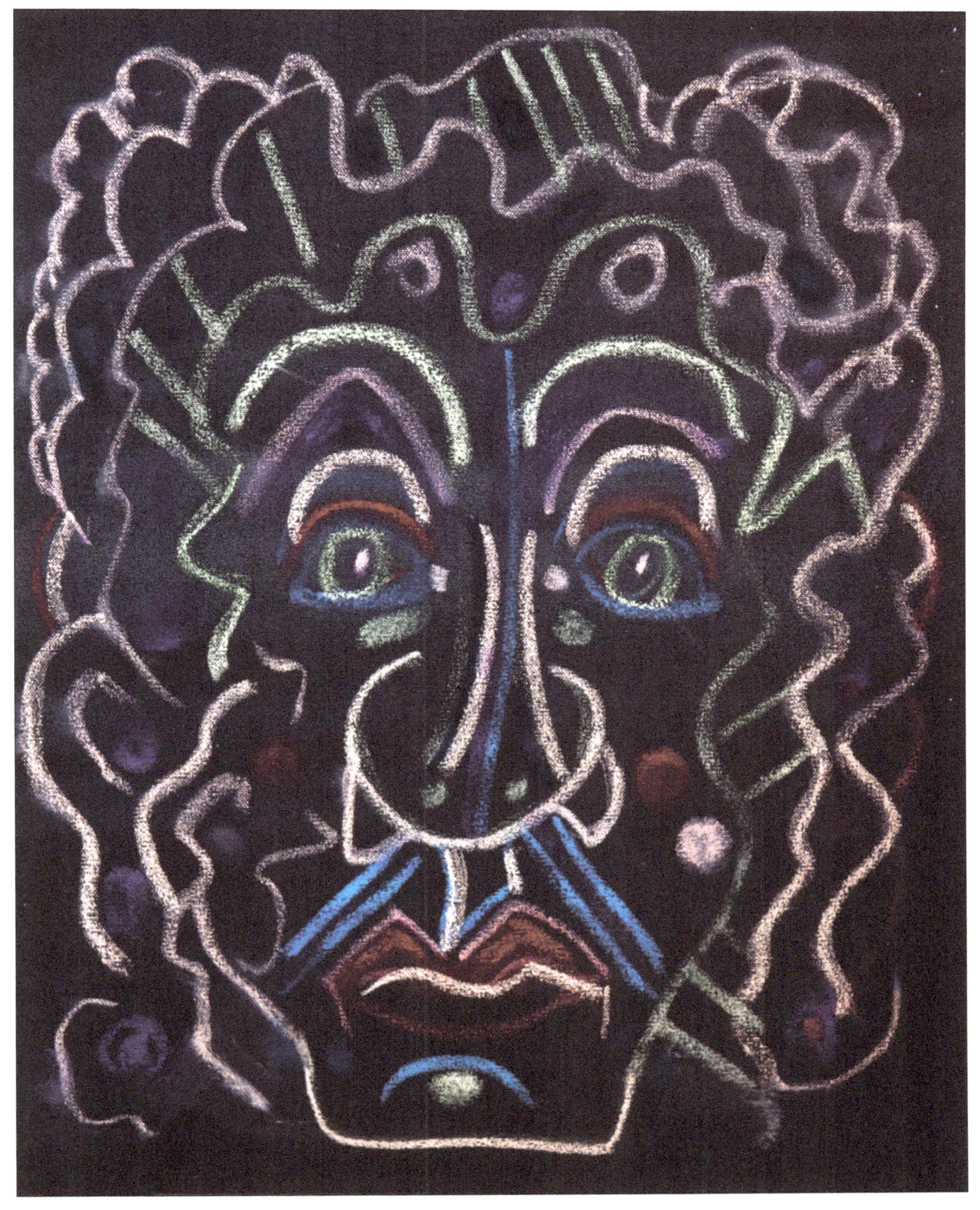

It's All See Through.
20 x 16. Pastel on black canvas. 2014.

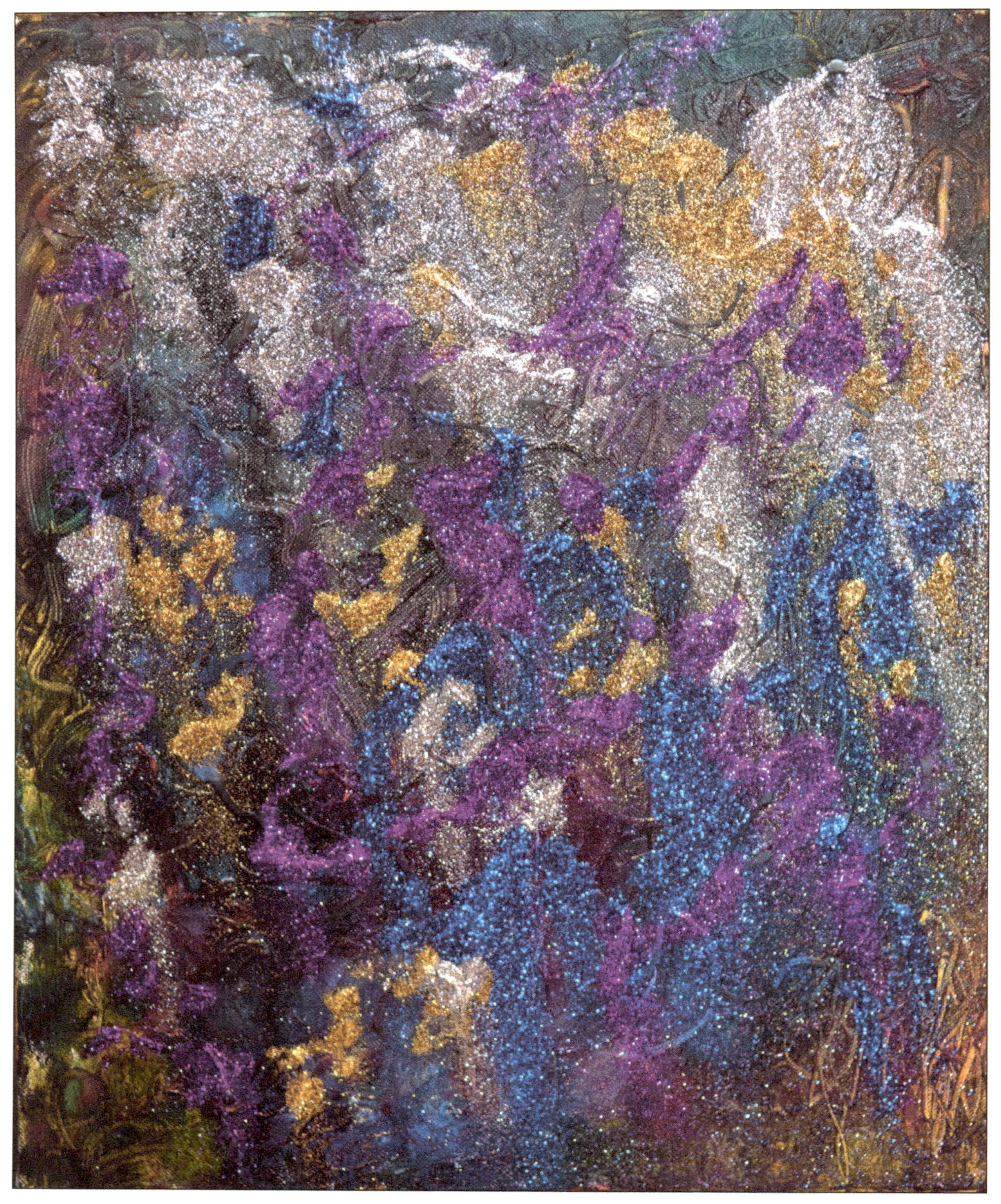

Beautiful Day on Uranus.
15 x 20. Oil, glitter. 2017.

      THE PAINTINGS OF DAVID DUBAL

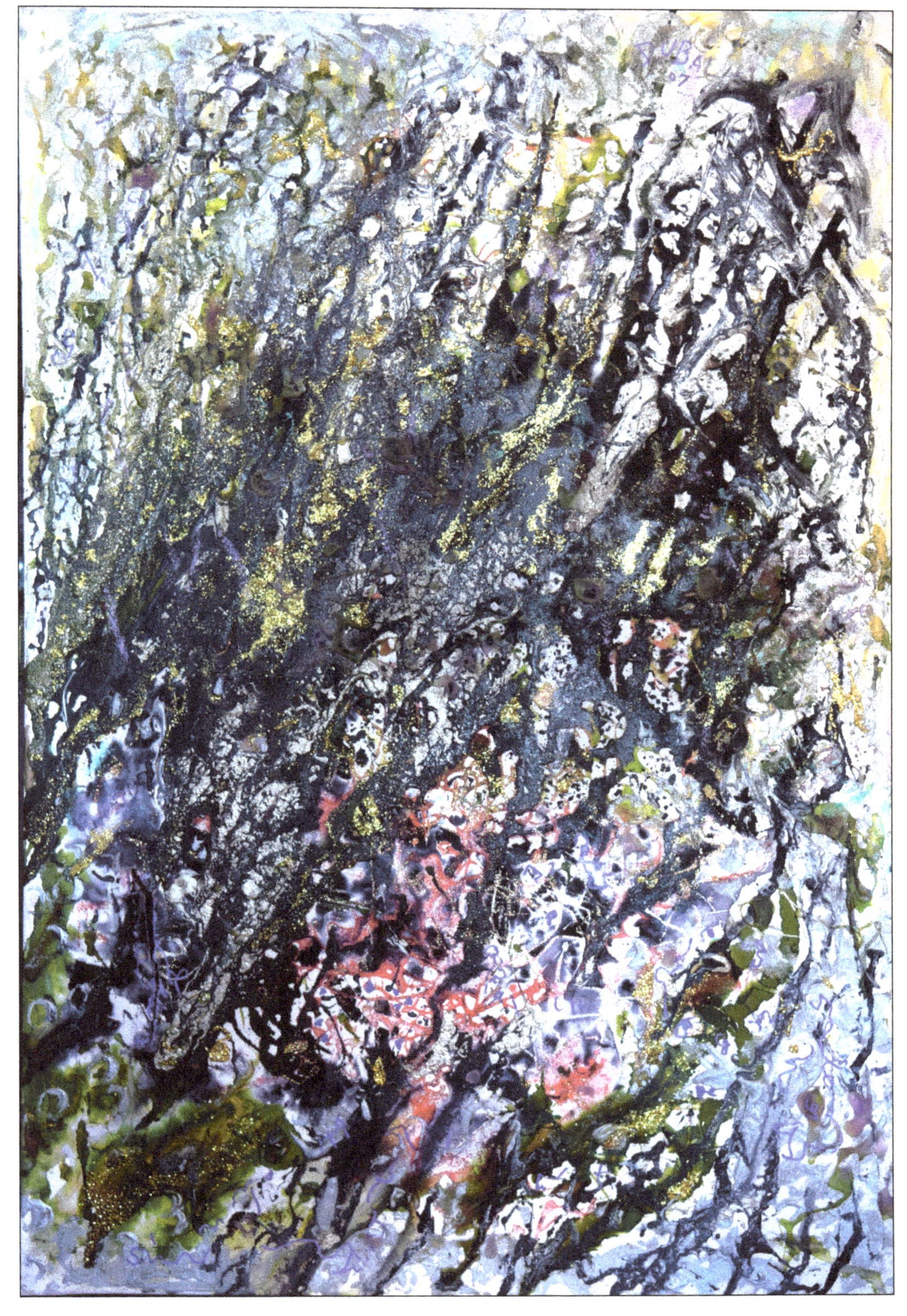

The Deluge.
36 x 24. Oil, glitter on canvas. 2008.

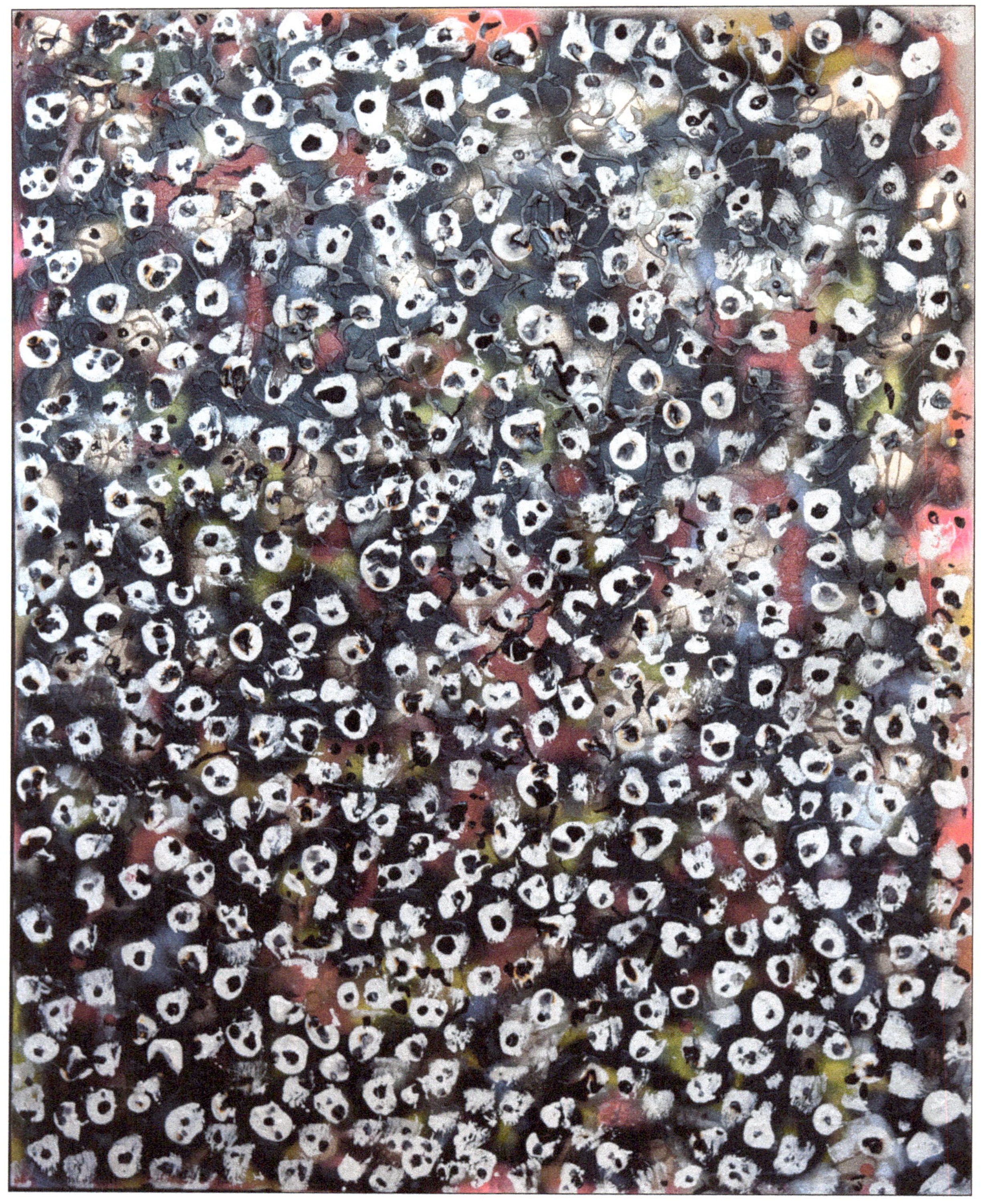

A Million Baby Blossoms.
28 x 20. Oil on Canvas. 2016.

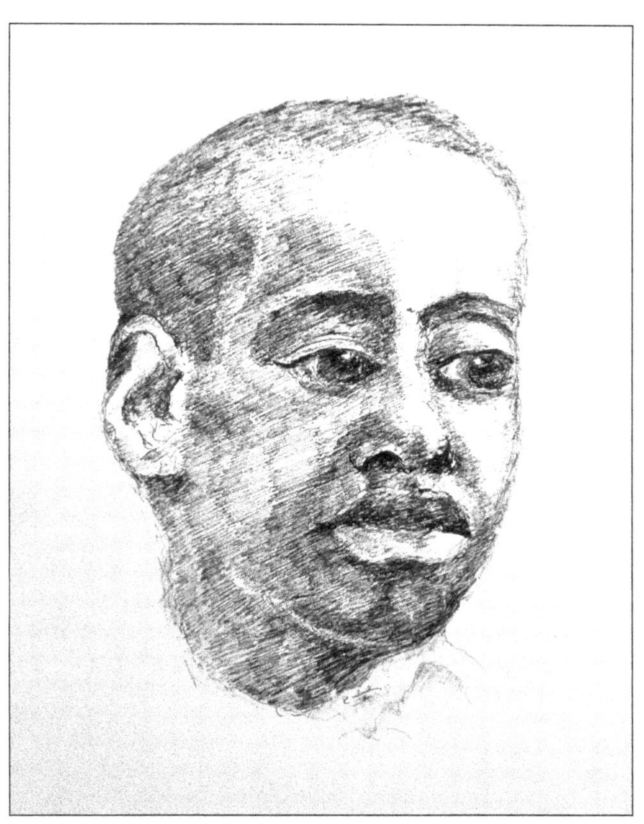

Brother One.
10 x 14. Pencil on paper. 2003.

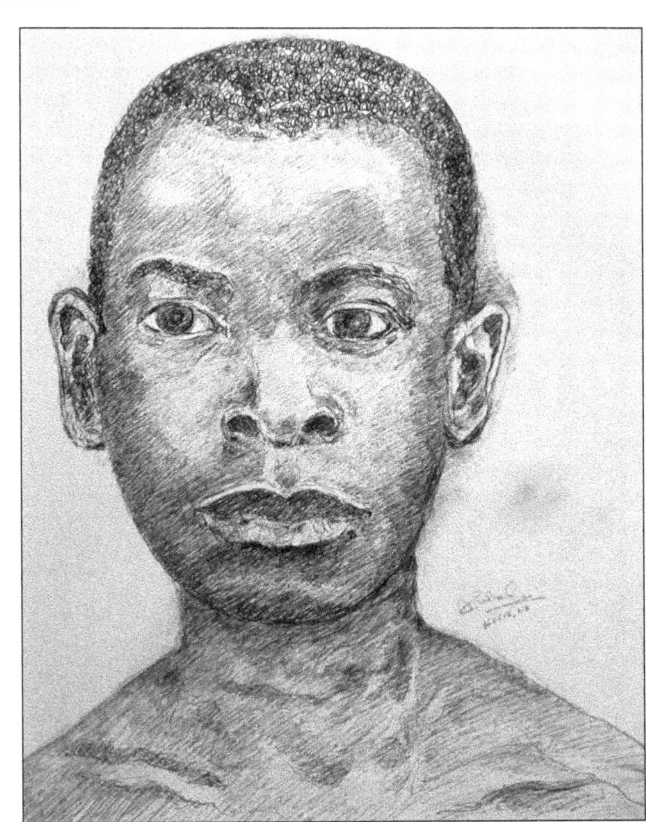

Brother Two.
10 x 14. Pencil on paper. 2003.

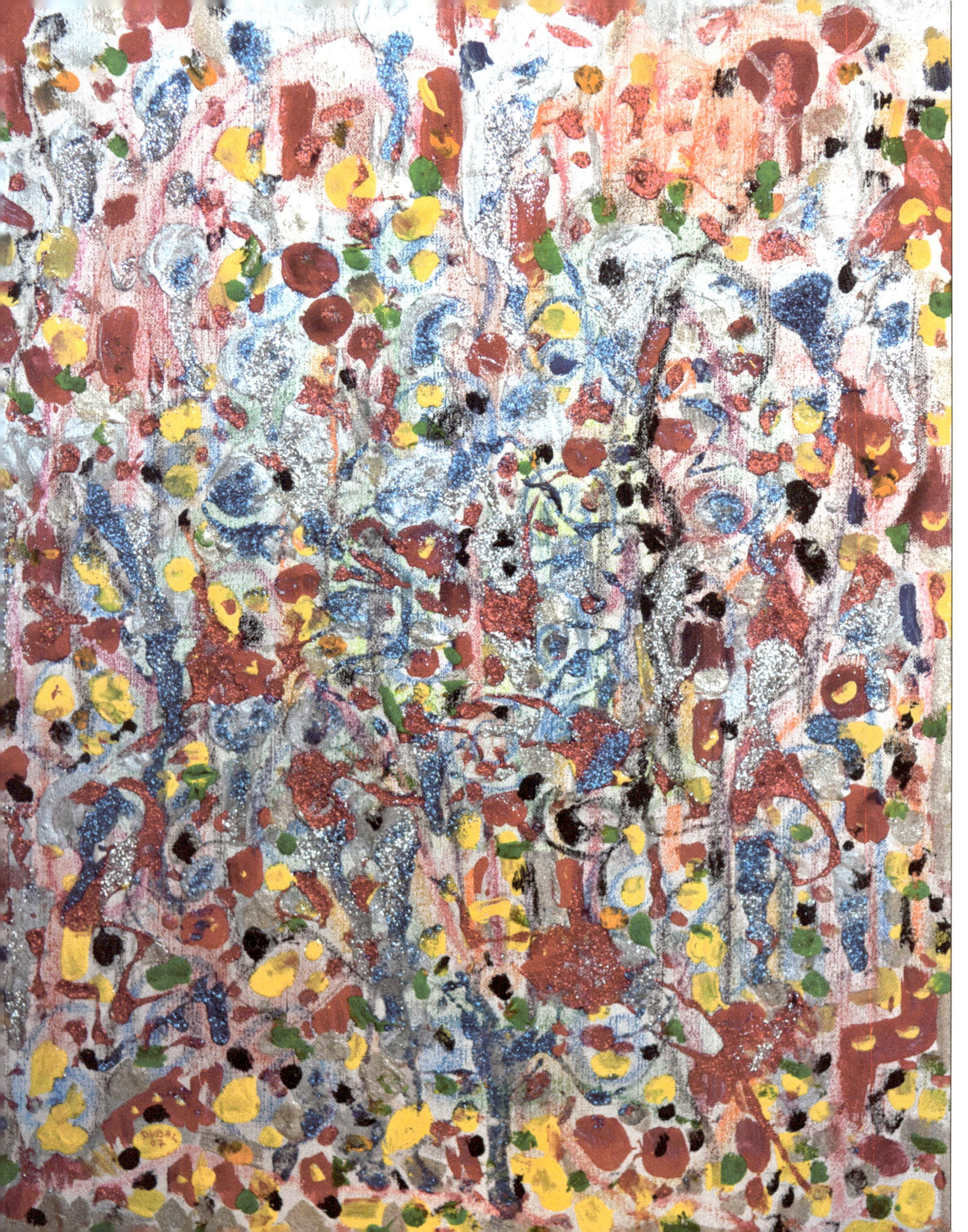

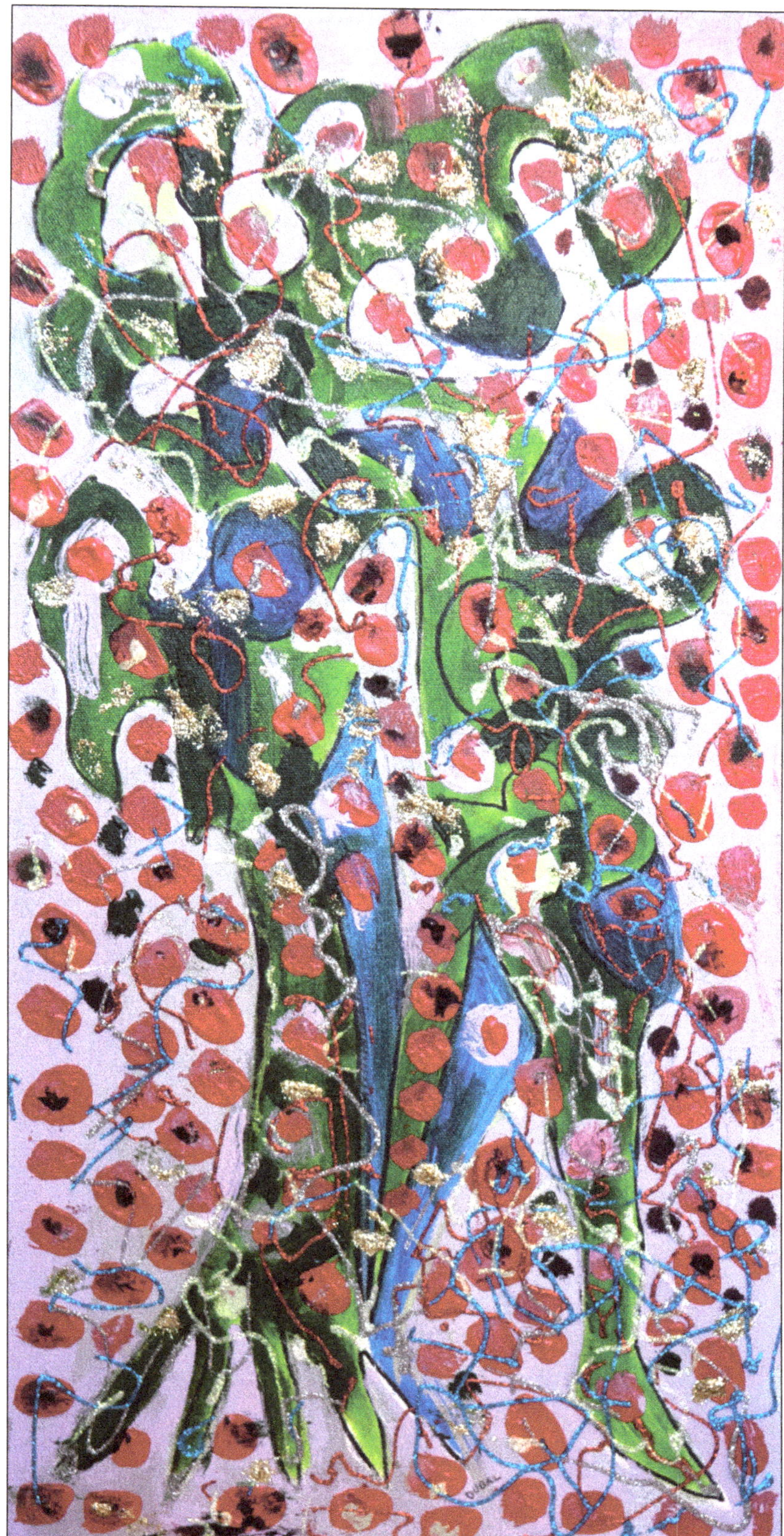

*The Jeweled Insect
Eating Cherries.*
24 x 12. Oil on Canvas.
2014.

(OPPOSITE)

Summer Garden.
25 x 17. Oil on canvas.
2007.

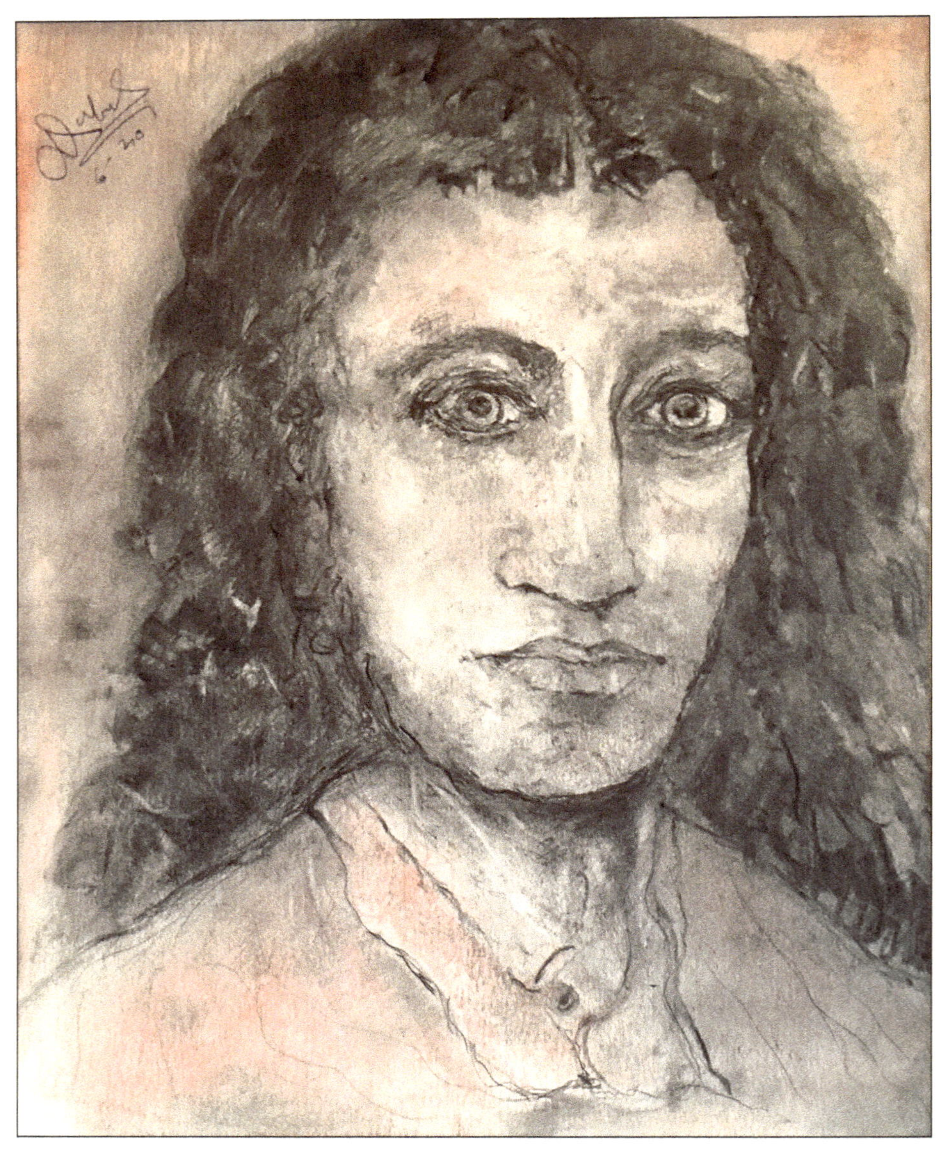

The Florentine Man.
11 x 14. Mixed media. 2020.

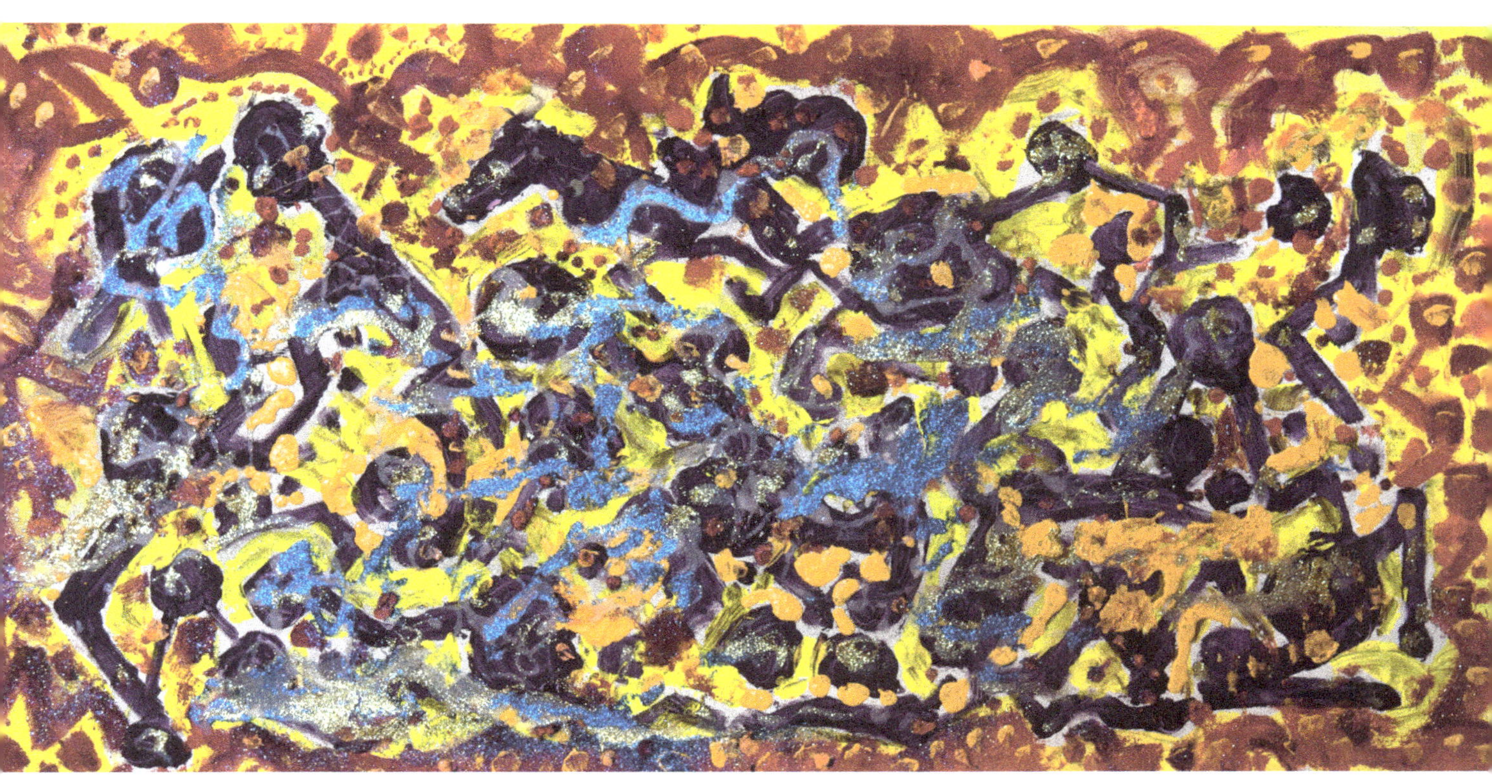

Battle on Horses, 45 BC.
18 x 36. Mixed media on canvas. 2013.

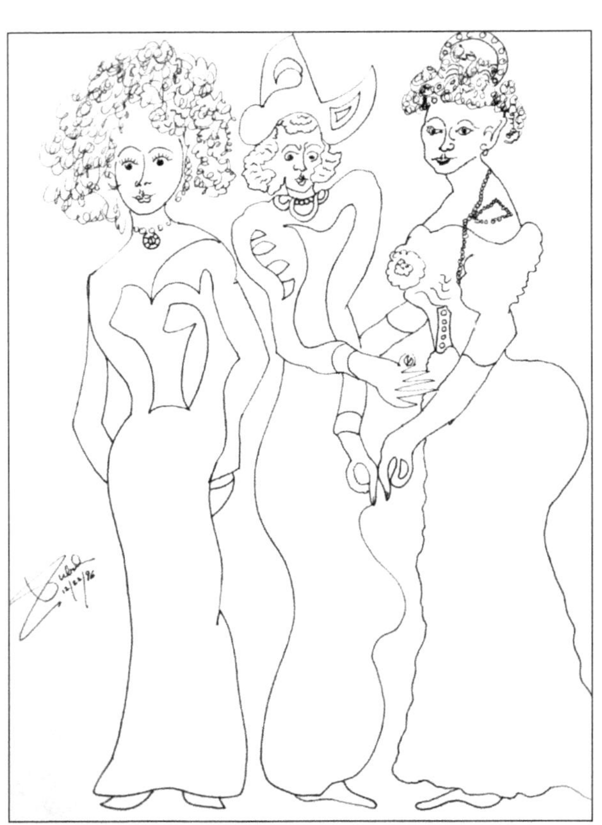

Three Terrific Women.
11 x 14. Pen and ink. 1991.

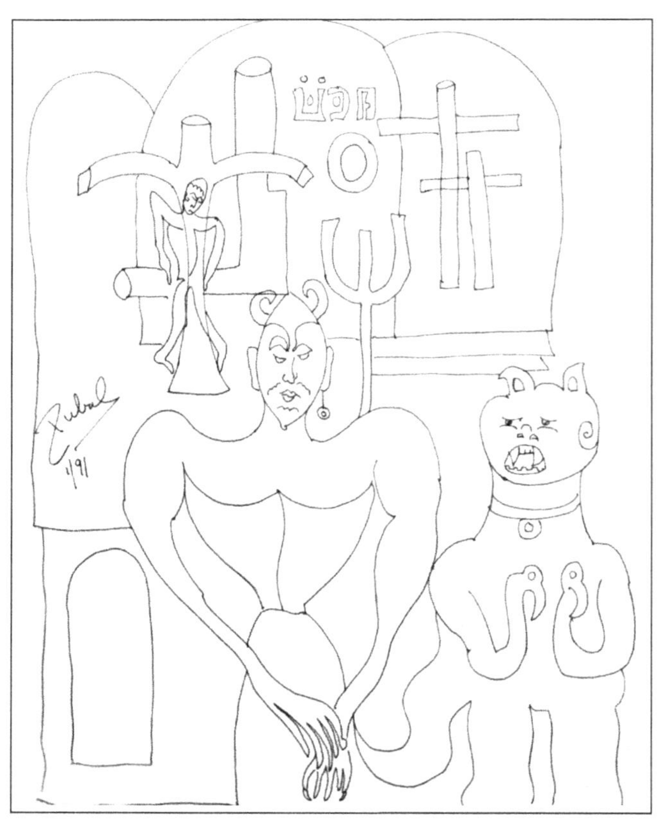

Devil and Crucifixion.
11 x 14. Pen and ink. 1991.

THE PAINTINGS OF DAVID DUBAL

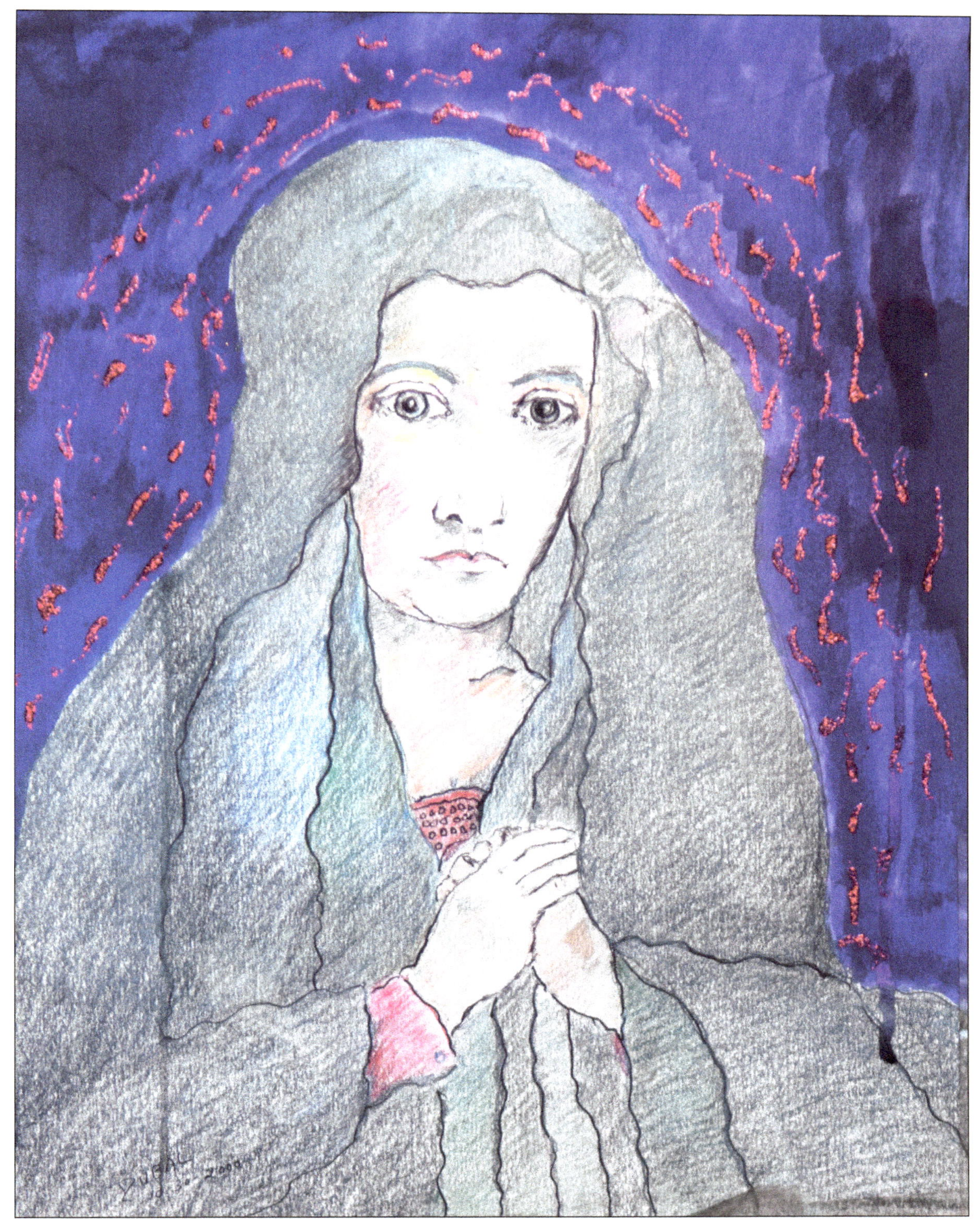

Madonna with Aura.
11 x 14. Colored pencils and red glitter. 1991.

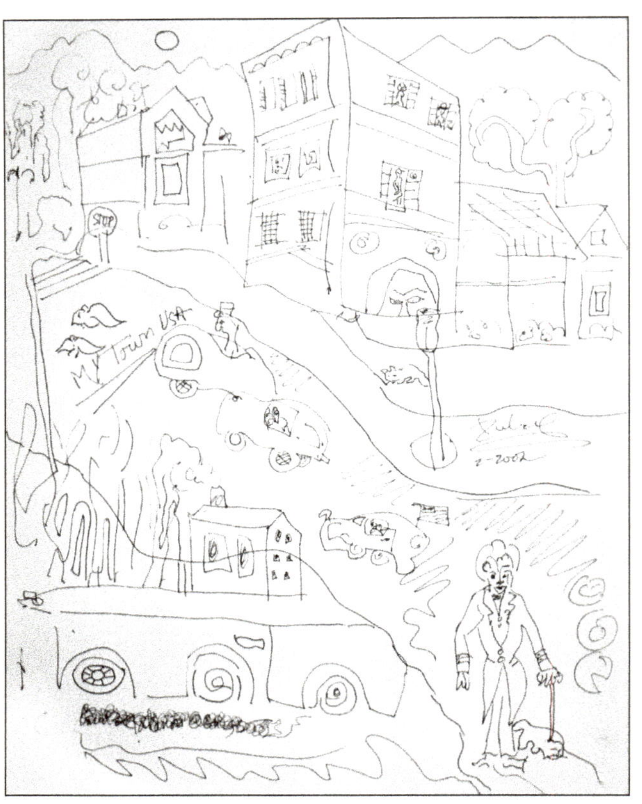

My Town.
11 x 14. Pen and ink on paper. 2002.

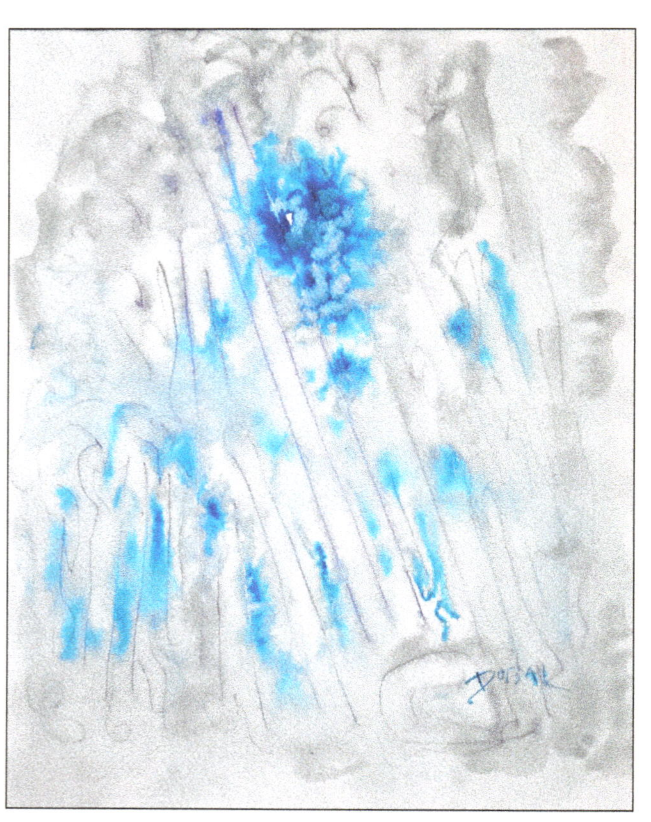

Angled Trees.
11 x 14. Watercolors. 2004.

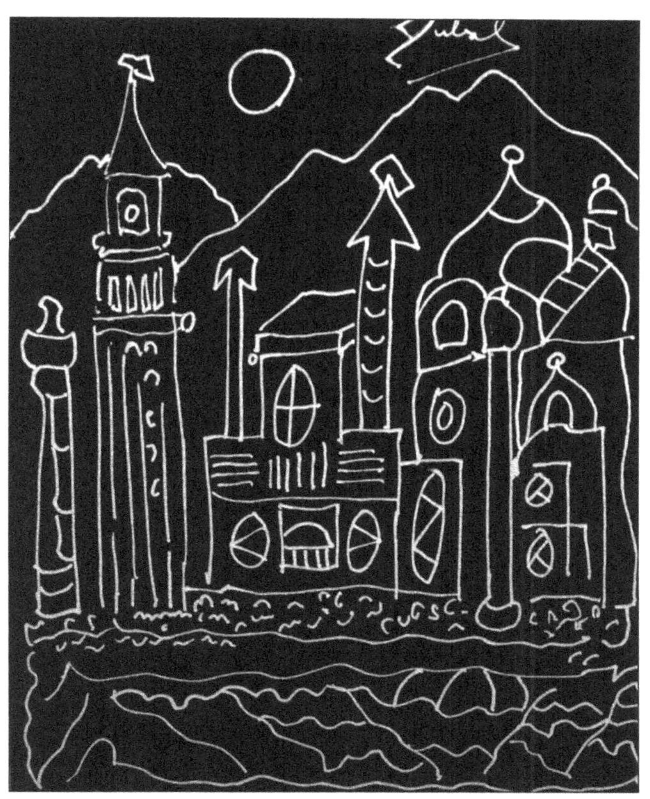

Moon, Mountain, and Town.
8 x 10. Silver ink on black board.
2010.

Quite a Fellow with Dog.
8 x 10. Silver ink on black board.
2010.

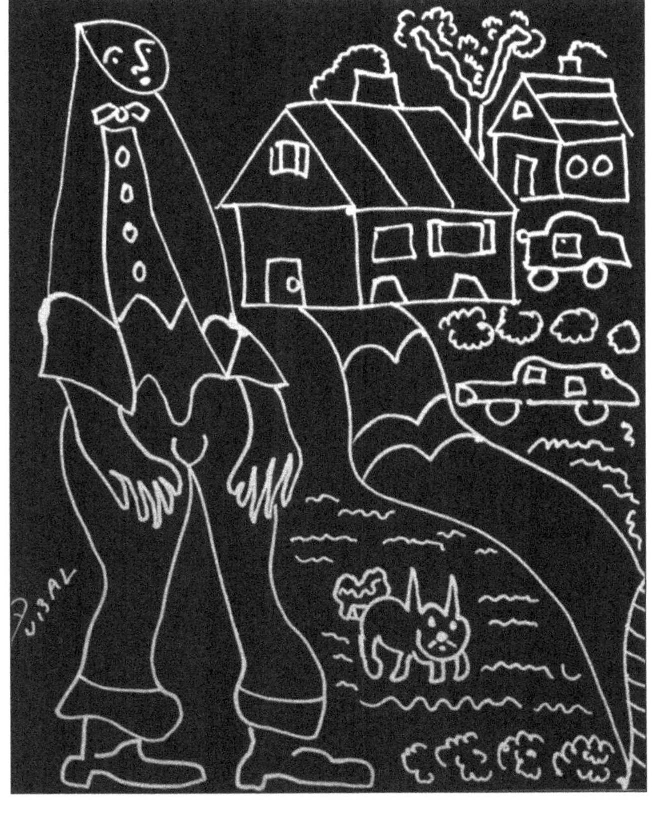

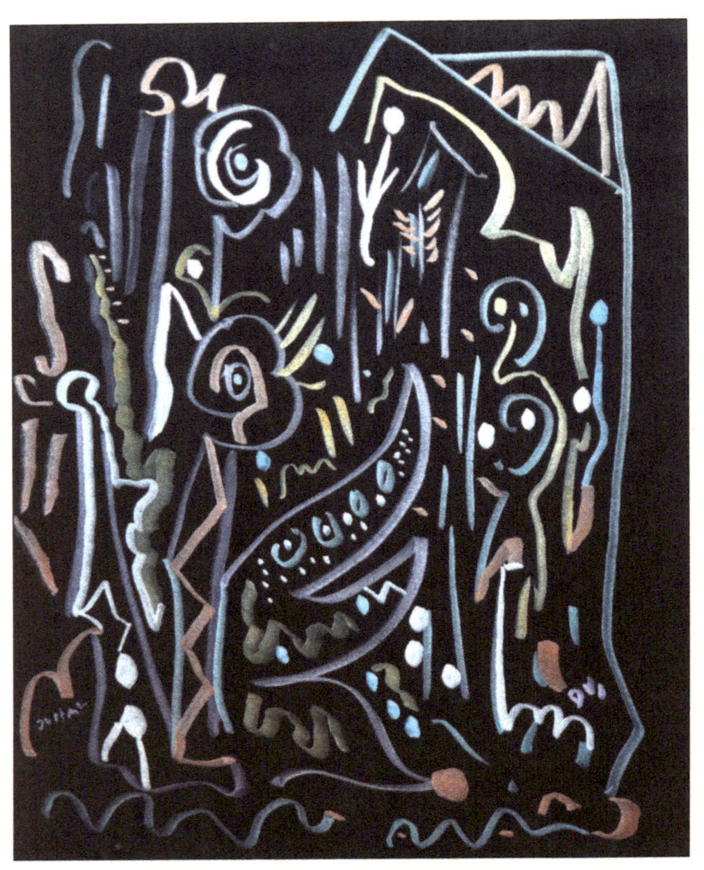

Plant Life on Pluto.
8 x 10. Pastel on black board.
2009.

Which Greek War.
8 x 10. Silver ink on
black board. 2009.

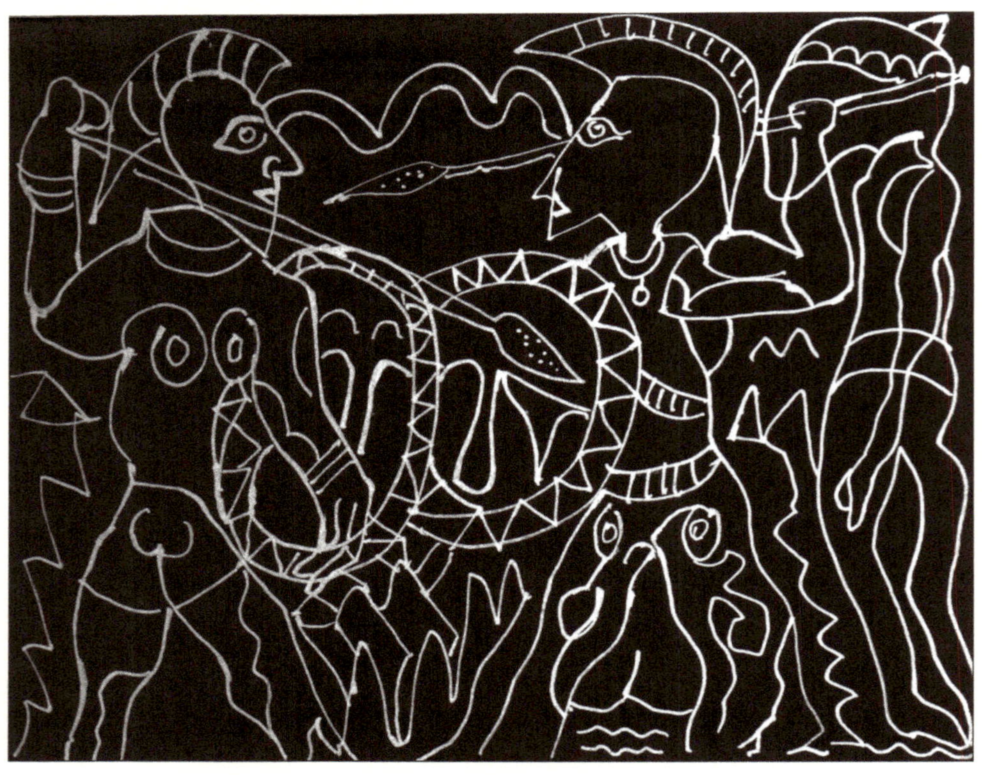

THE PAINTINGS OF DAVID DUBAL

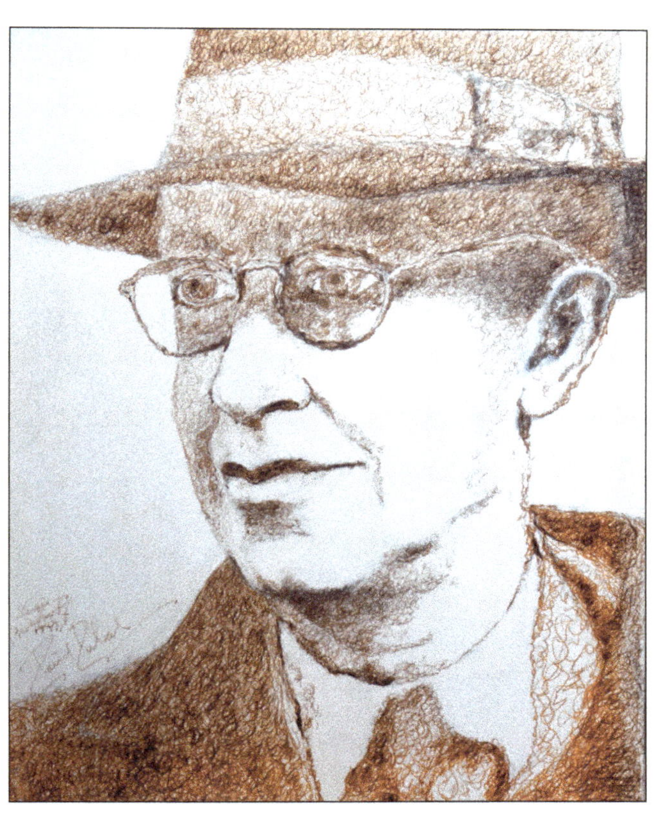

Prokofiev after Photo.
11 x 14. Brown ink on paper.
1989.

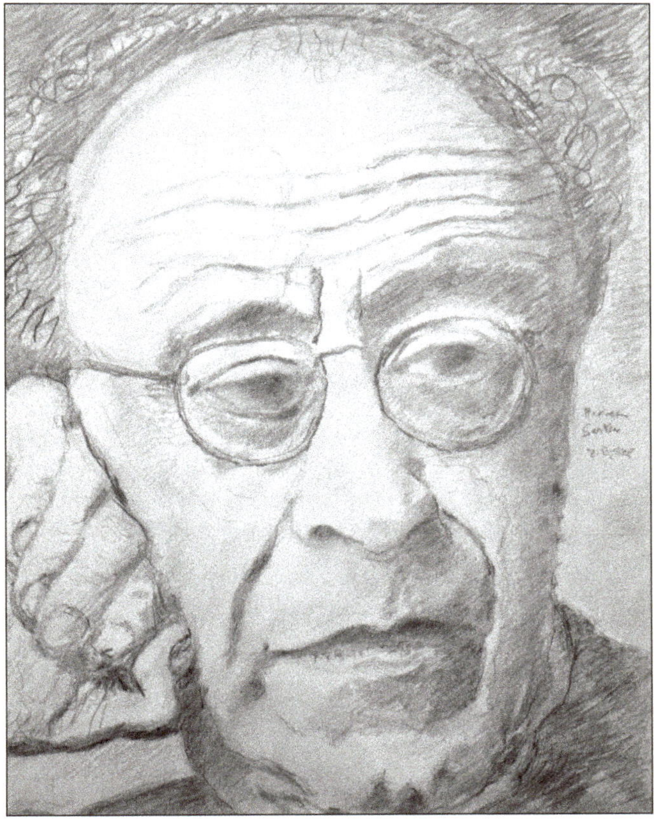

Rudolf Serkin after Photo.
11 x 14. Pencil. 2001.

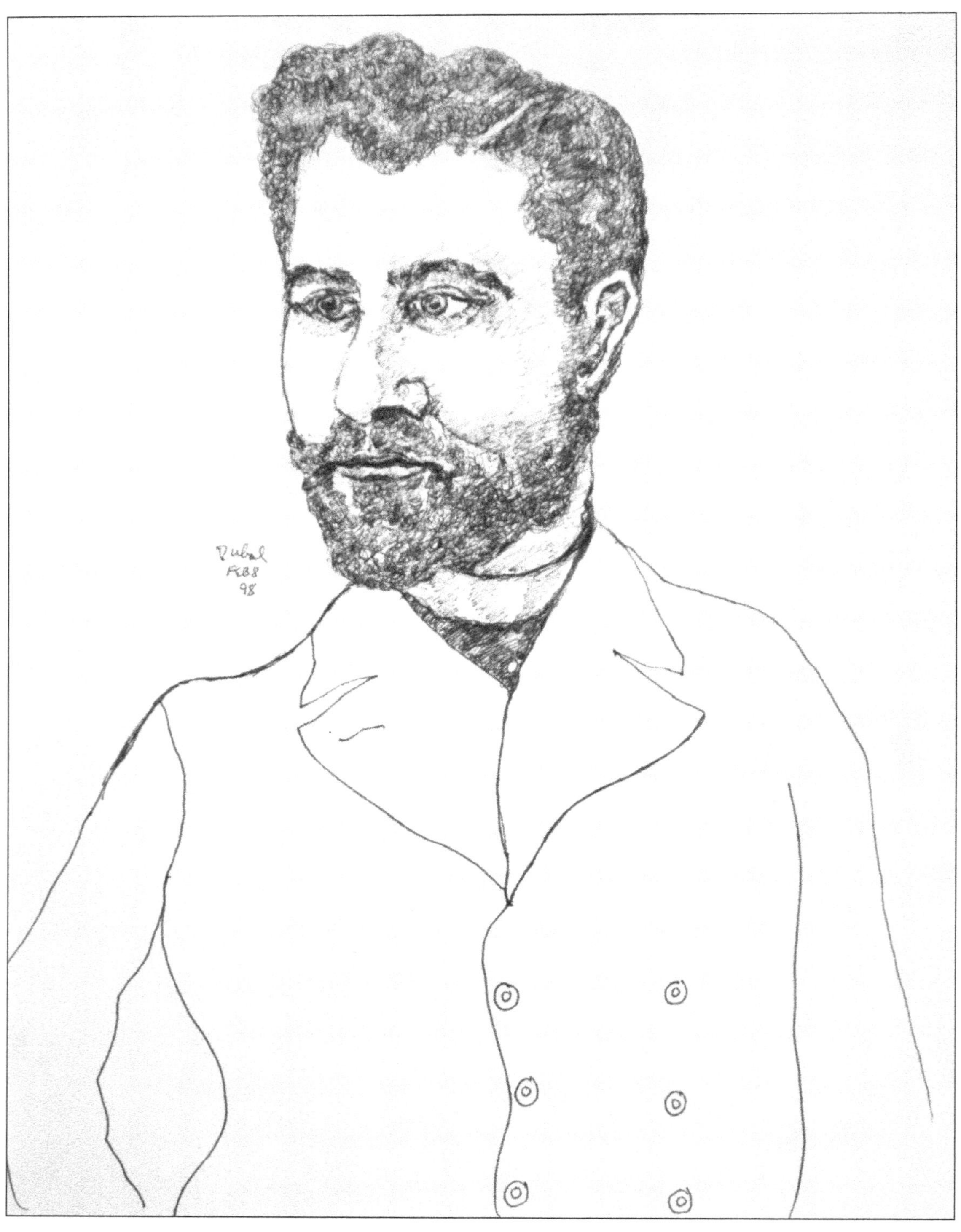

Portrait of a Man.
11 x 14. Pen and ink. 2005.

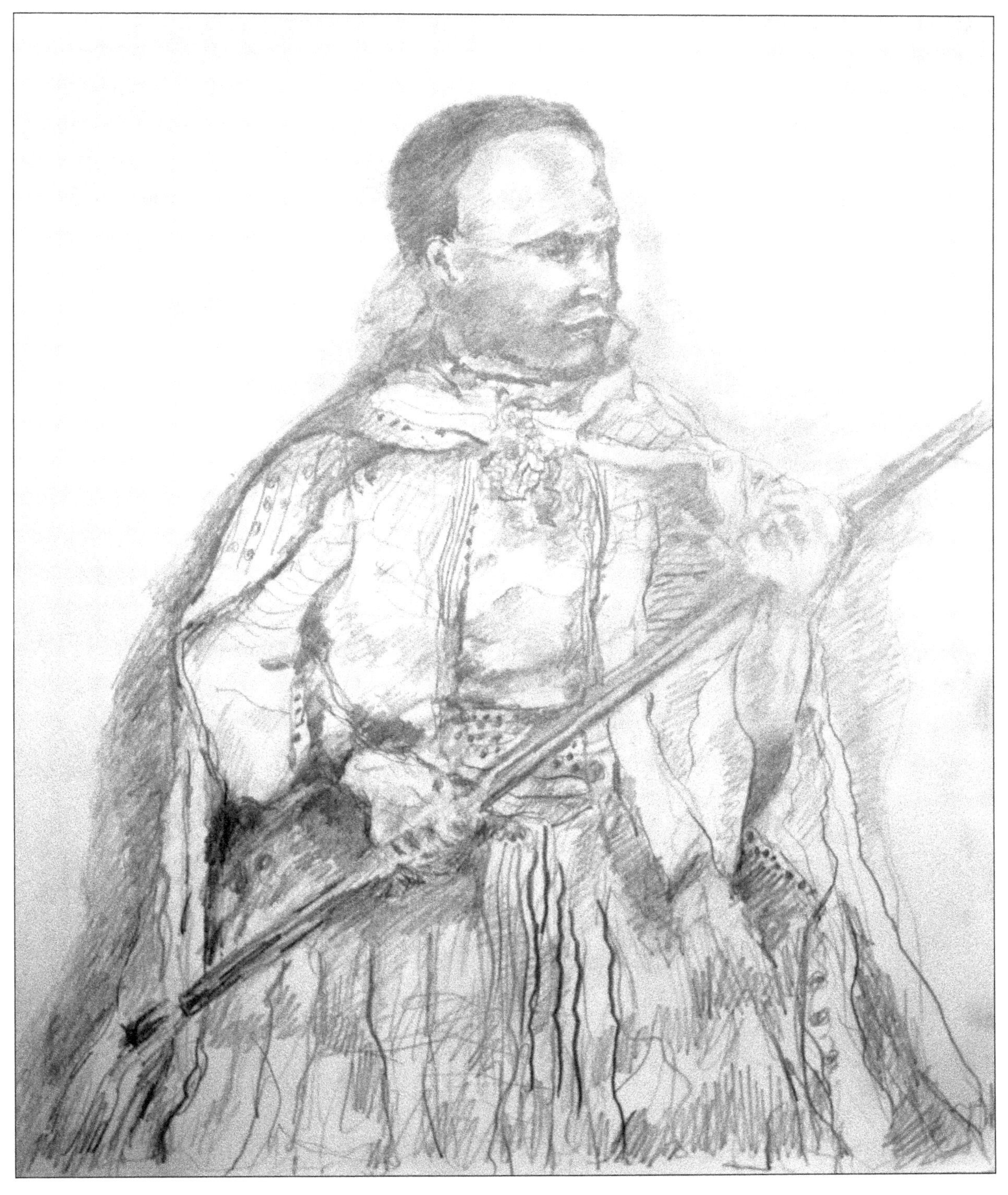

Warrior with Lance after Géricault.
14 x 17. Pencil on paper. 2005.

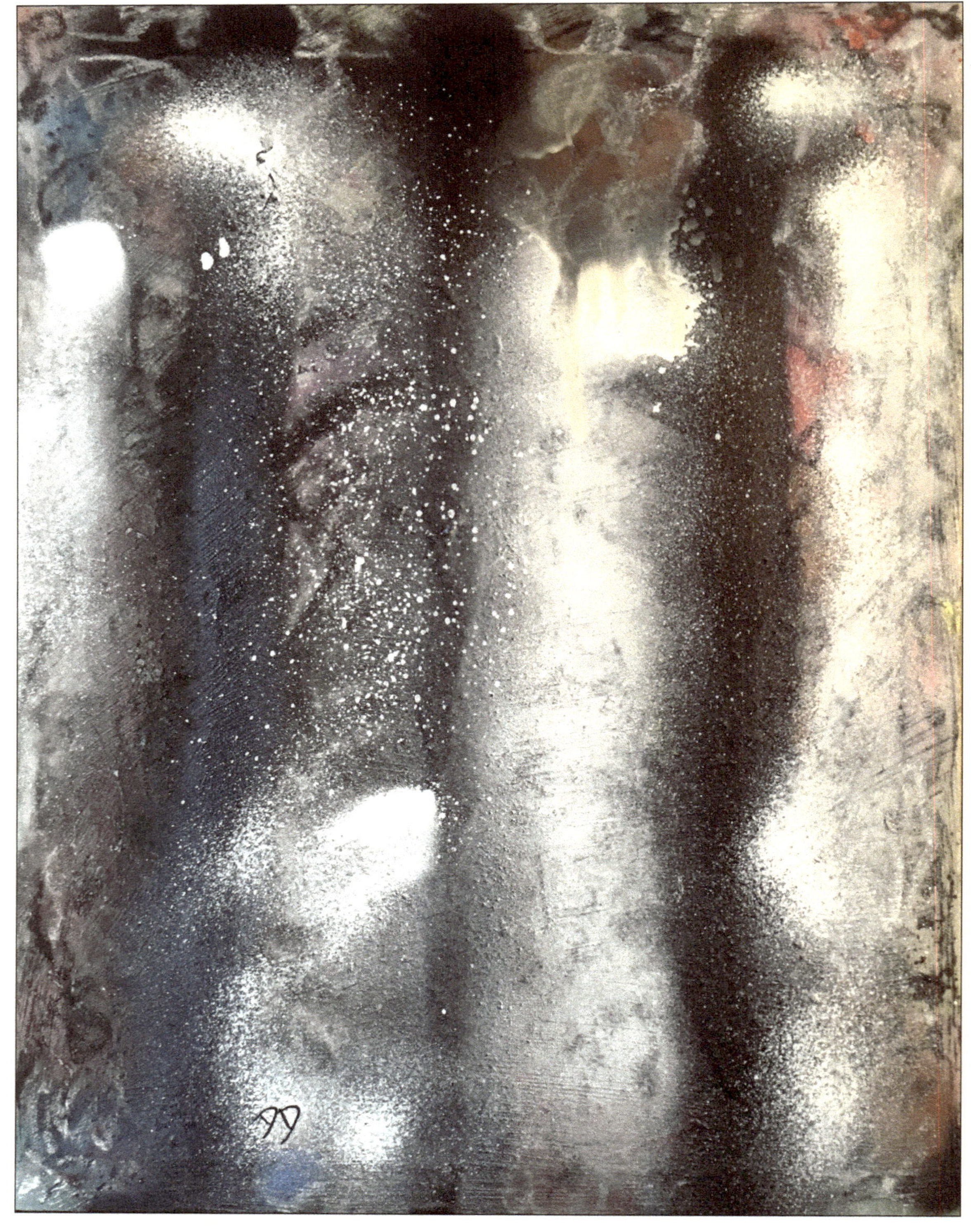

Hazy Elephant Dream.
16 x 12. Spray paint on canvas. 2017.

     THE PAINTINGS OF DAVID DUBAL

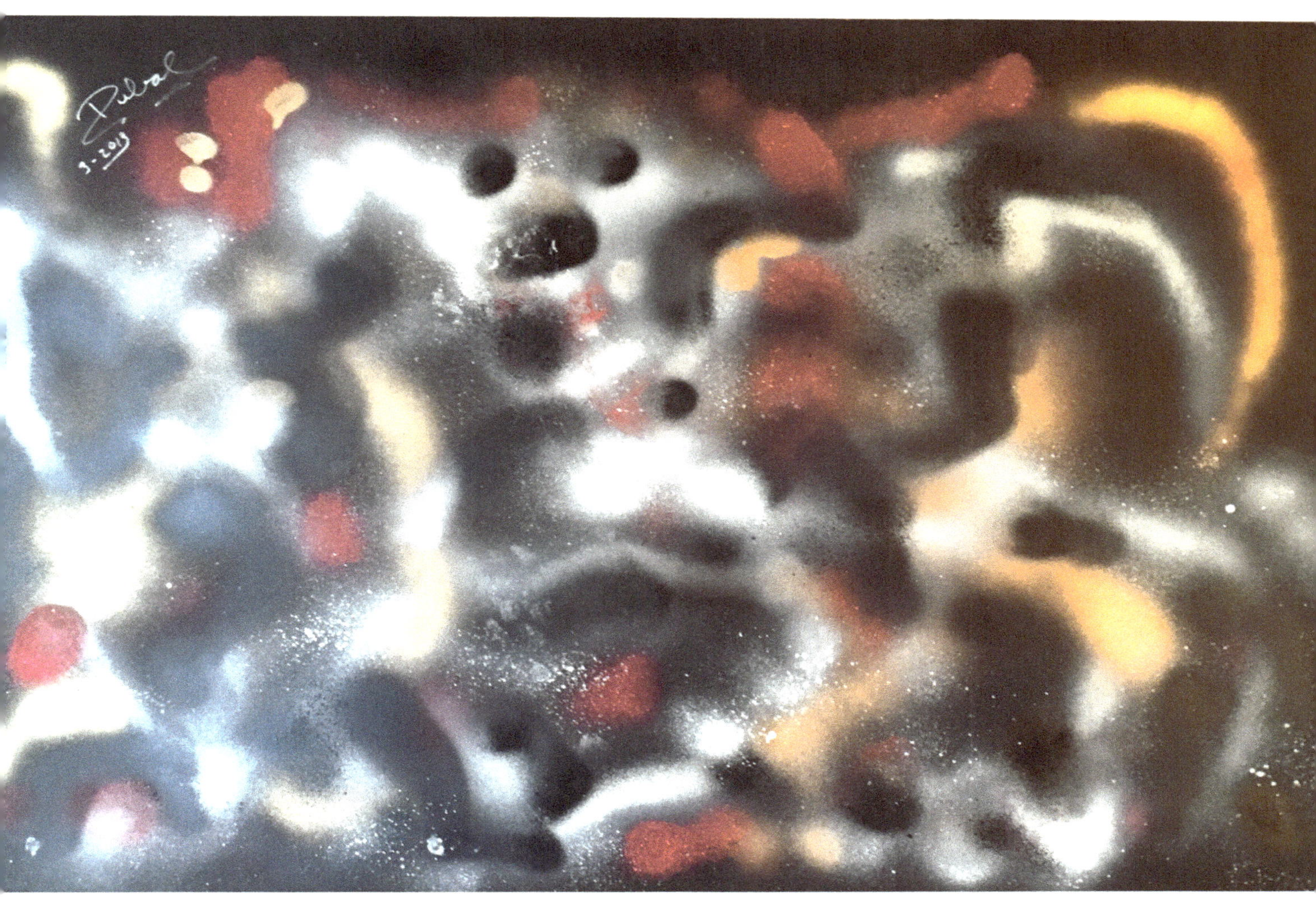

A Display.
20 x 30. Spray paint on black board. 2019.

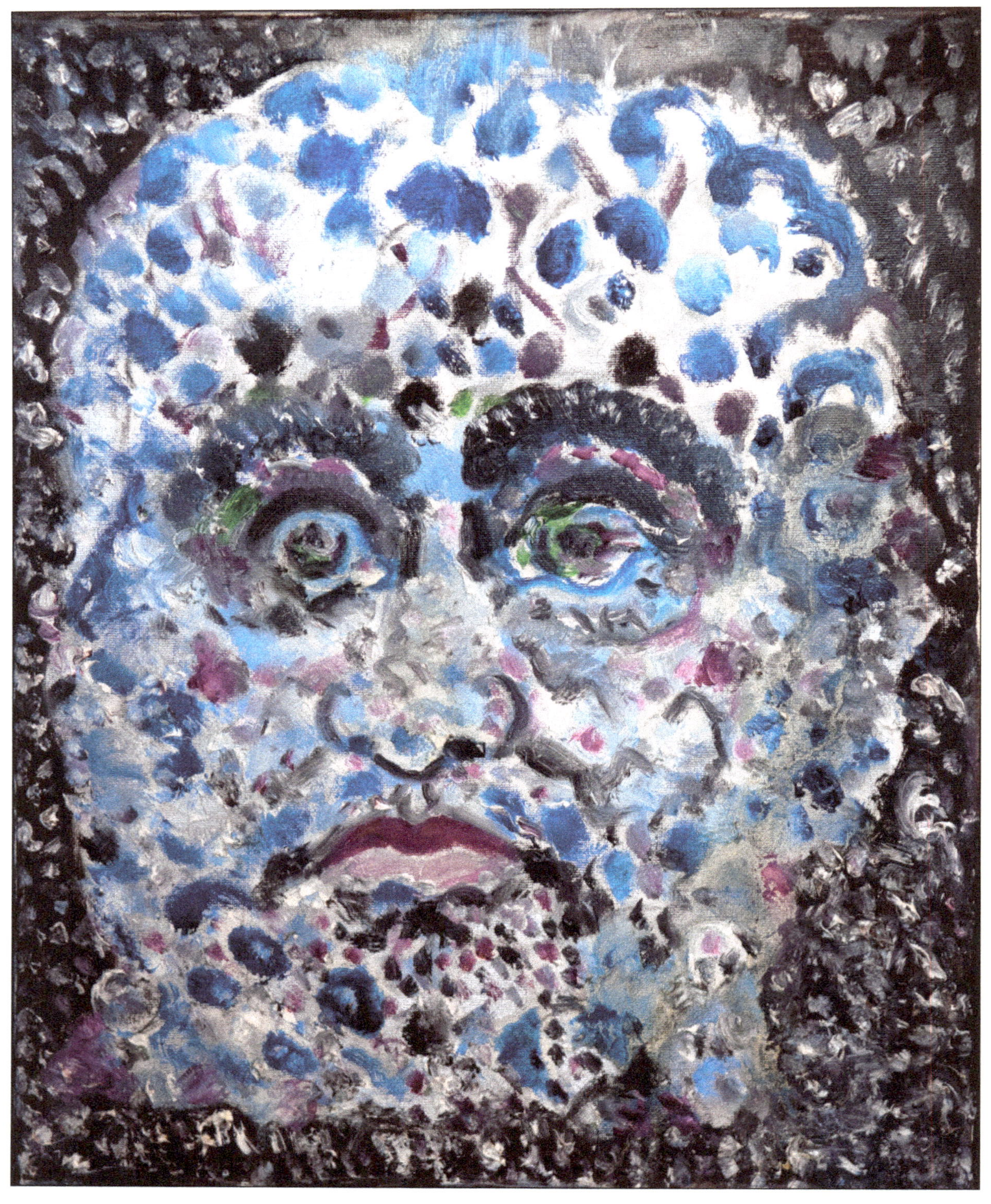

Quite a Face.
20 x 16. Oil on canvas. 2015.

THE PAINTINGS OF DAVID DUBAL

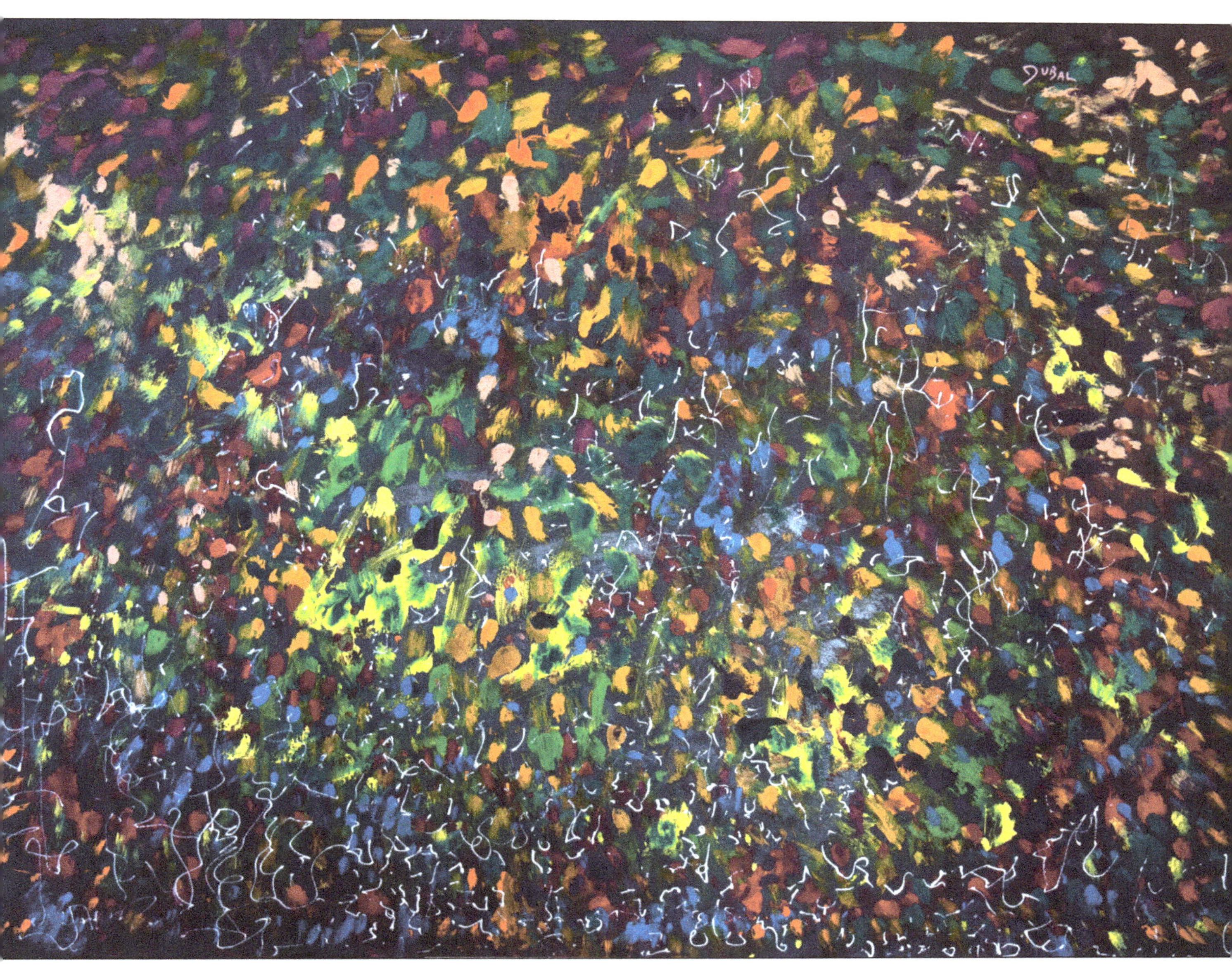

After I Blinked.
29 x 40. Oil on black board. 2008.

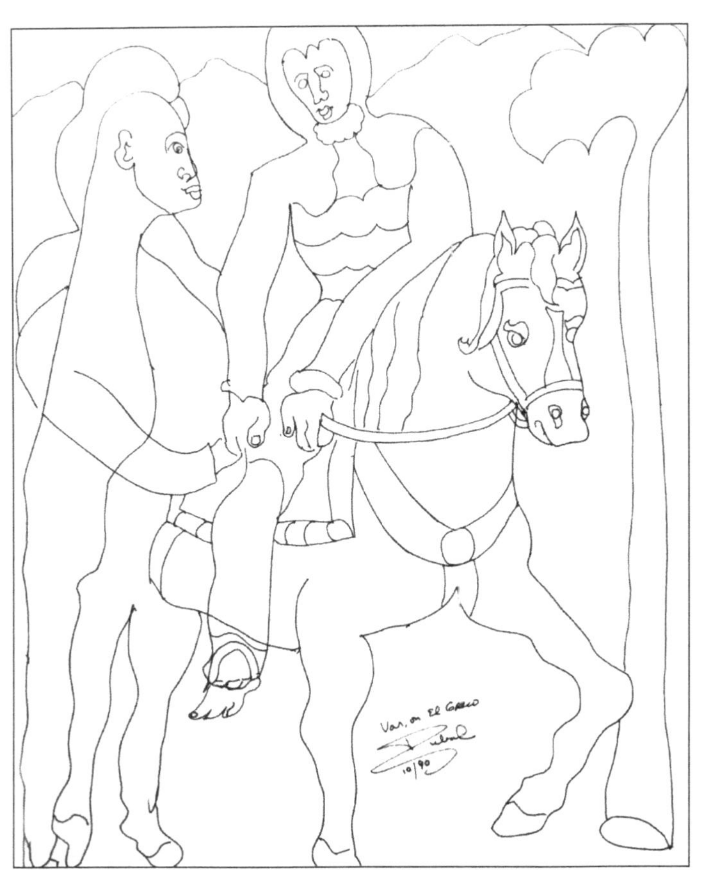

Variation on El Greco.
11 x 14. Pen and ink. 1990.

*The Poor Monkey
with Sabertooth Tiger.*
8 x 10. Silver ink on
black board. 2009.

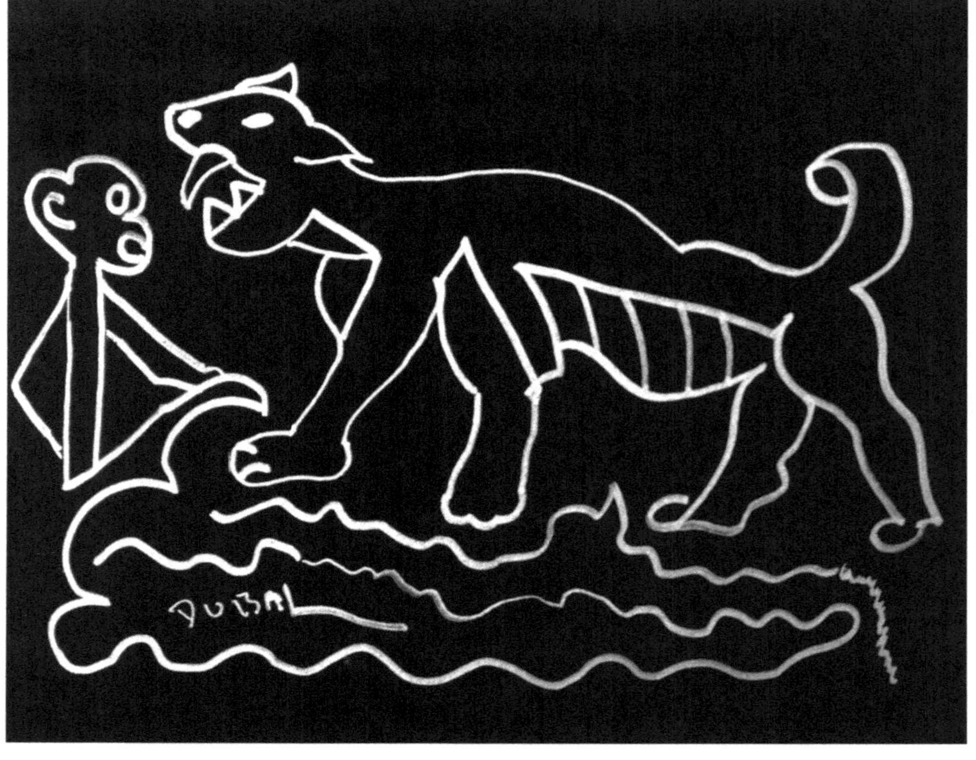

THE PAINTINGS OF DAVID DUBAL

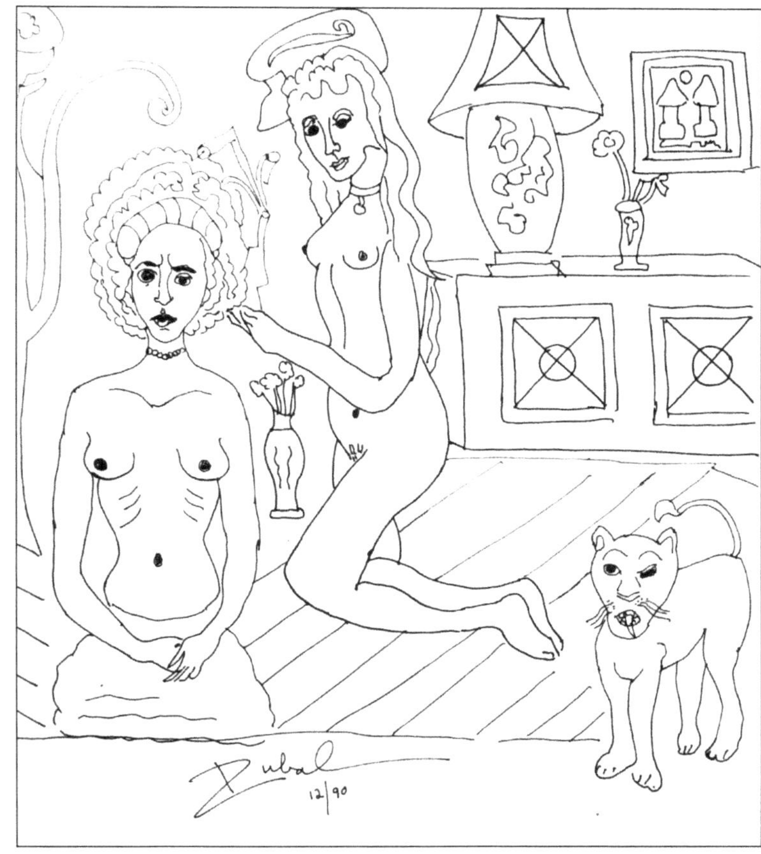

Two Fun Girls on Bed, Small Mountain Lion.
14 x 10. Pen and ink. 1990.

Appassionata: Sonata no. 23.
14 x 17. Pen and ink on paper. 2016.

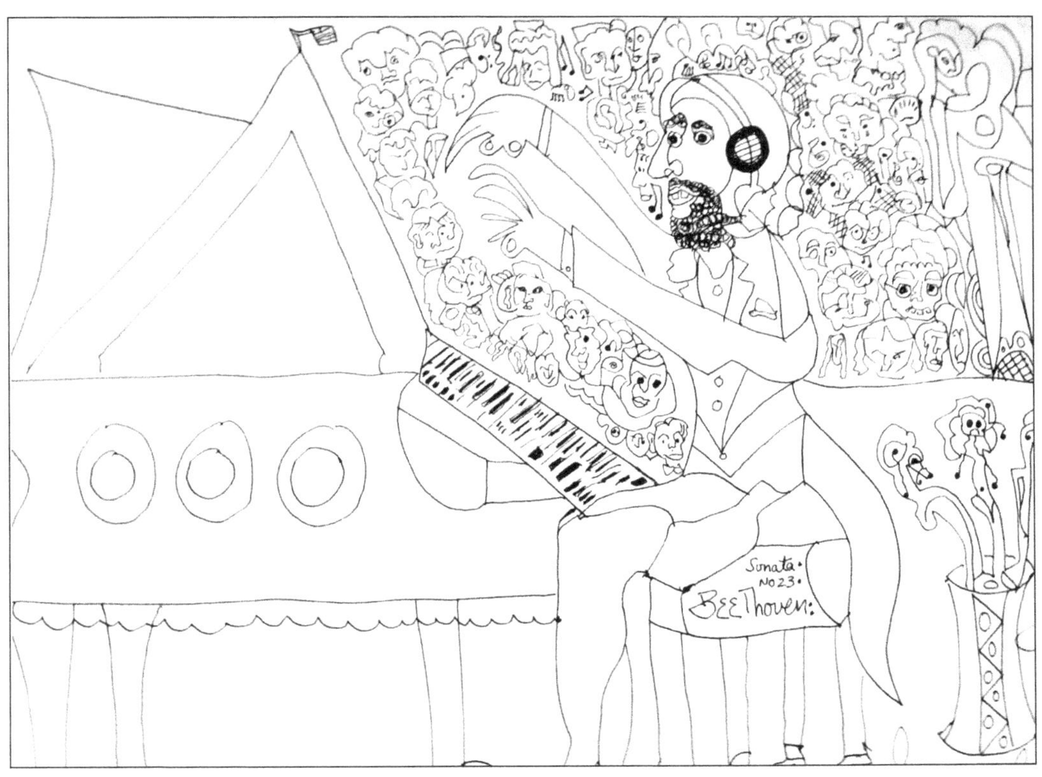

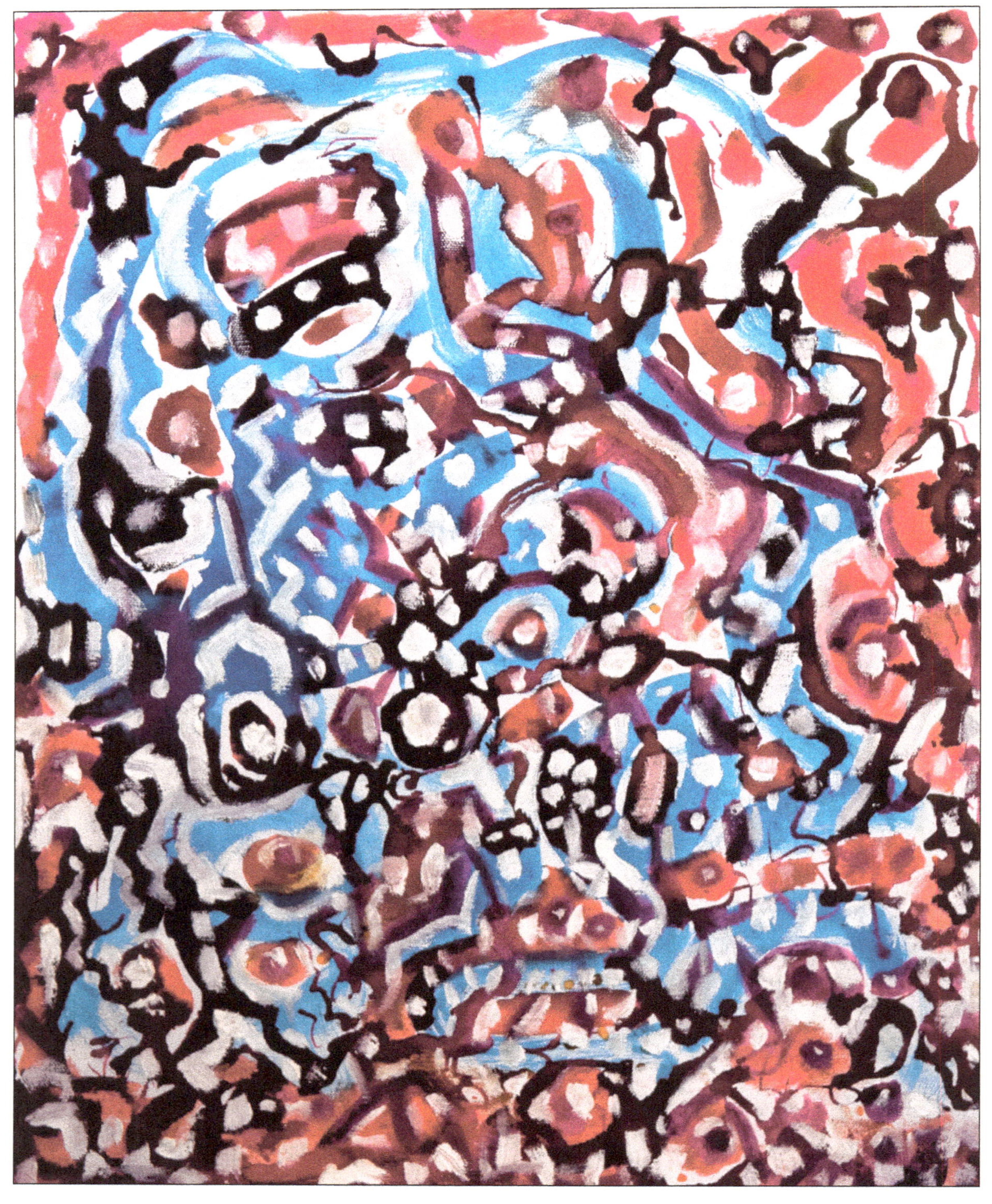

Abstract 30.
23 x 16. Oil on canvas. 2014.

 THE PAINTINGS OF DAVID DUBAL

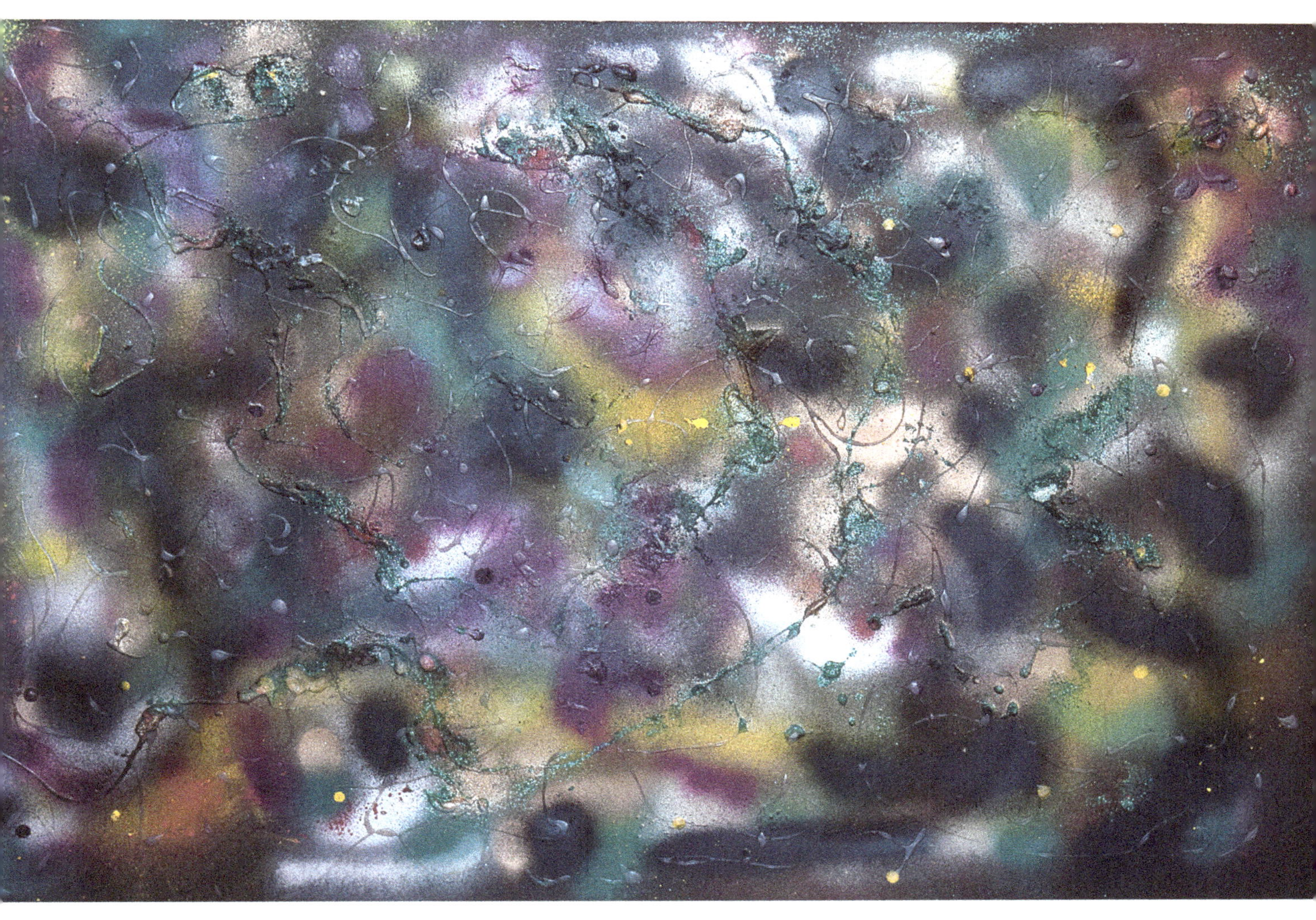

Beautifully Textured.
20 x 30. Mixed Media. 2013.

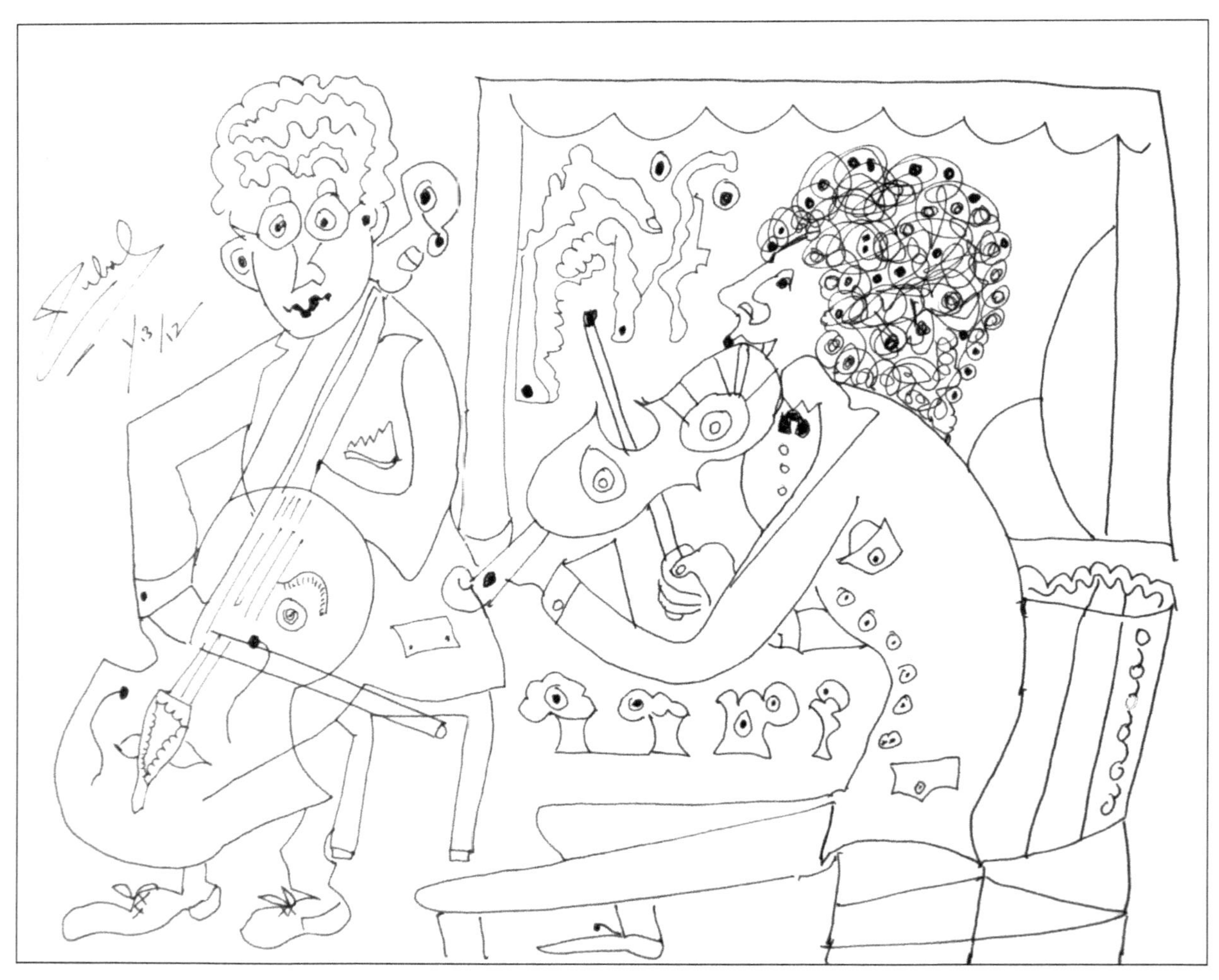

String Duo.
11 x 14. Pen and ink. 2012.

 THE PAINTINGS OF DAVID DUBAL

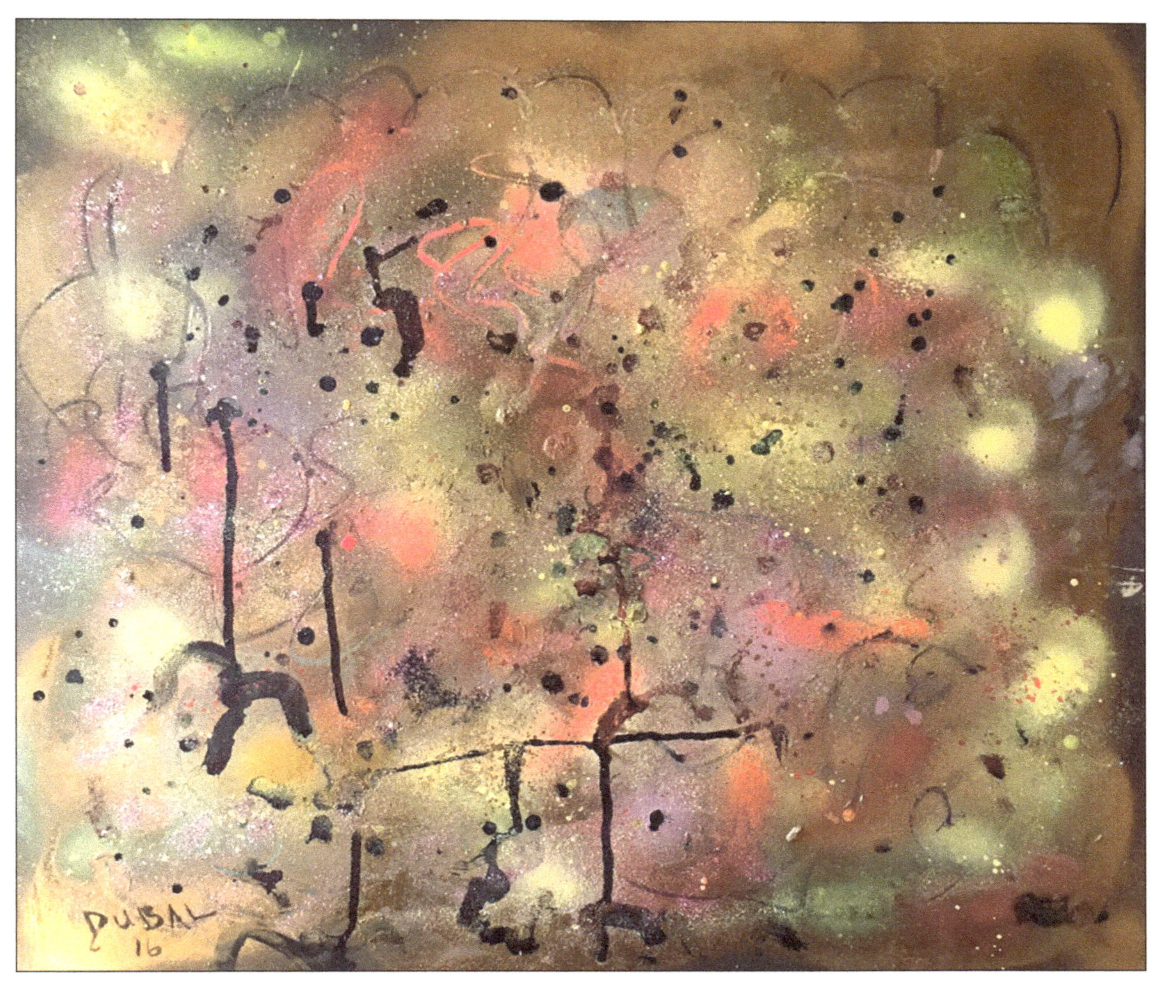

Sadda Ratta Dumpling.
16 x 18. Mixed media on board. 2016.

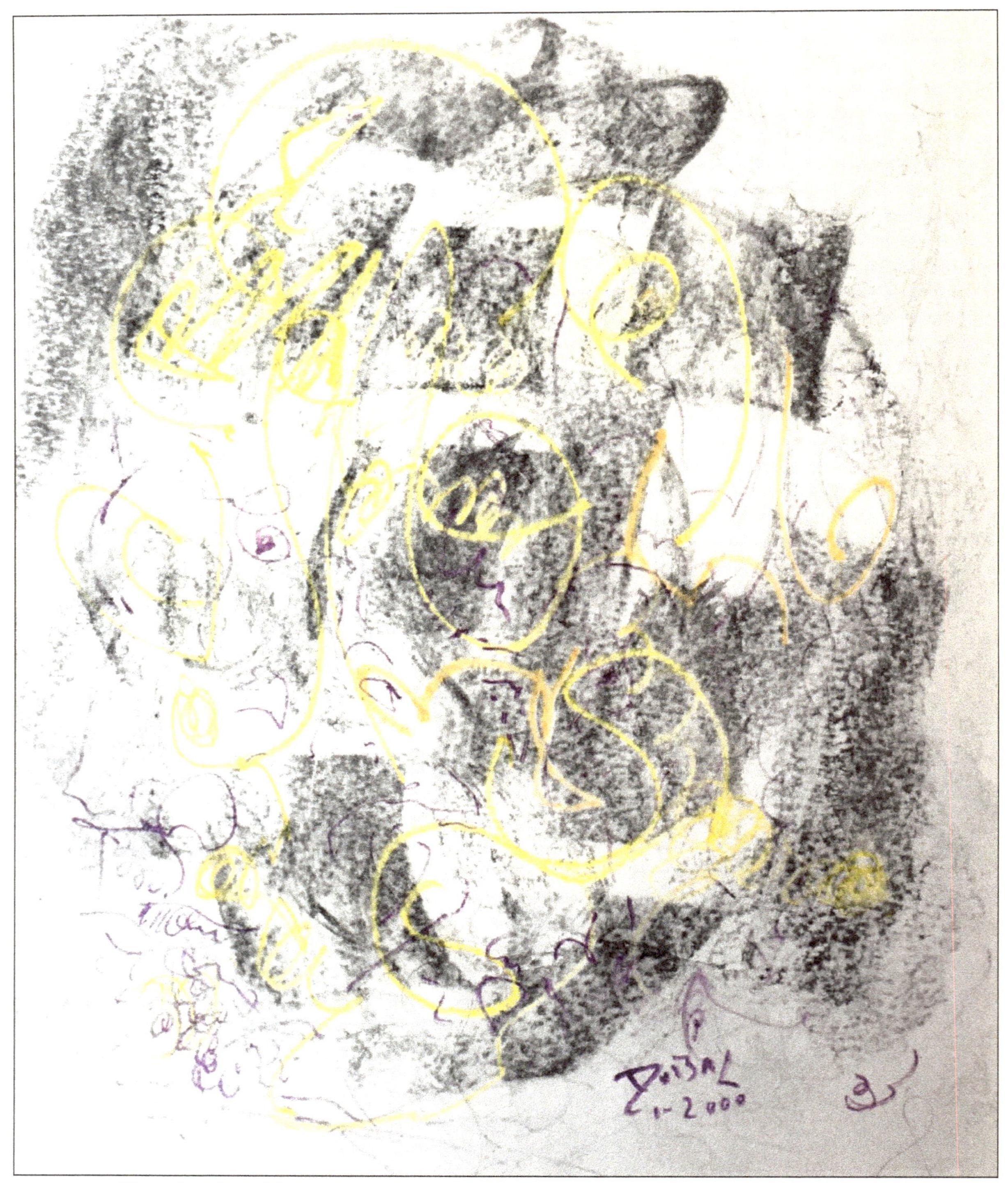

Many Things.
11 x 14. Charcoal and yellow pastel. 2000.

THE PAINTINGS OF DAVID DUBAL

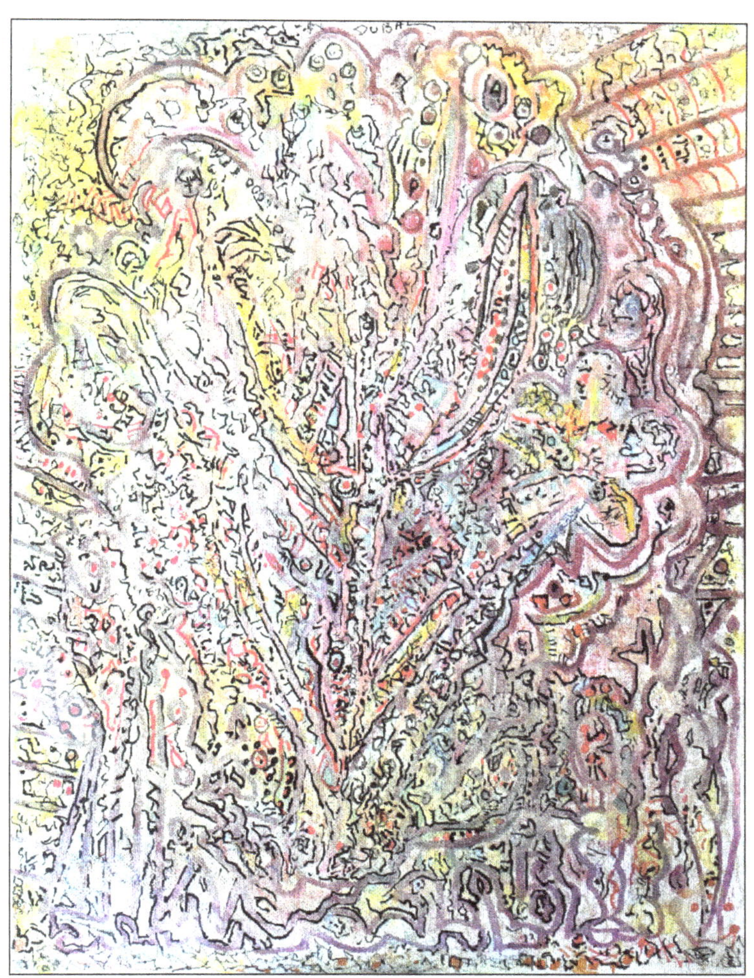

Deep Inside.
14 x 10. Inks on paper. 2000.

All Going Well.
13 x 11. Colored inks
on wood. 2015.

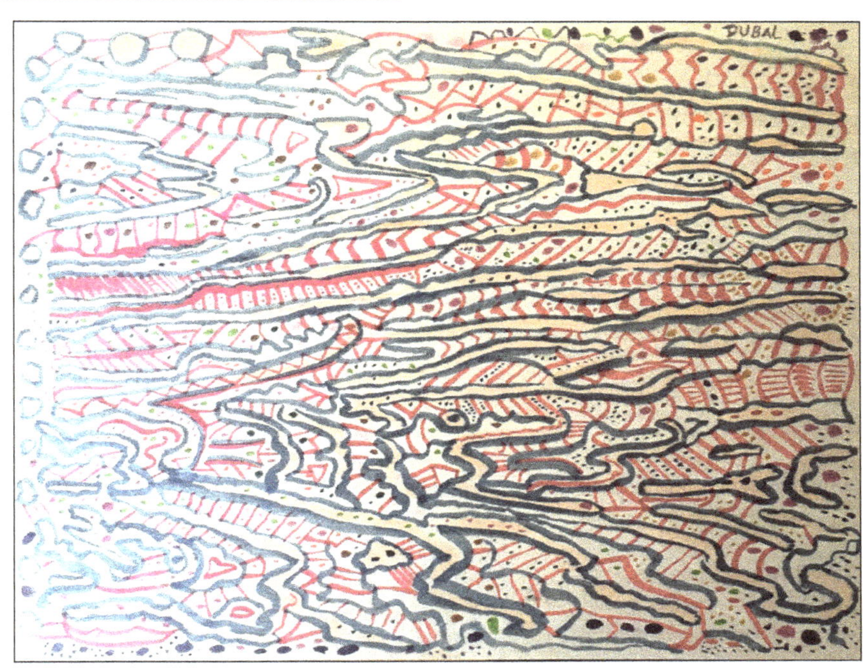

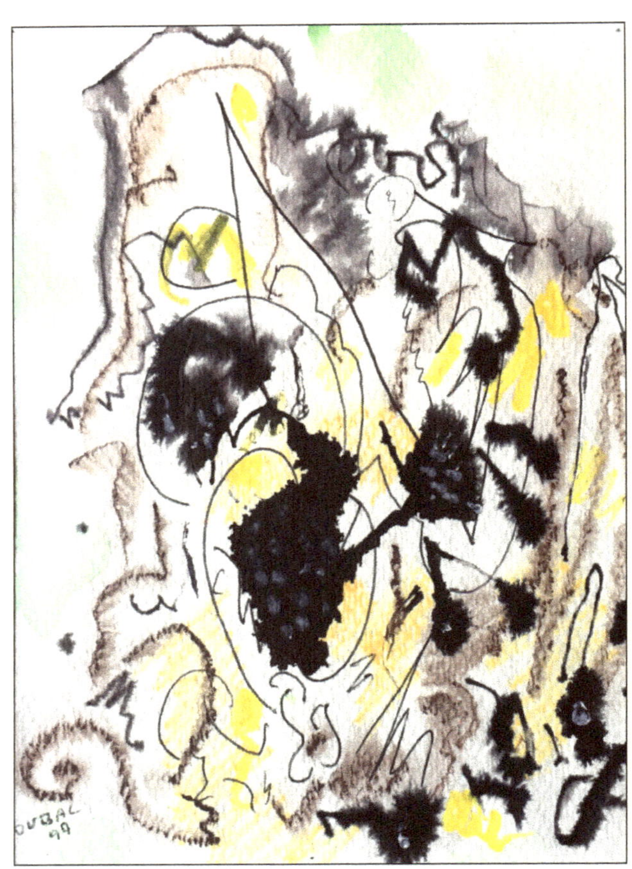

Hanging Grapes.
7 x 5. Watercolor. 1999.

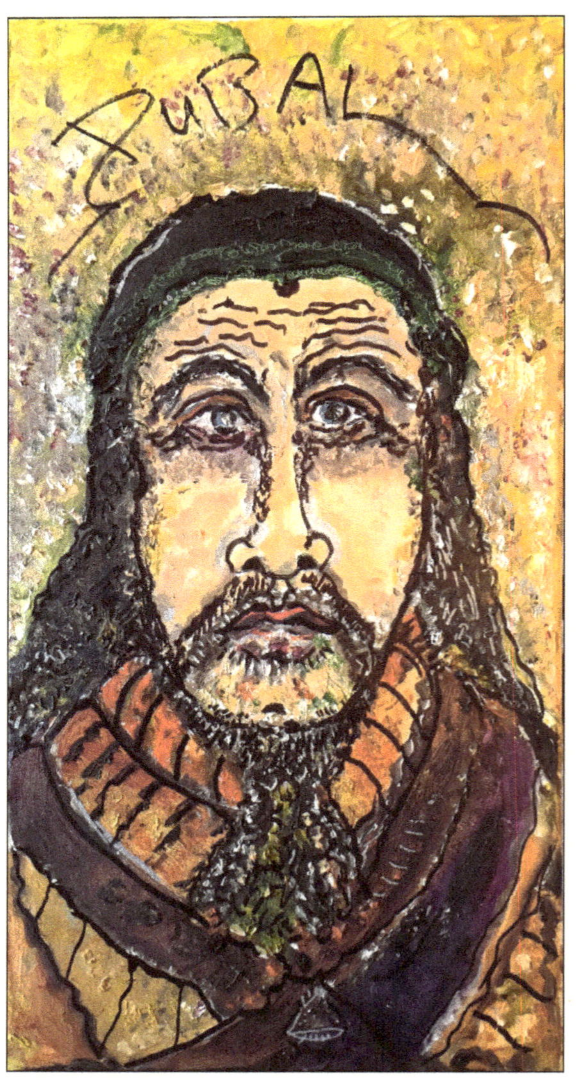

Genghis Khan.
24 x 12. Oil on canvas. 2012.

THE PAINTINGS OF DAVID DUBAL

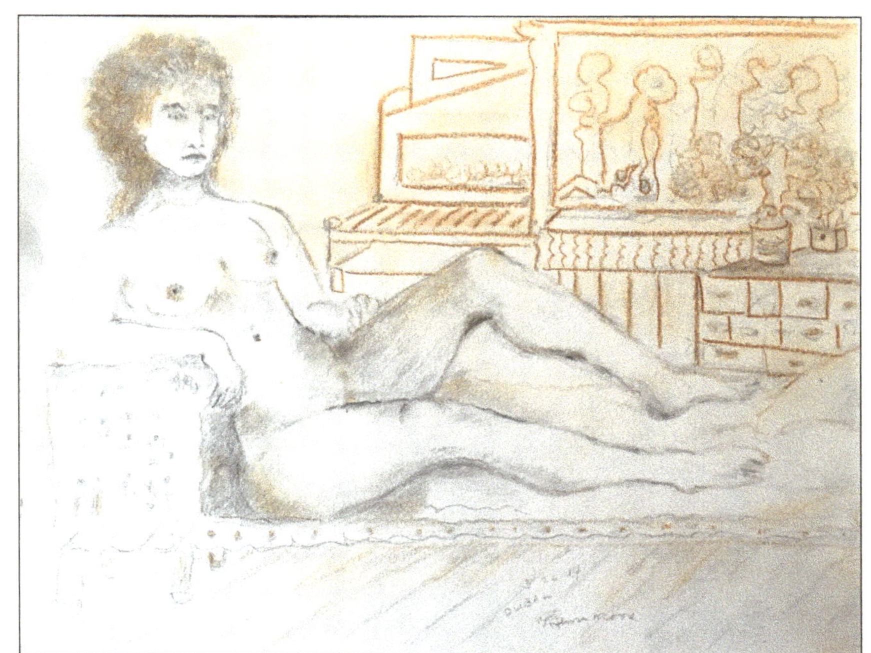

Nude Girl after Henry Moore.
11 x 14. Pencil on paper. 2016.

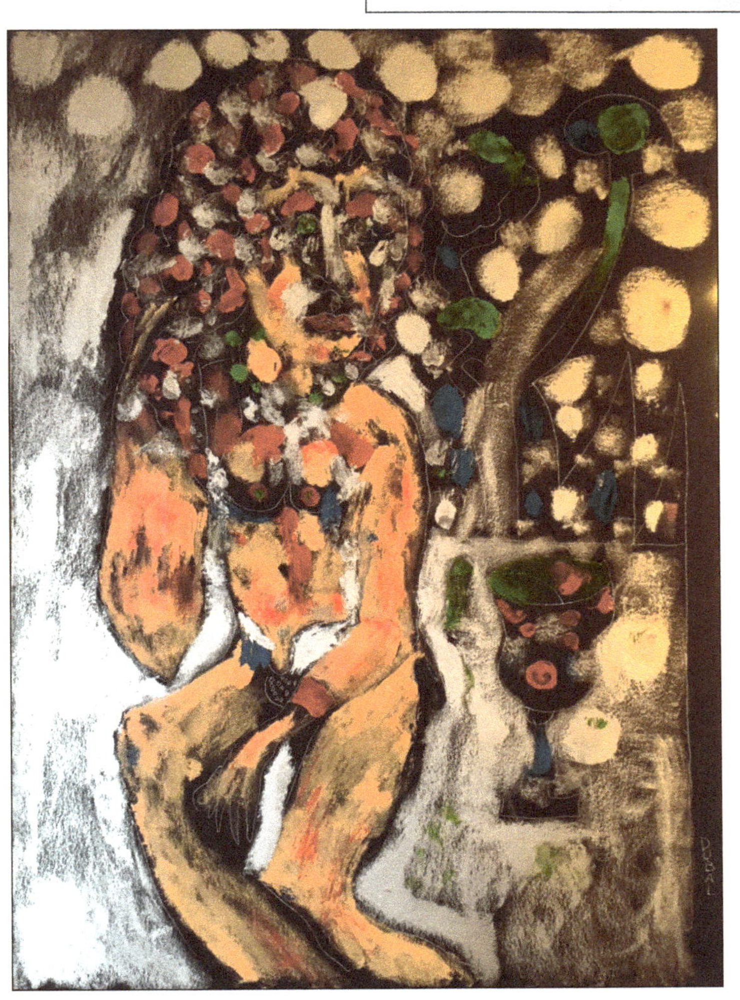

Ideal Woman.
30 x 20. Mixed media on black board. 2014.

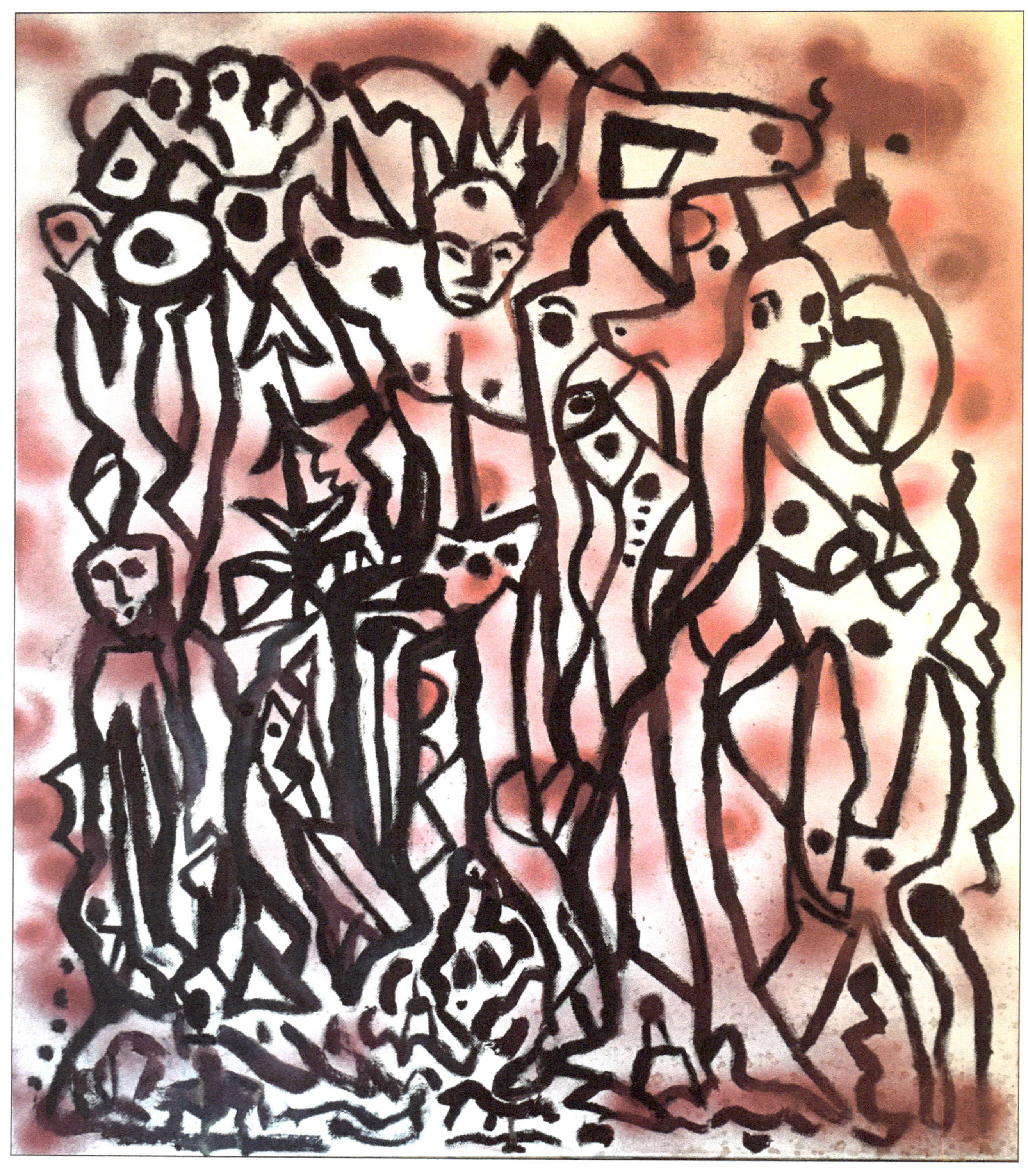

Agony.
29 x 23. Red spray paint and black oil paint. 2015.

THE PAINTINGS OF DAVID DUBAL

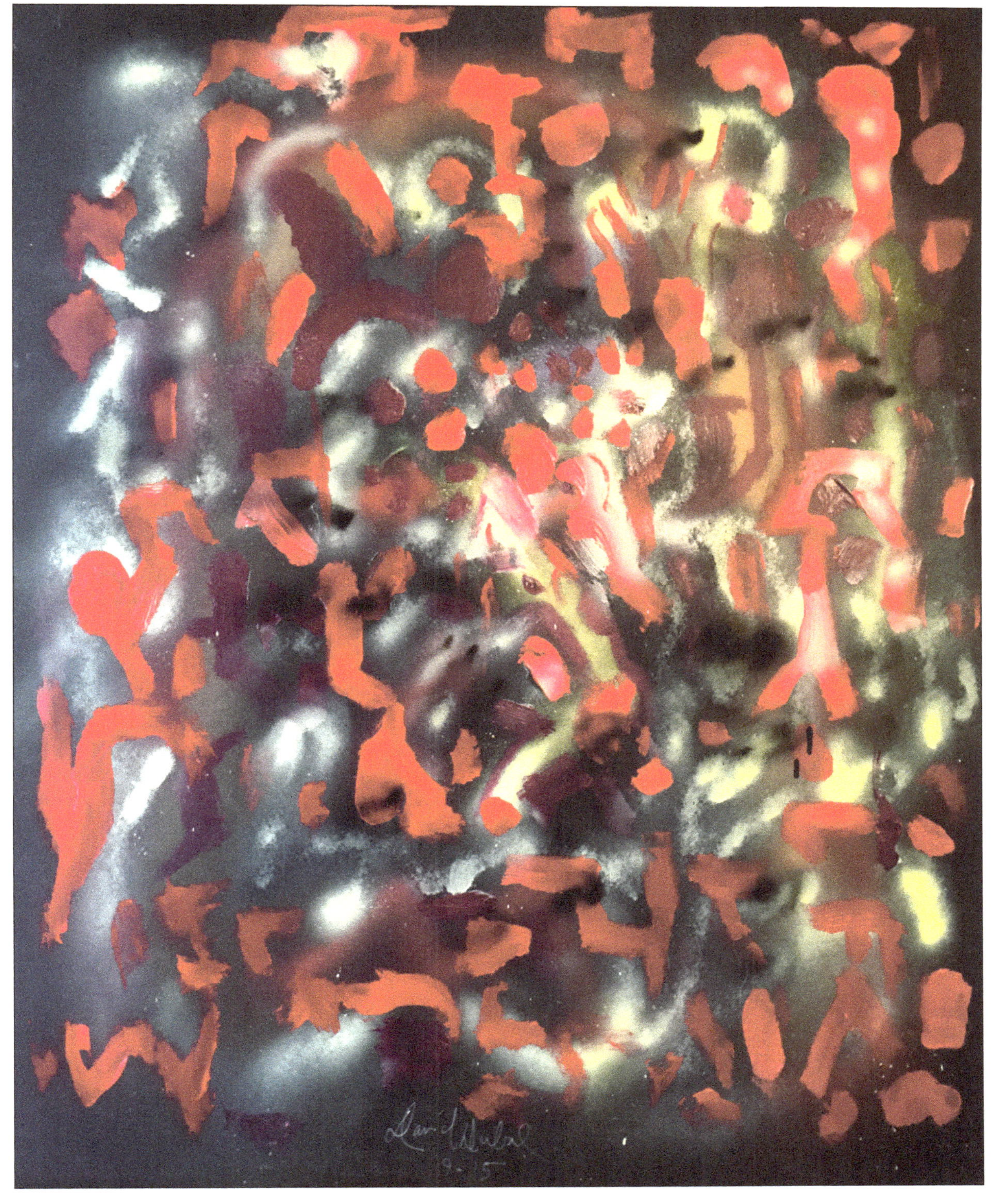

A Call to the Field.
40 x 30. Spray paint and oil on black board. 2013.

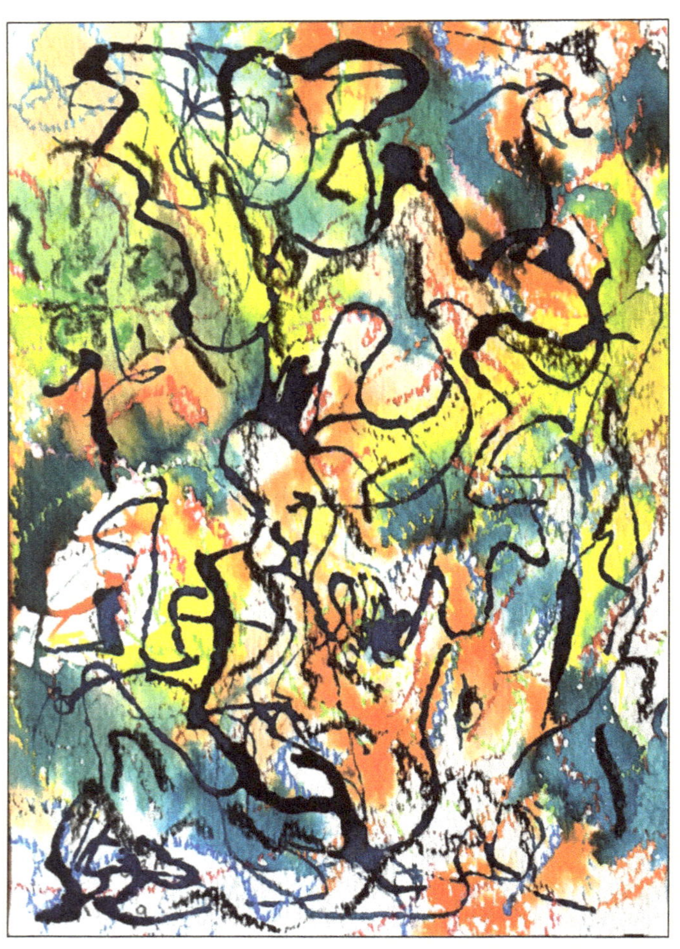

Good Day.
6 x 9. Watercolor on paper.
1999.

My Yellow.
6 x 9. Watercolor on paper.
1999.

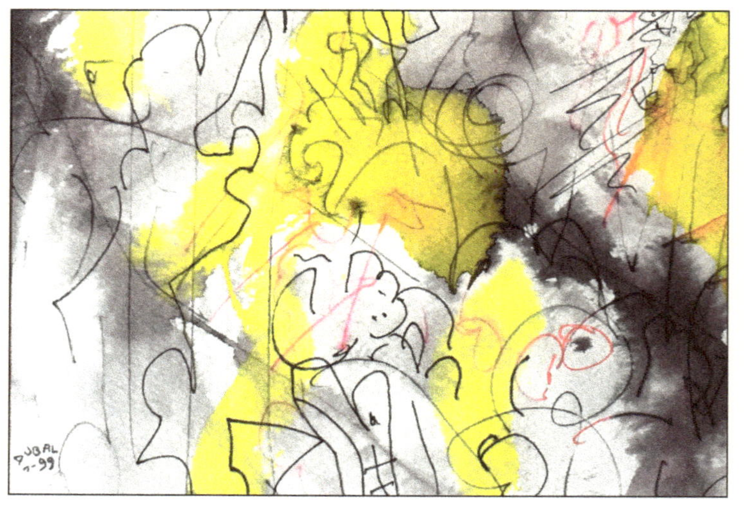

THE PAINTINGS OF DAVID DUBAL

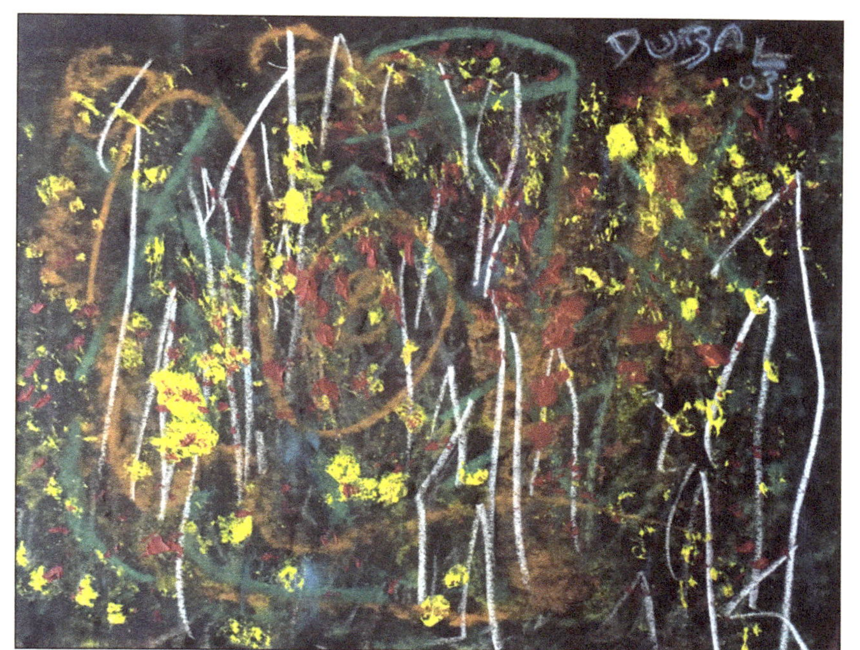

The White Blade.
8 x 12. Mixed media on black board. 2003.

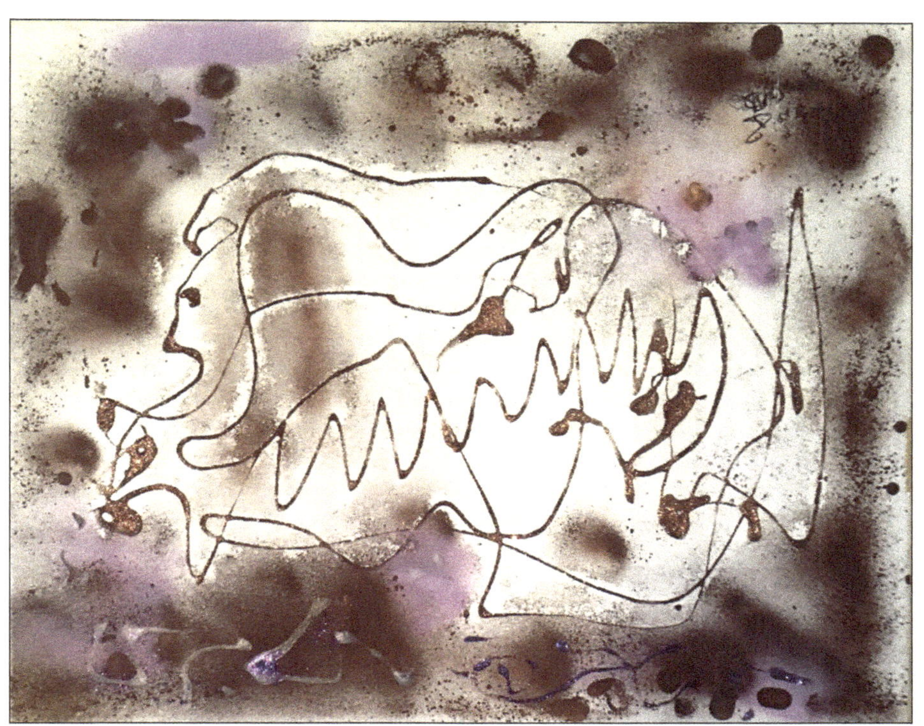

The Best Bull.
16 x 20. Mixed media on canvas. 2017.

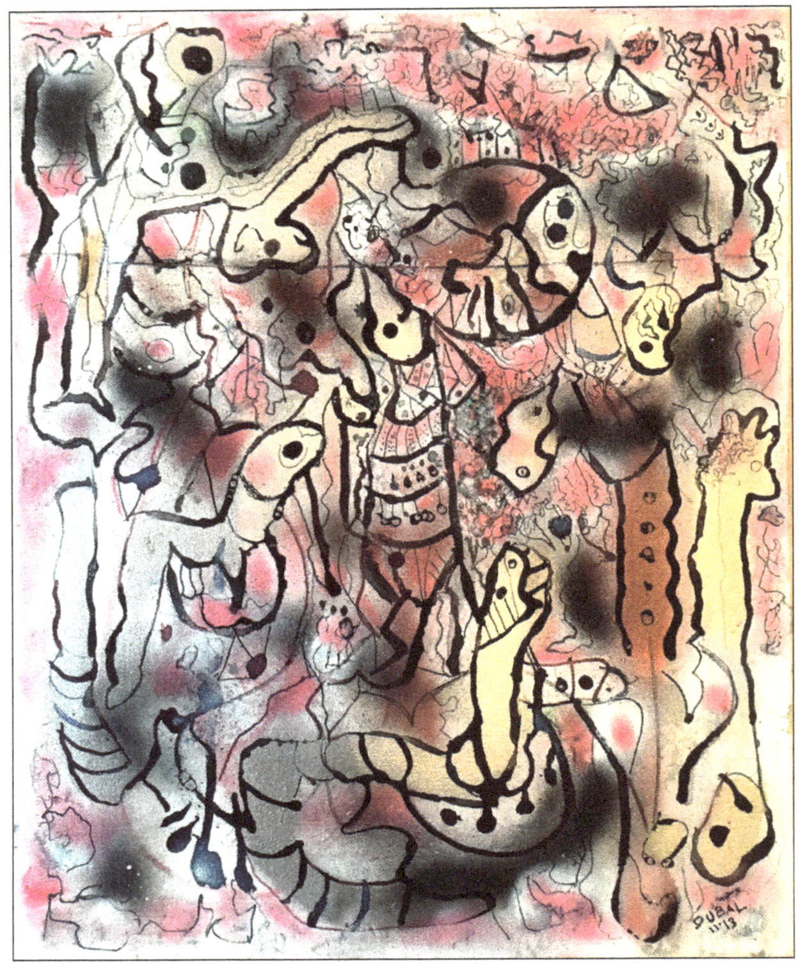

The Congregation.
16 x 20. Mixed media on canvas. 2013.

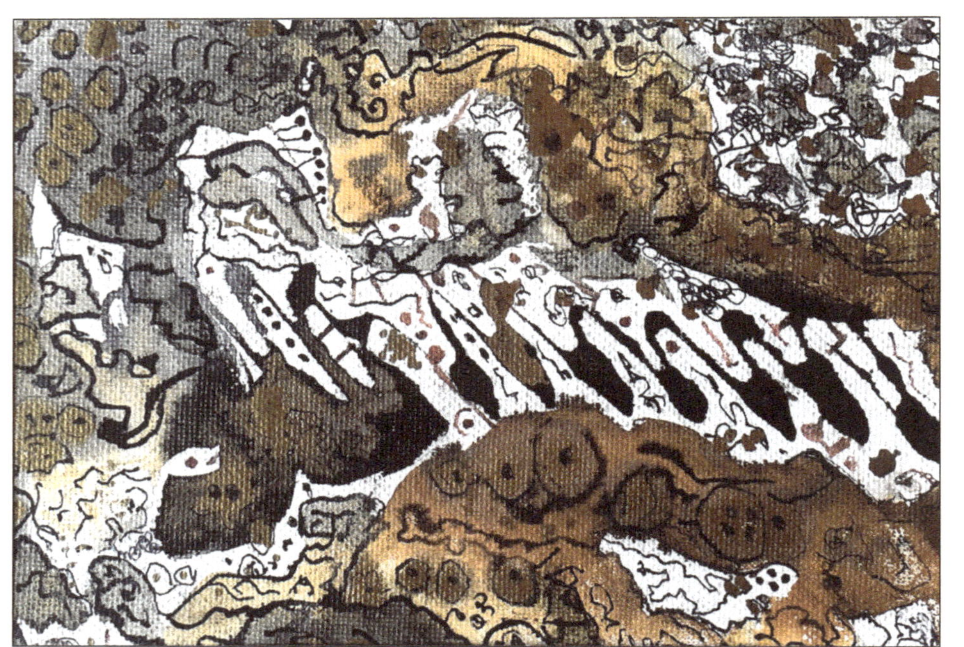

From the Caves of Pensacola.
9 x 12. Watercolor on canvas and board. 2013.

THE PAINTINGS OF DAVID DUBAL

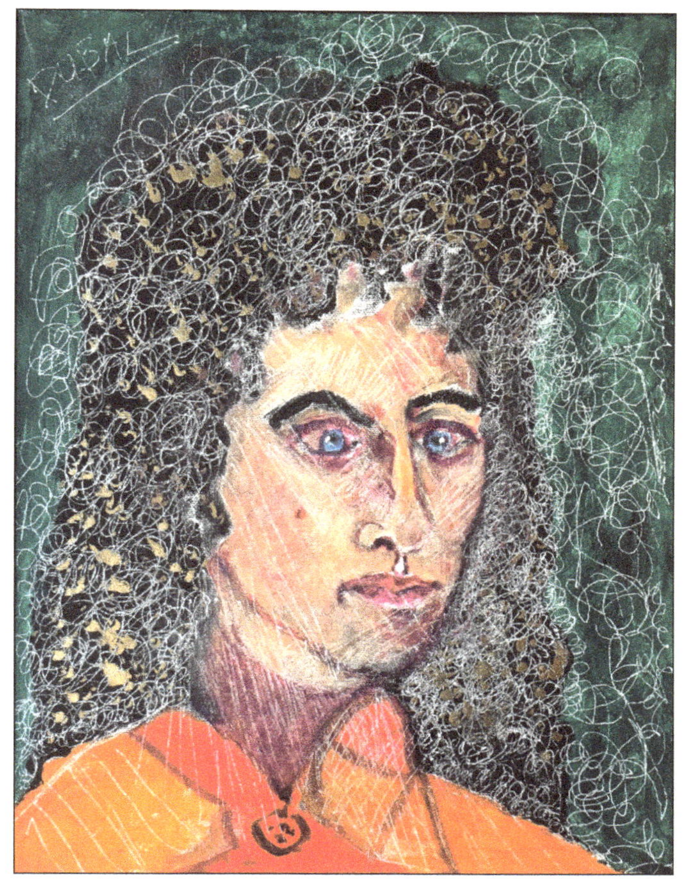

Blue Eyes and Off-center Collar.
22 x 16. Mixed media. 2015.

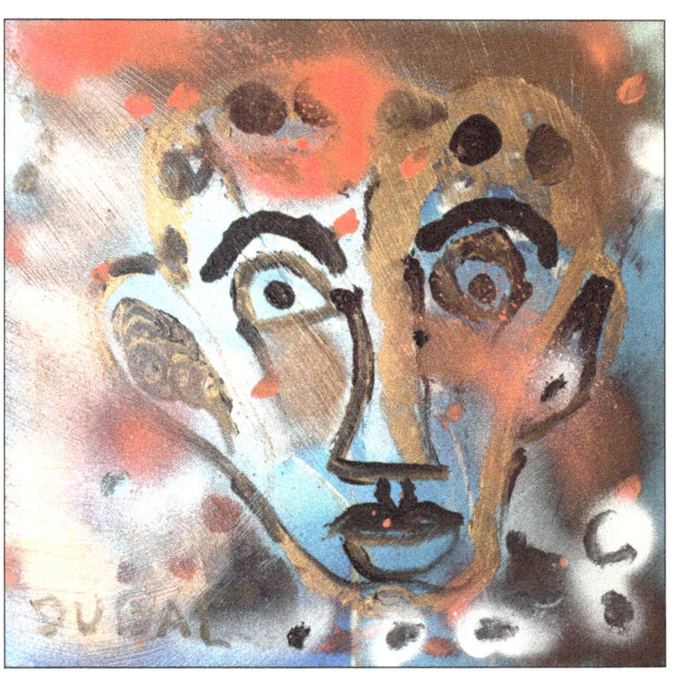

Homage to Picasso.
15 x 15. Oil and spray on canvas. 2018.

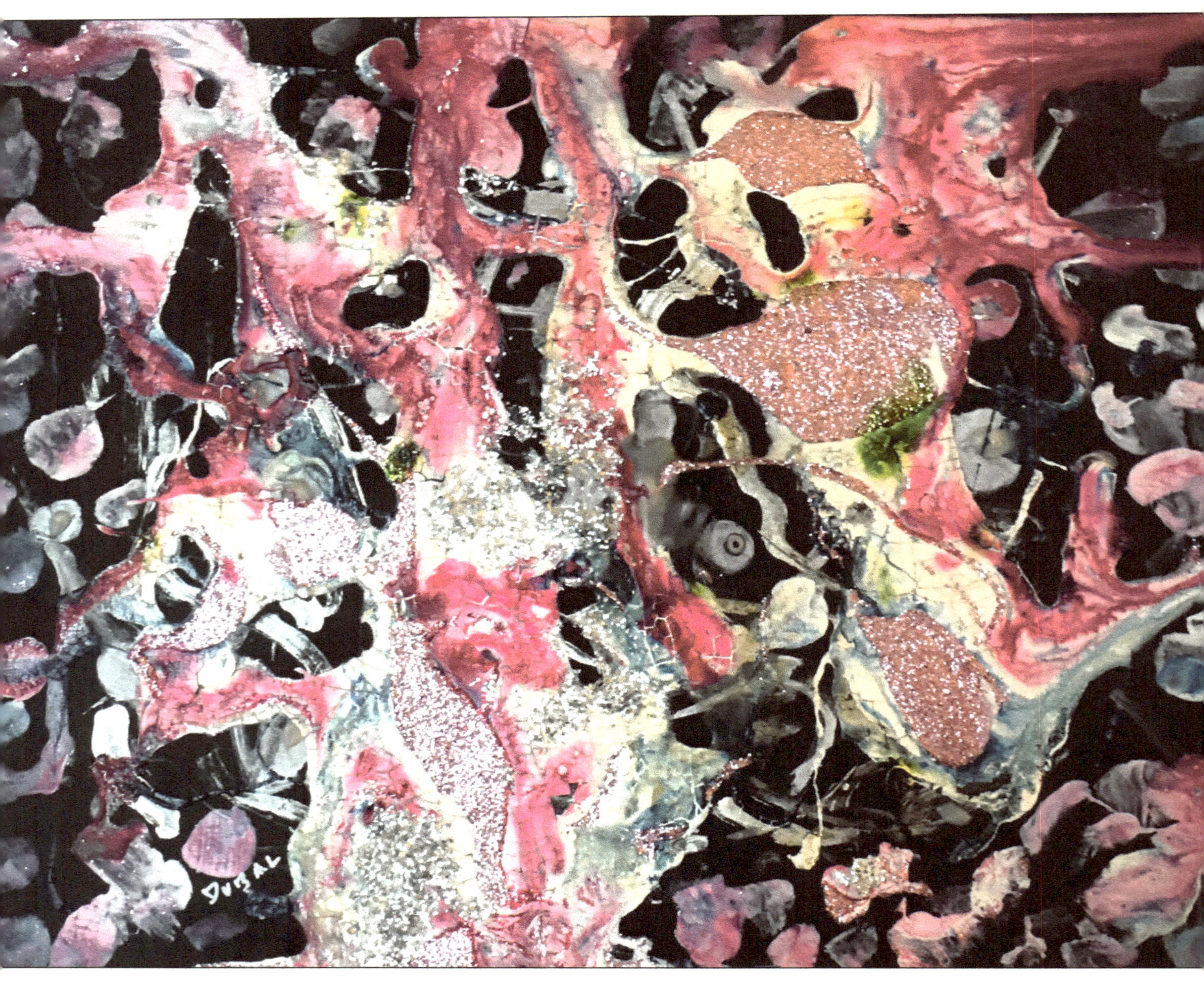

Gloriana.
16 x 20. Glitter, paste. 2013.

THE PAINTINGS OF DAVID DUBAL

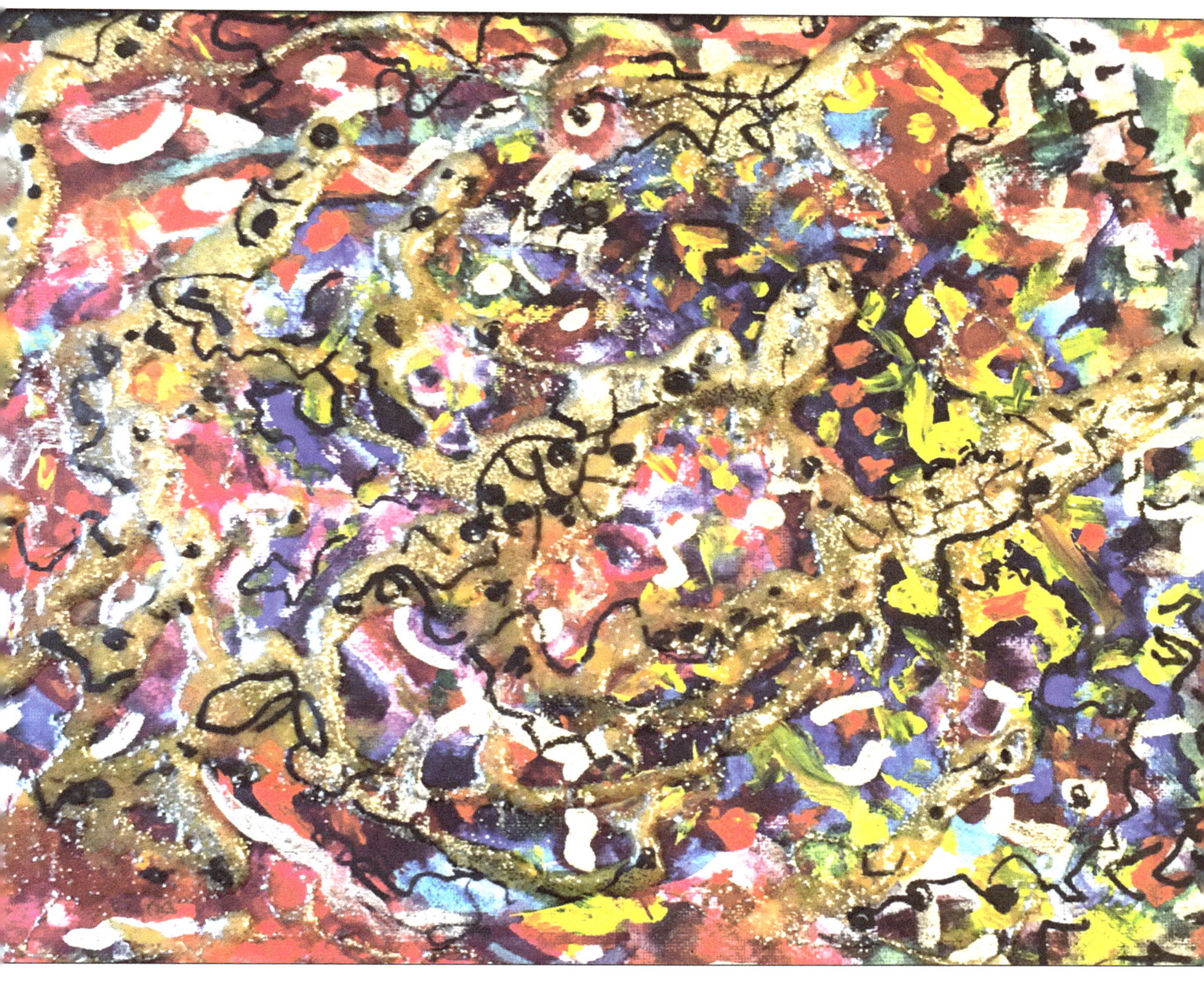

Color Scream.
18 x 18. Mixed media on board. 2014.

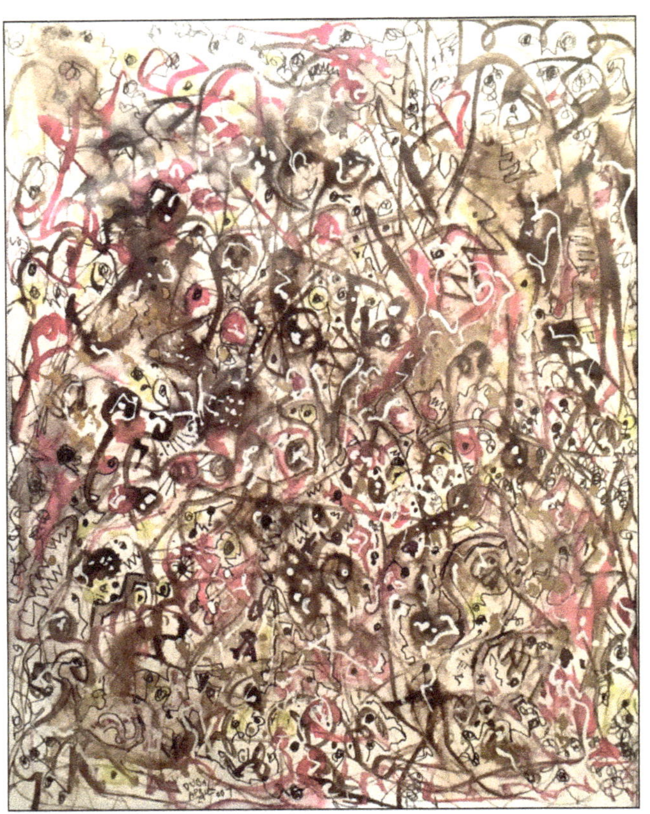

No Title.
14 x 12. Watercolor on
paper. 2007.

The Mind Works.
30 x 24. Spray and
colored inks on canvas.
2013.

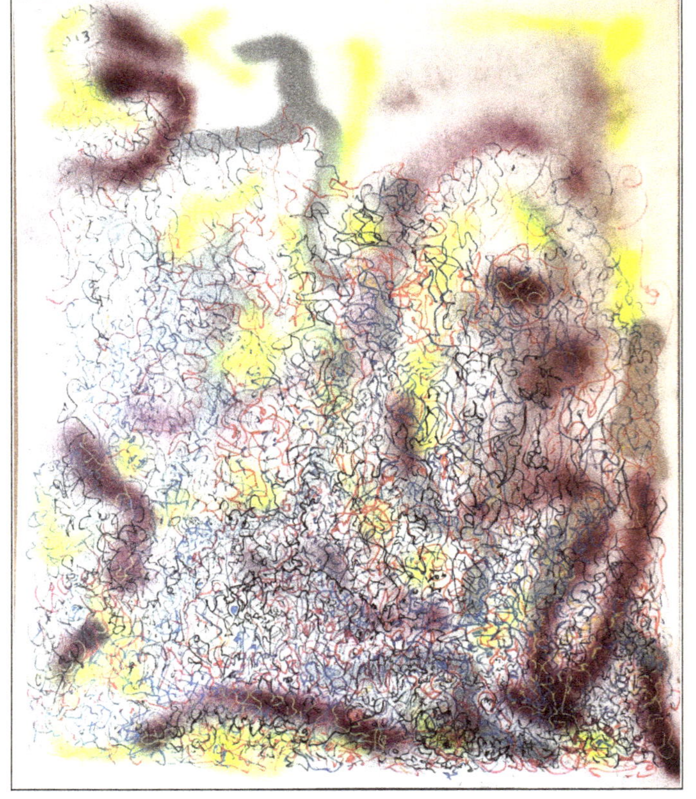

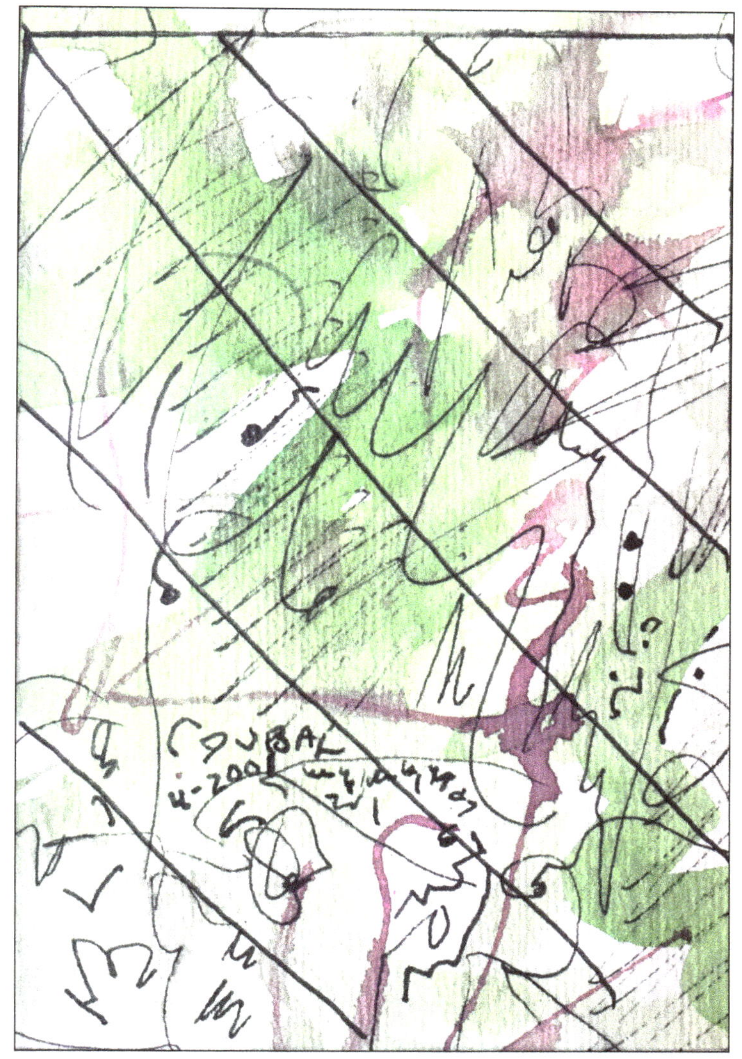

5 Lines.
3 x 5. Watercolor. 1999.

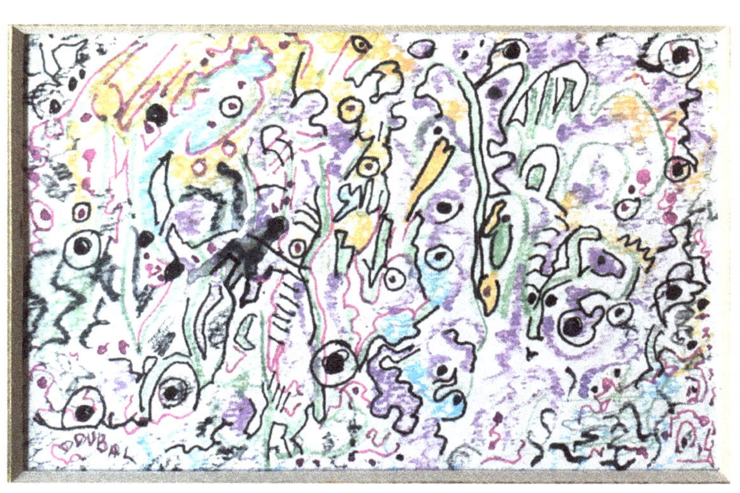

Good Looking.
3 x 4½. Watercolor. 1999.

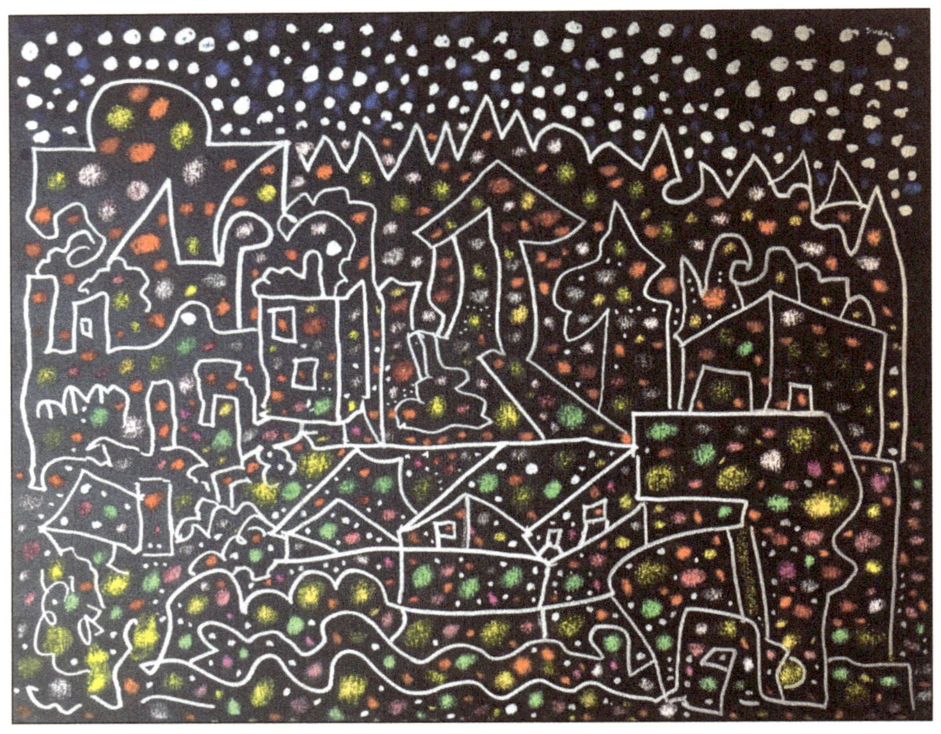

City Streets at Night.
16 x 20. Ink and pastel on black canvas. 2013.

Your Galaxy.
14 x 17. Mixed media on black board. 1998.

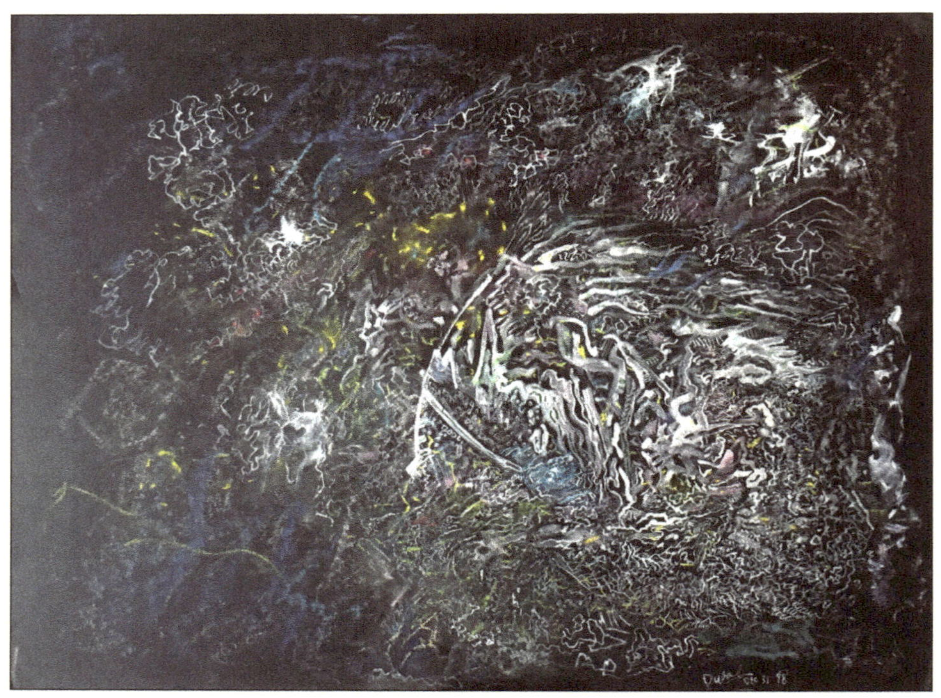

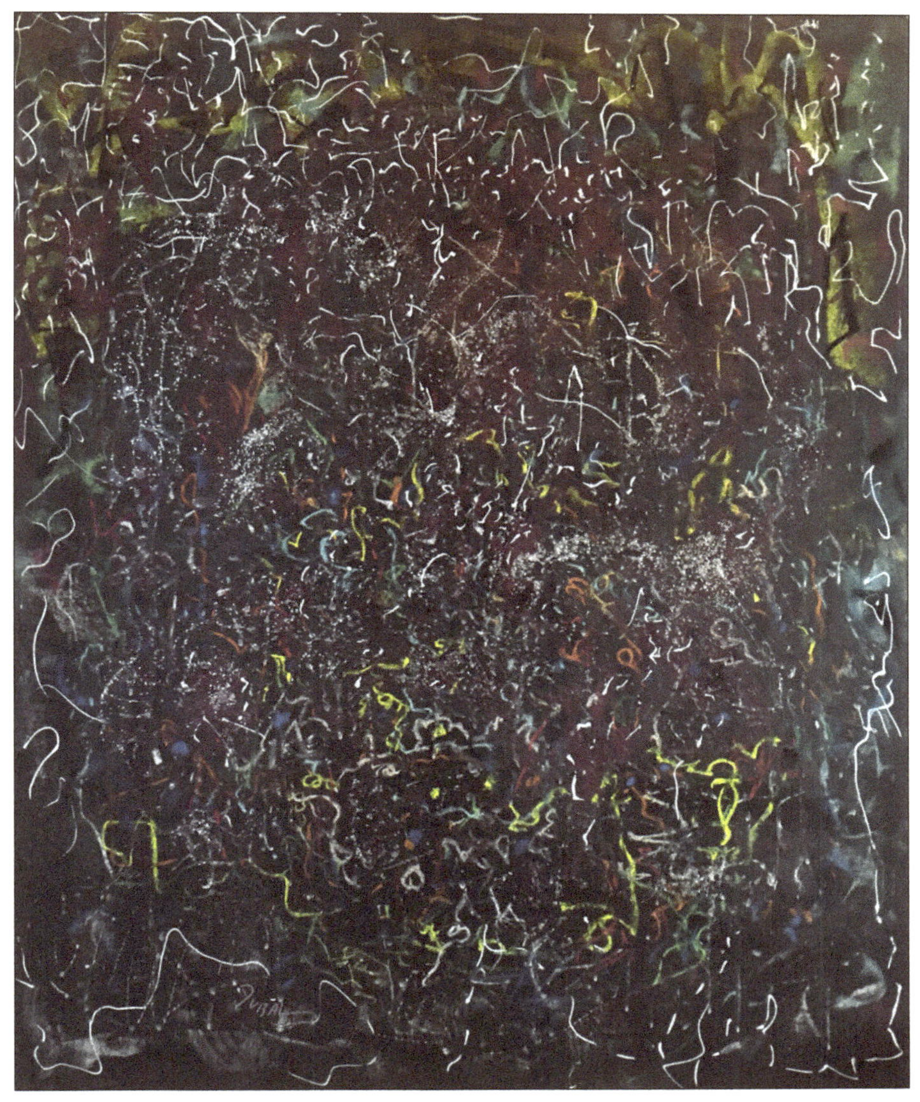

Full of Life.
40 x 30. Mixed media on black board. 2009.

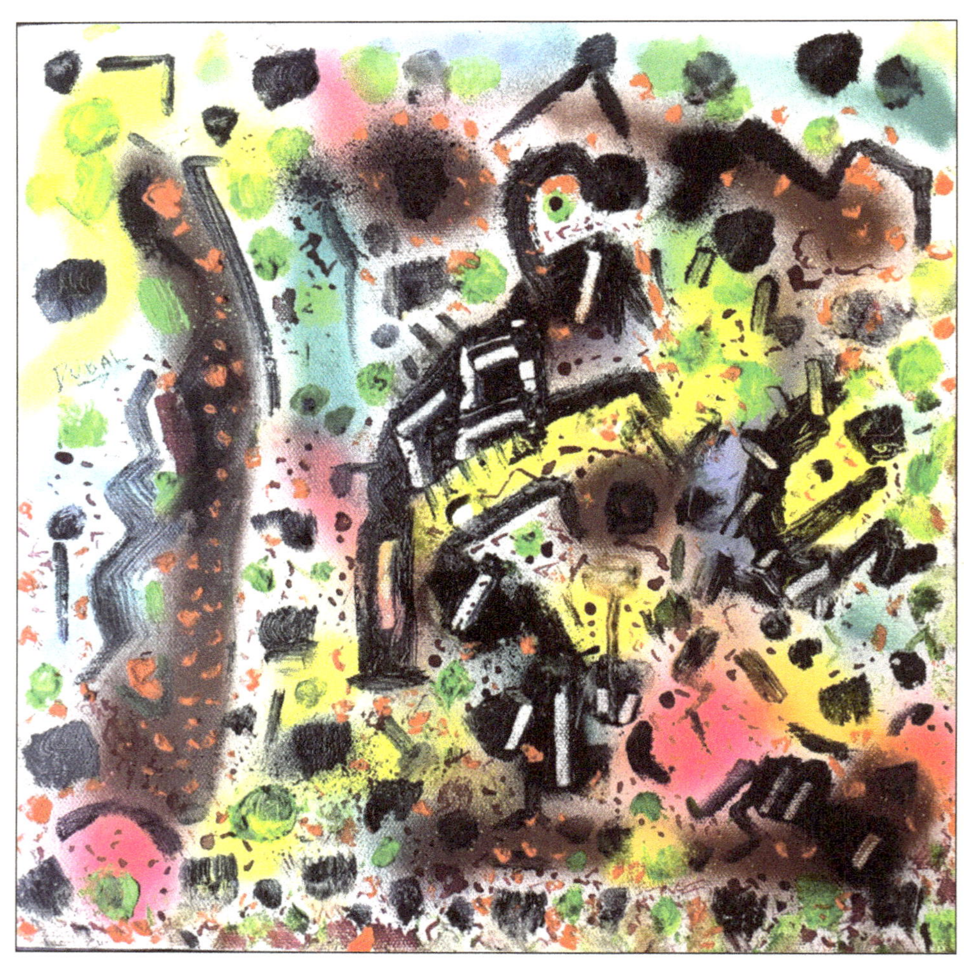

French Village.
12 x 12. Mixed media on canvas. 2014.

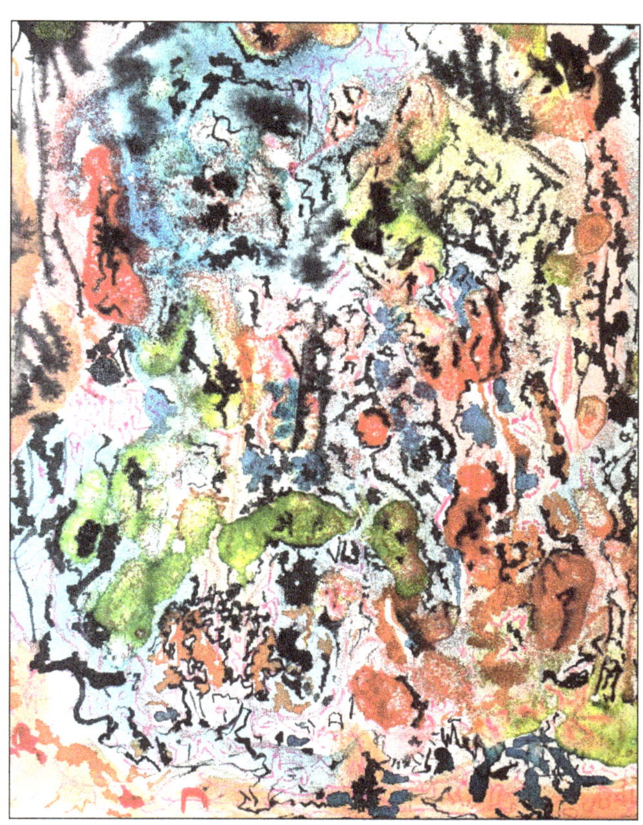

Feel the Texture.
12 x 16. Mixed media on
canvas board. 2006.

Some Yellow.

12 x 16. Mixed media.
Charcoal and watercolor
on paper. 2015.

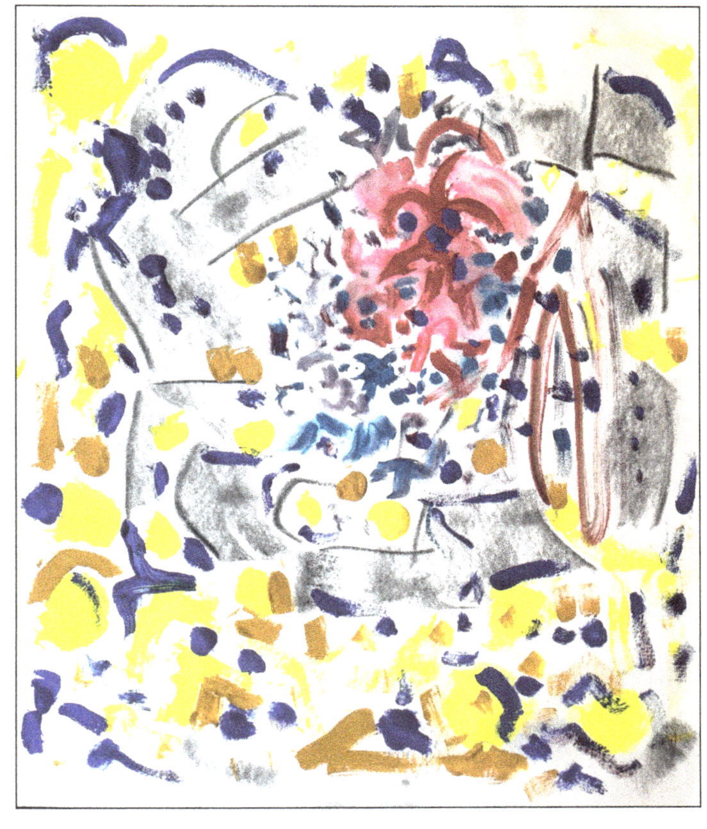

Delicious Fruit.

7 x 5. Watercolor on paper. 1999.

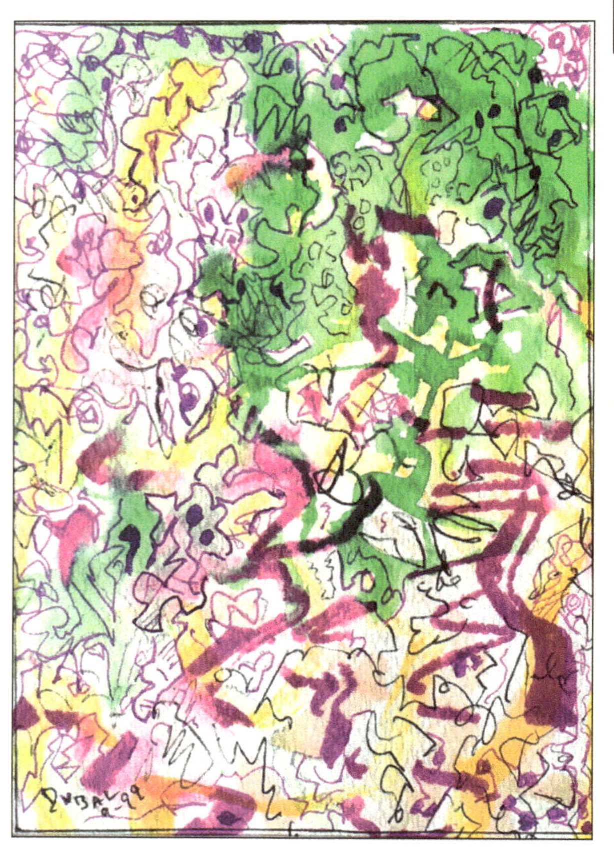

Full Sprout.

7 x 5. Watercolor on paper. 1999.

THE PAINTINGS OF DAVID DUBAL

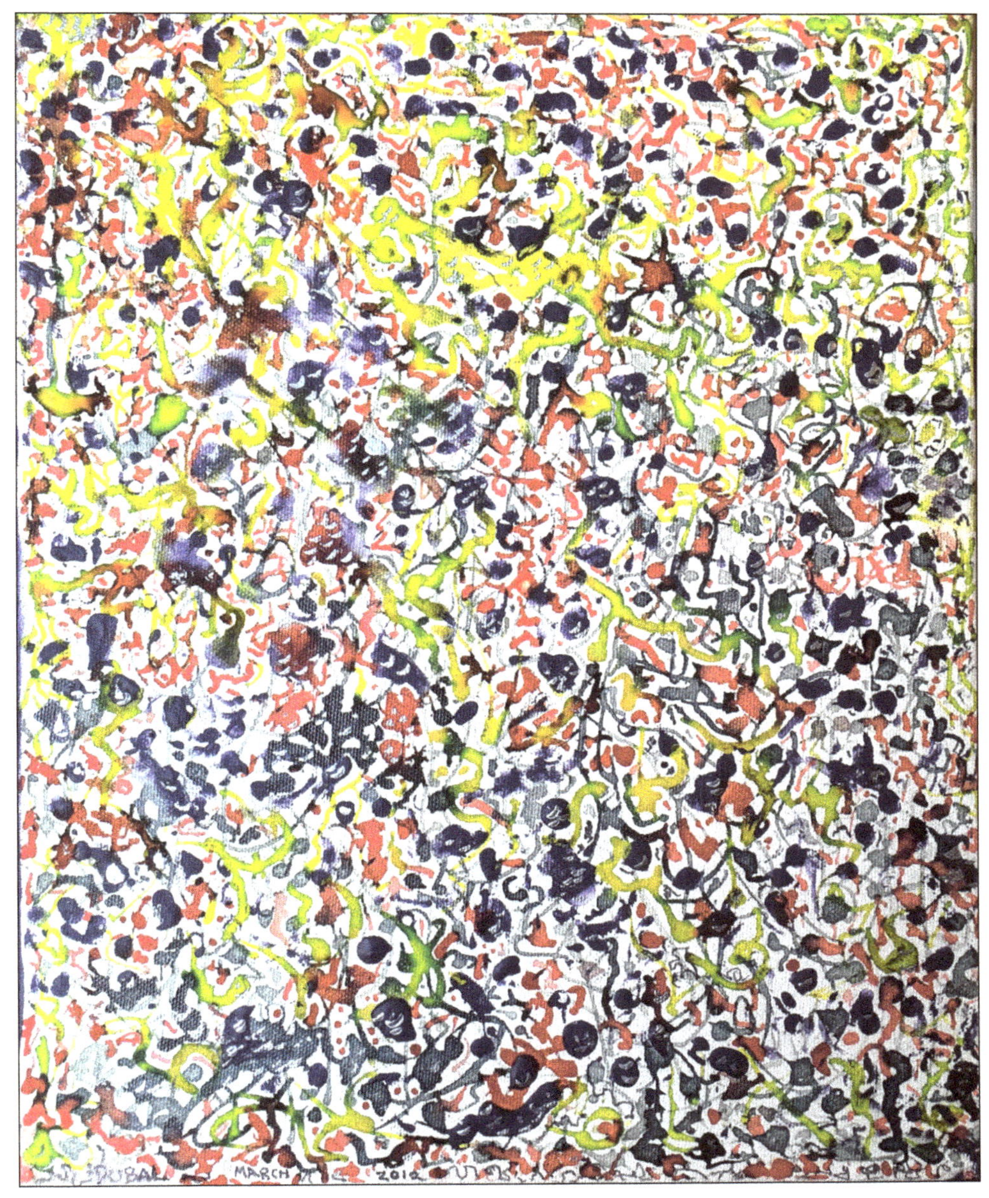

Euphony.
14 x 11. Oil on canvas. 2016.

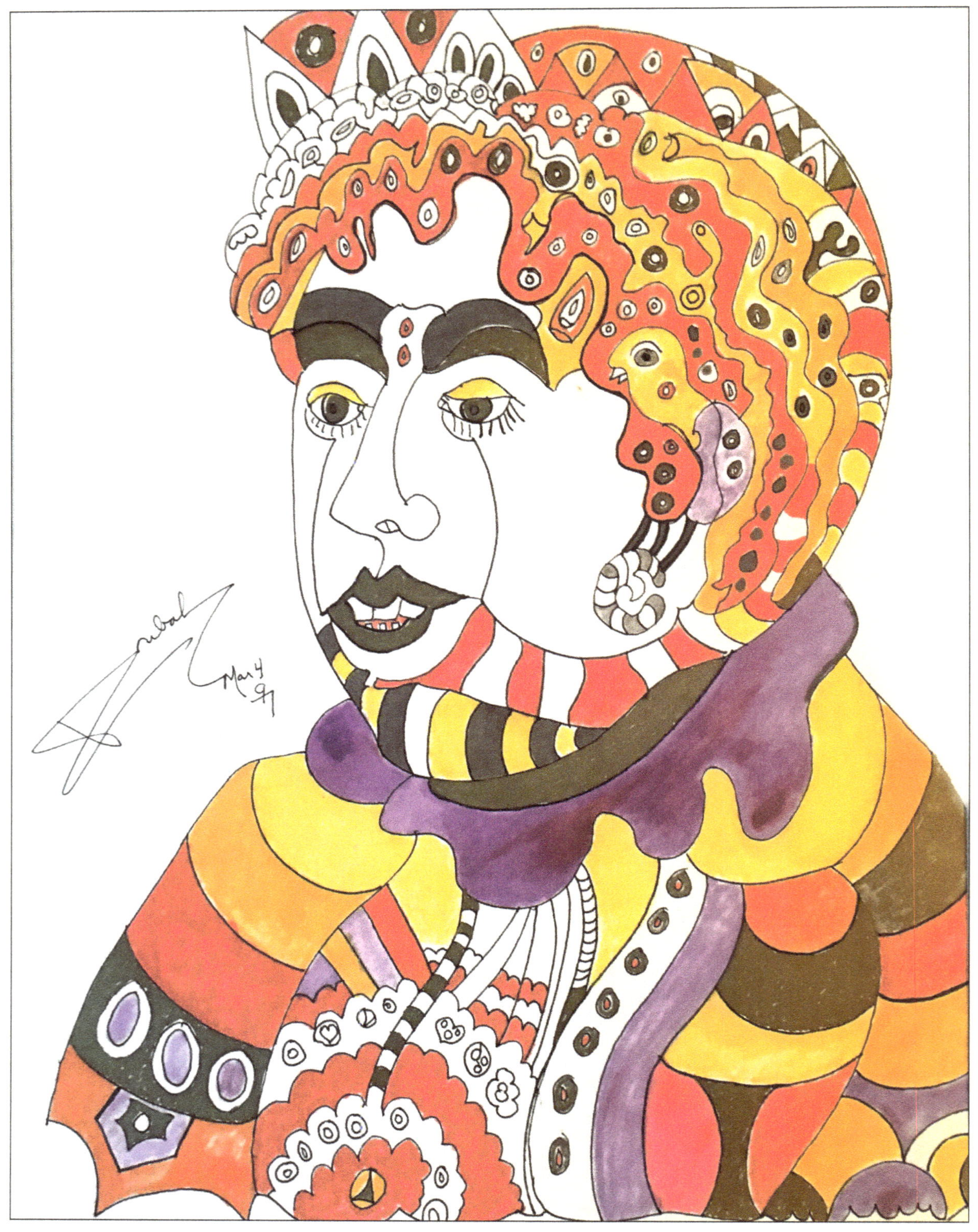

Grand Leader in Full Regalia.
10½ x 14. Colored ink on paper. 1997.

THE PAINTINGS OF DAVID DUBAL

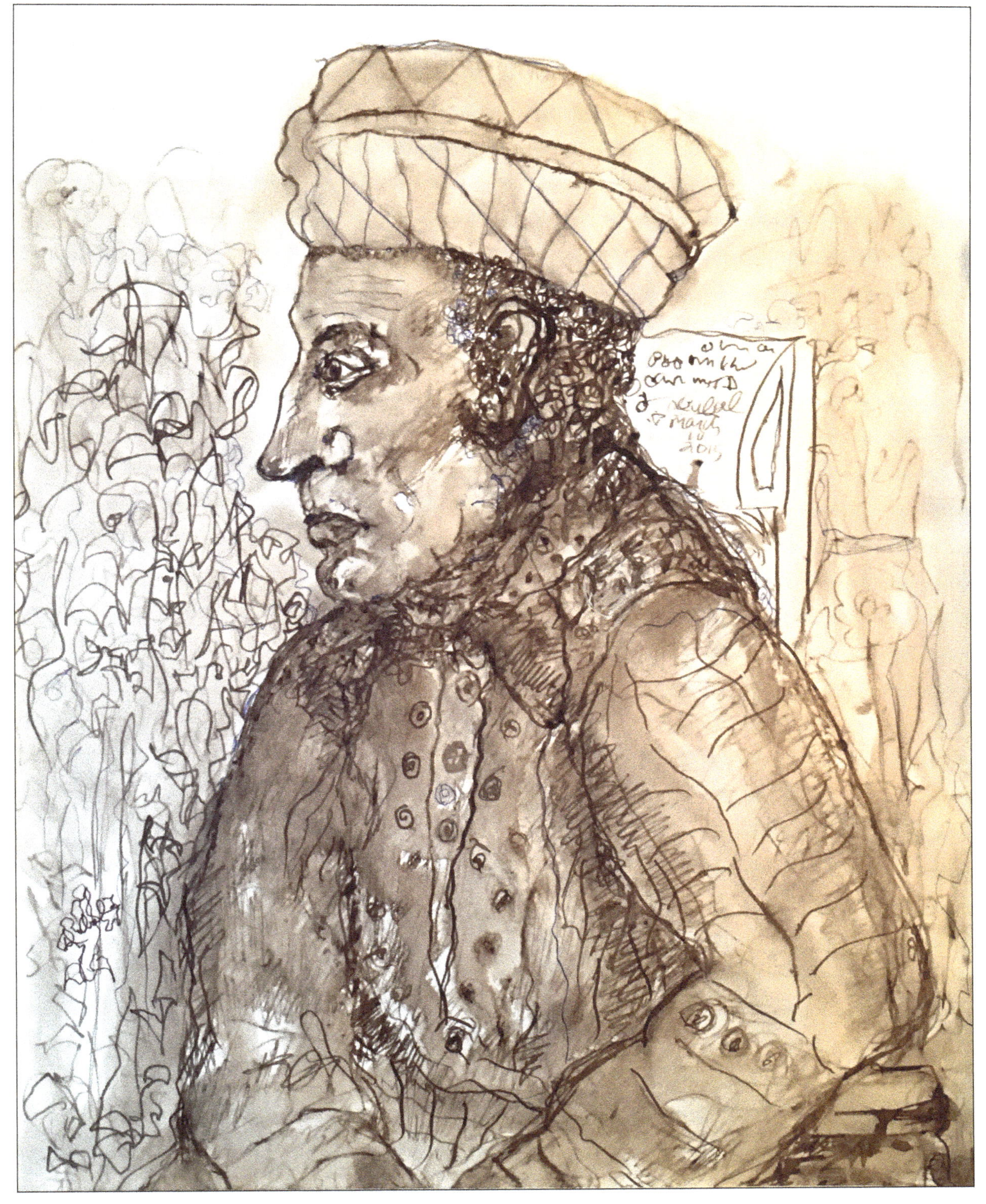

Humanist Scholar.

11 x 14. Bister ink and pen. 2015.

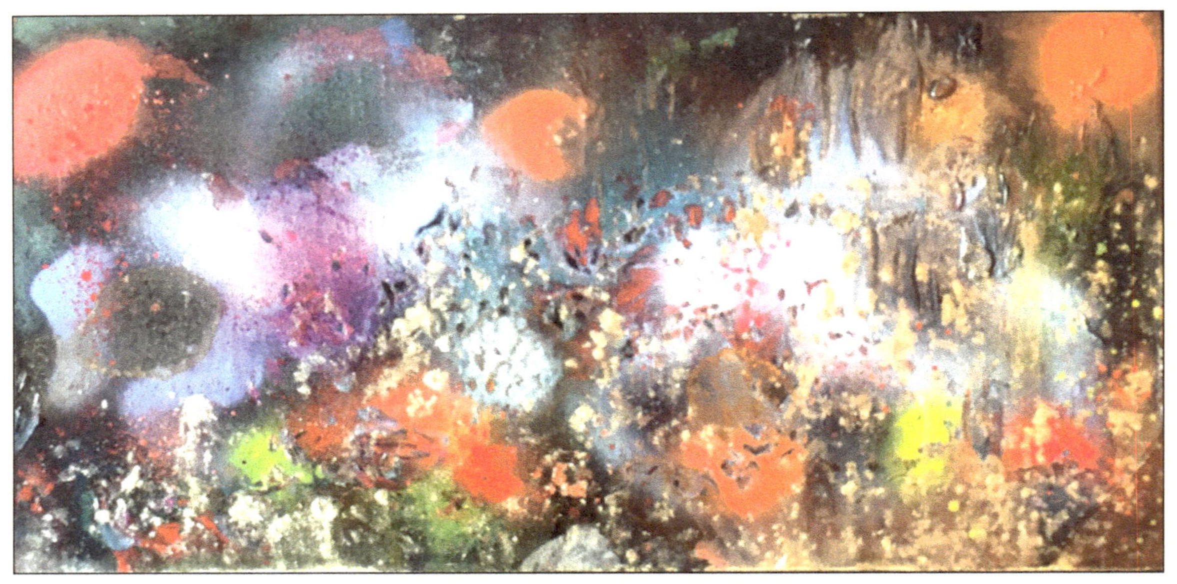

The Suns of Summer.
5 x 11. Spray paint on wood. 2013.

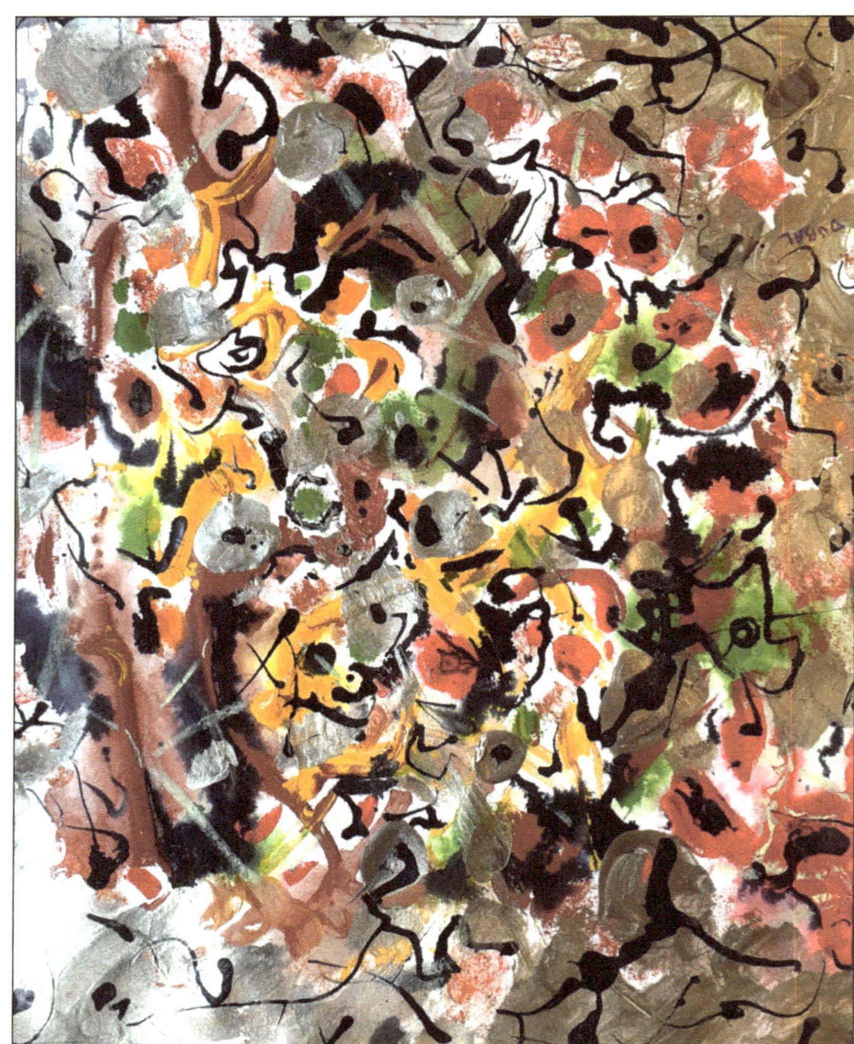

Gold is Everywhere.
11 x 14. Mixed media on paper. 2011.

THE PAINTINGS OF DAVID DUBAL

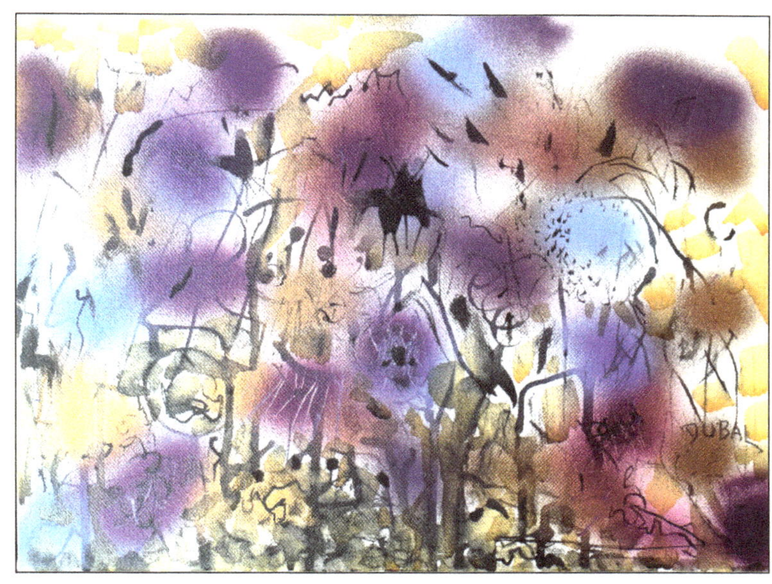

Purple Sage.
11 x 14. Mixed media
on canvas. 2017.

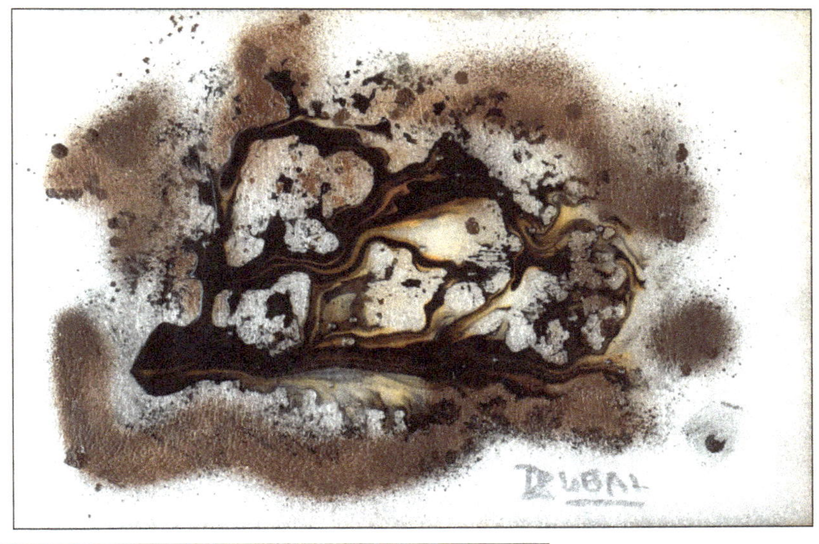

*Beautiful
Browns.*
8 x 12. Mixed
media on
Styrofoam.
2017.

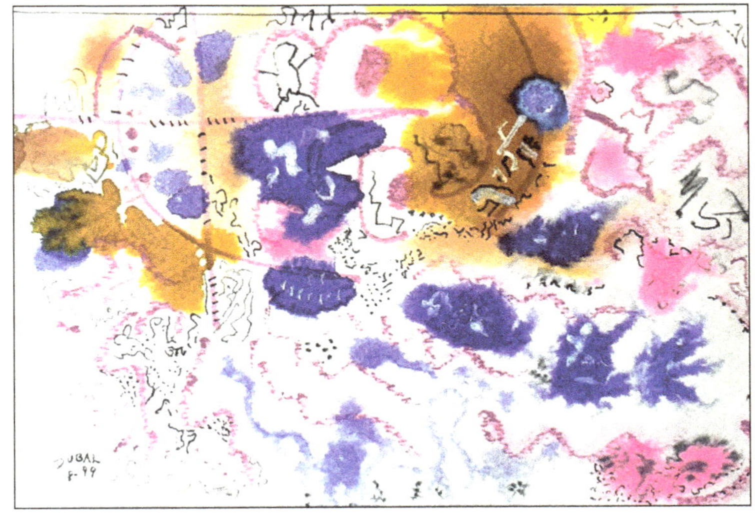

*Calm Sea and
Prosperous Voyage.*
5 x 7. Mixed media.
1999.

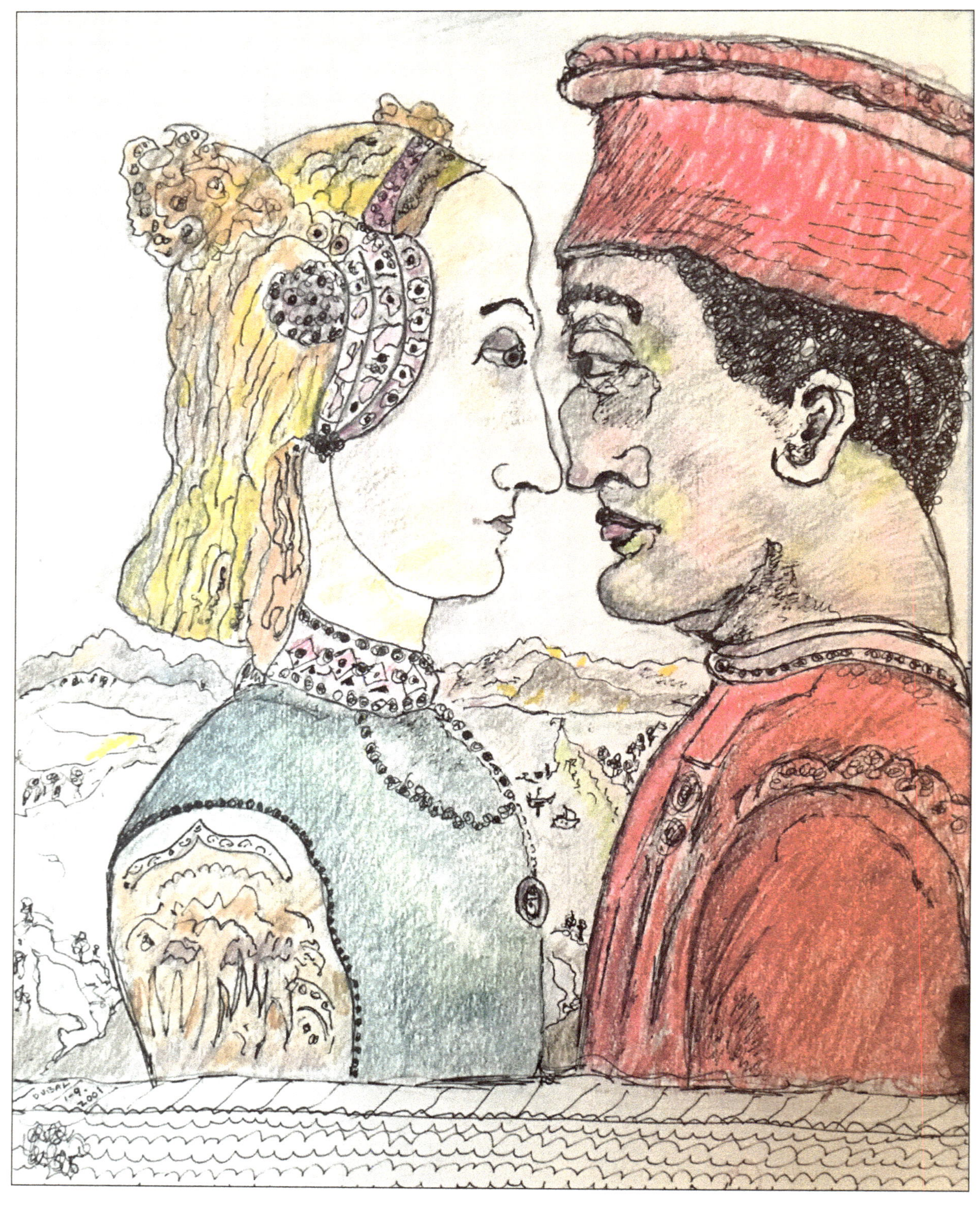

Two famous heads touching noses.
11 x 14. Colored pencils on paper. 2001.

THE PAINTINGS OF DAVID DUBAL

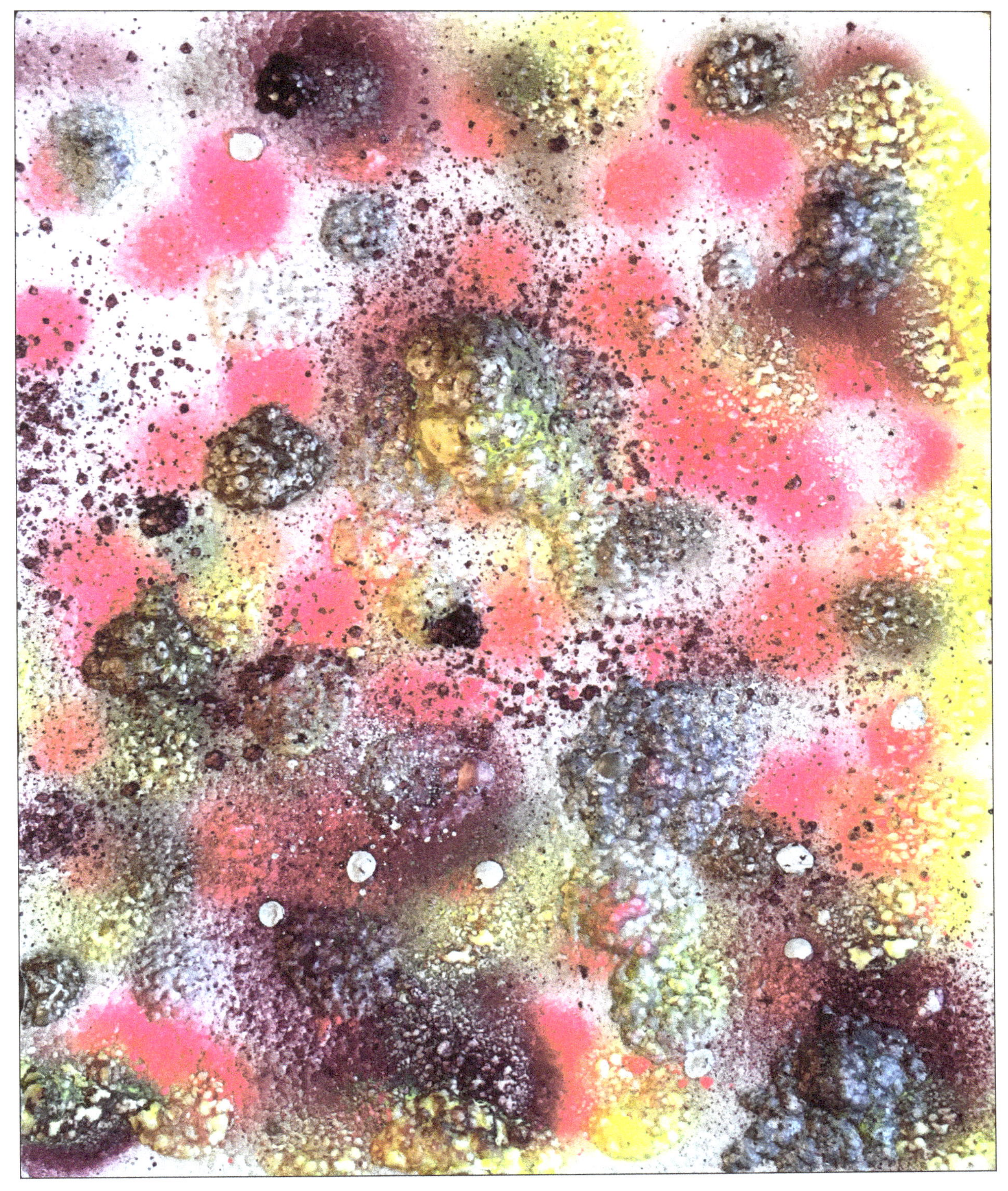

Styrofoam 31.
12 x 12. Spray paint on Styrofoam. 2018.

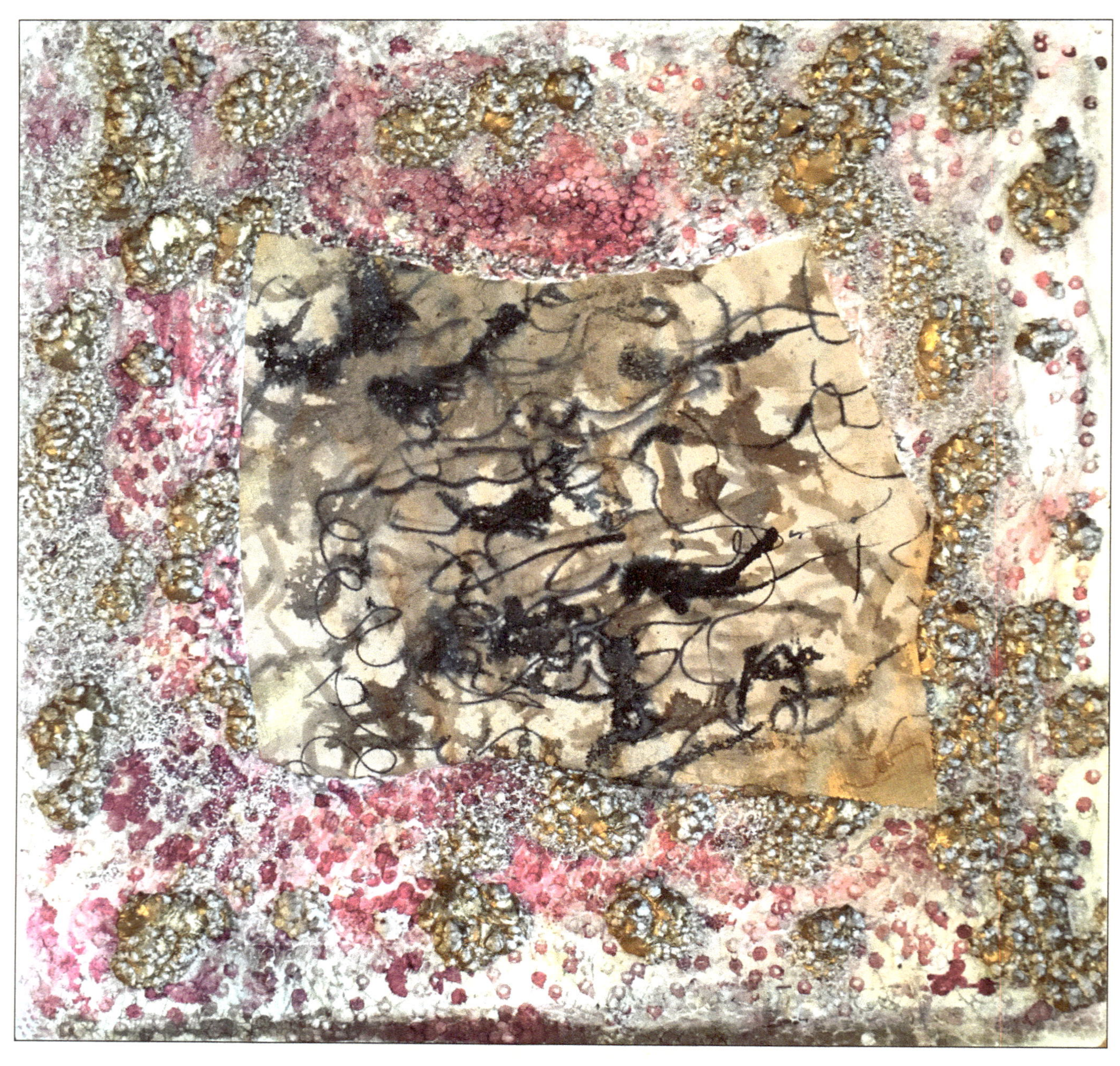

Collage in F sharp.
12 x 12. Mixed media on Styrofoam. 2017.

THE PAINTINGS OF DAVID DUBAL

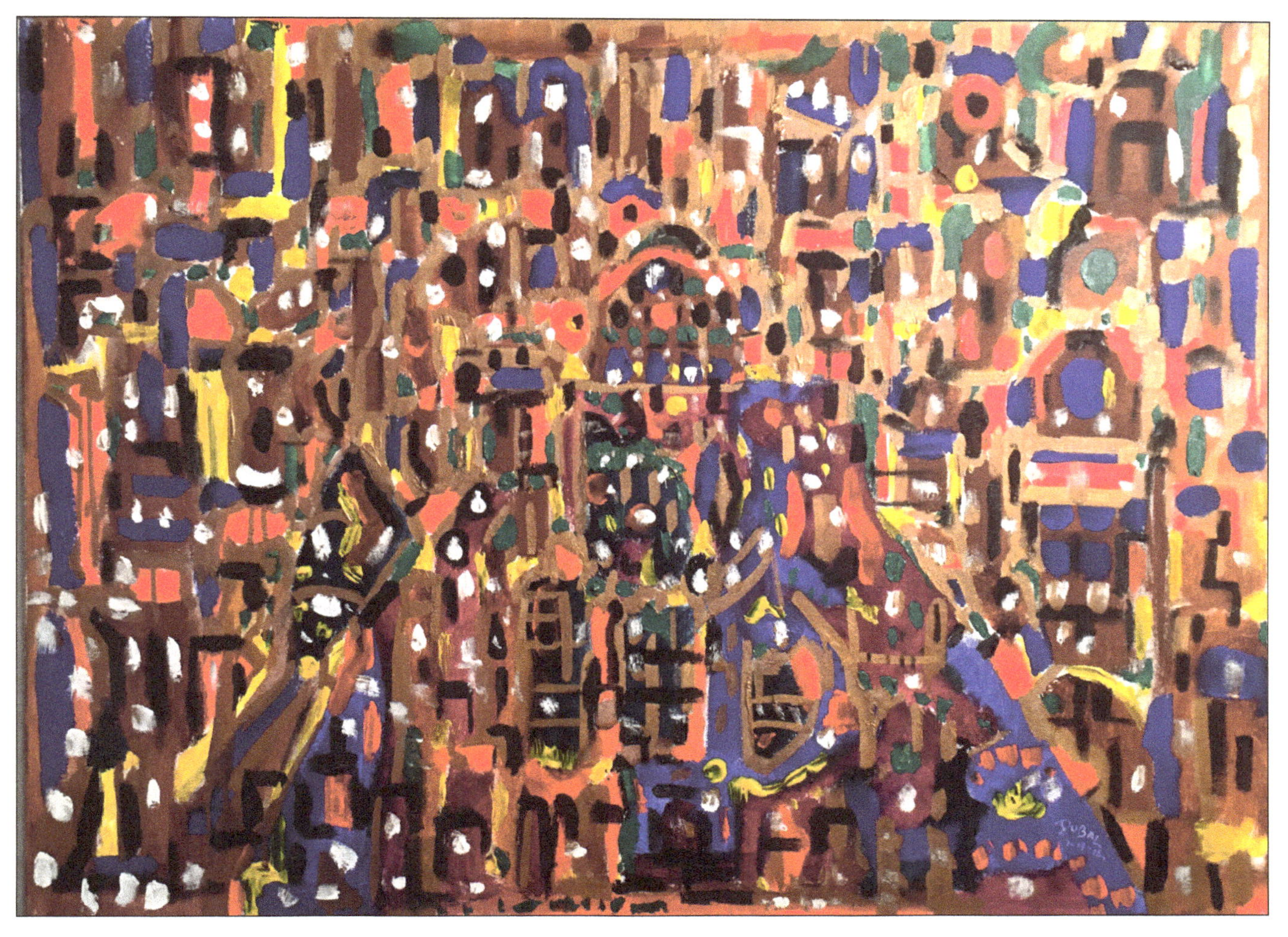

Venice at Night.
30 x 40. Oil on canvas. 2012.

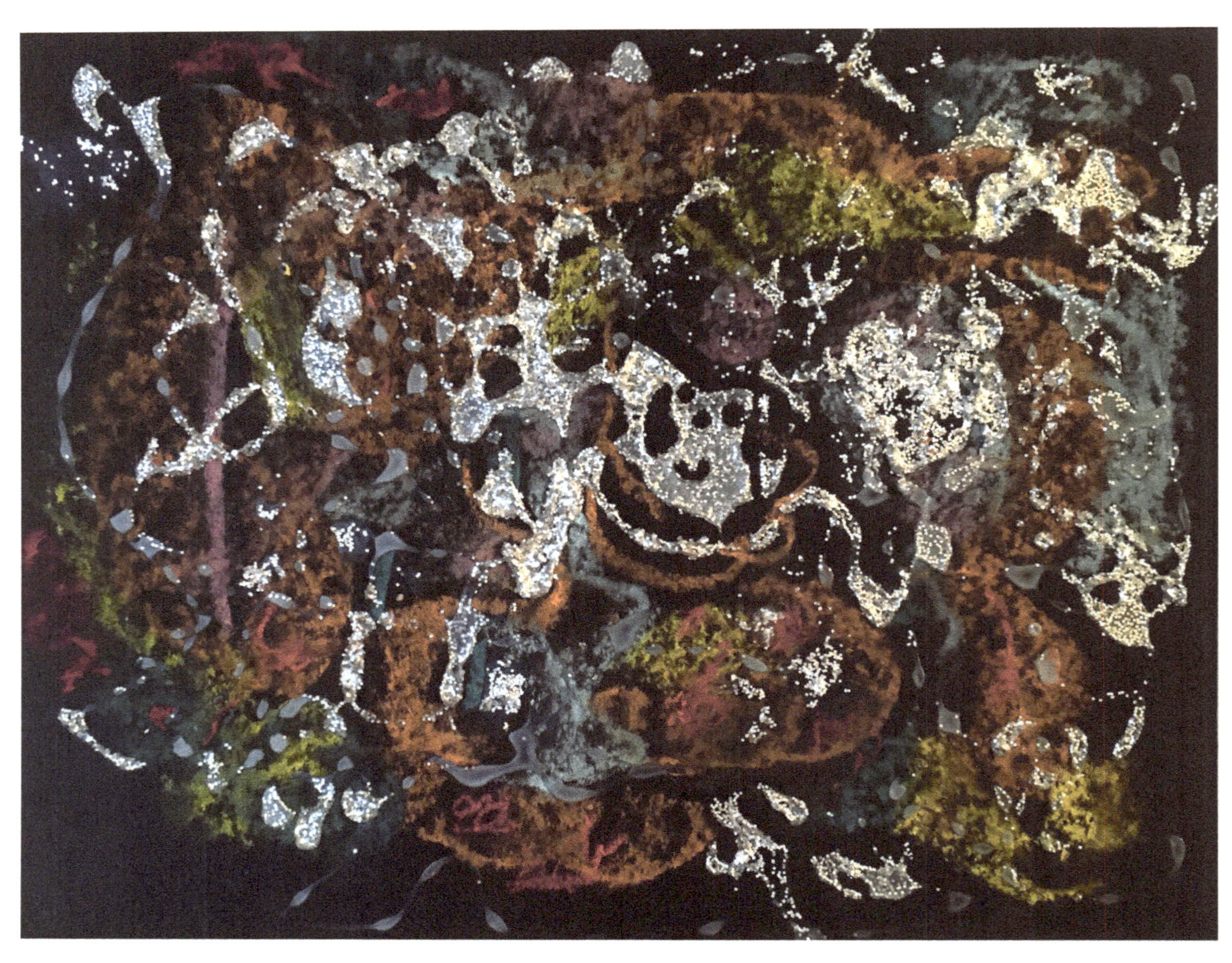

Inside a Star.
12 x 16. Silver paint and pastel. 2003.

     THE PAINTINGS OF DAVID DUBAL

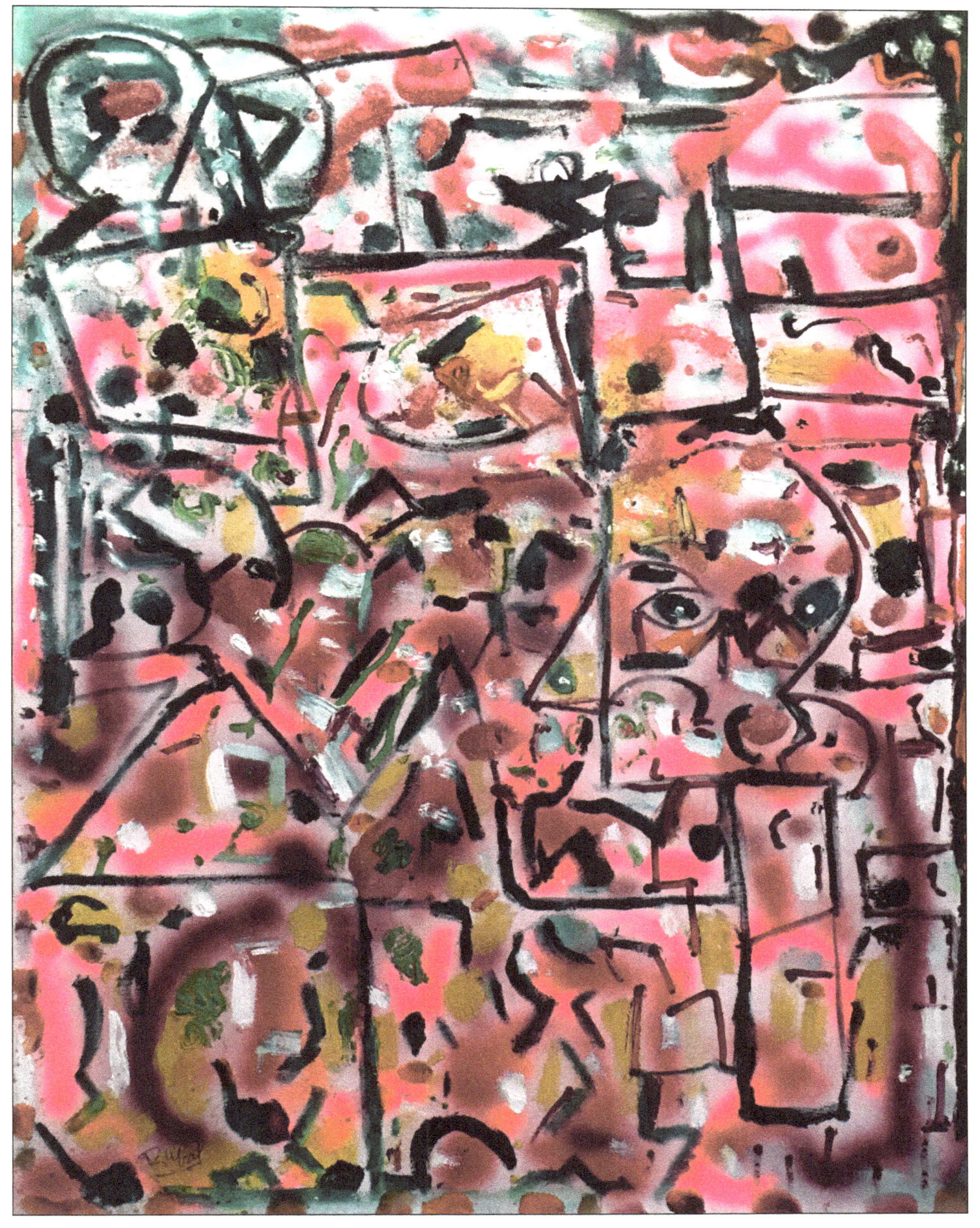

All The Things You Are.
40 x 30. Oil on canvas. 2013.

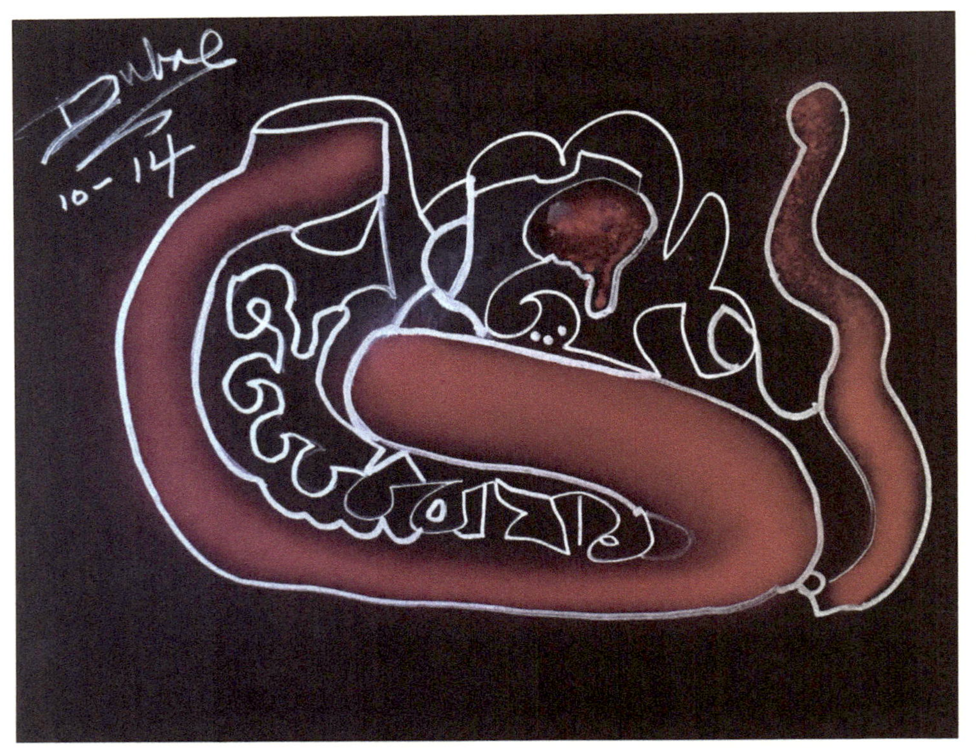

The New Worm.
14 x 14. Silver and red spray paint. 2014.

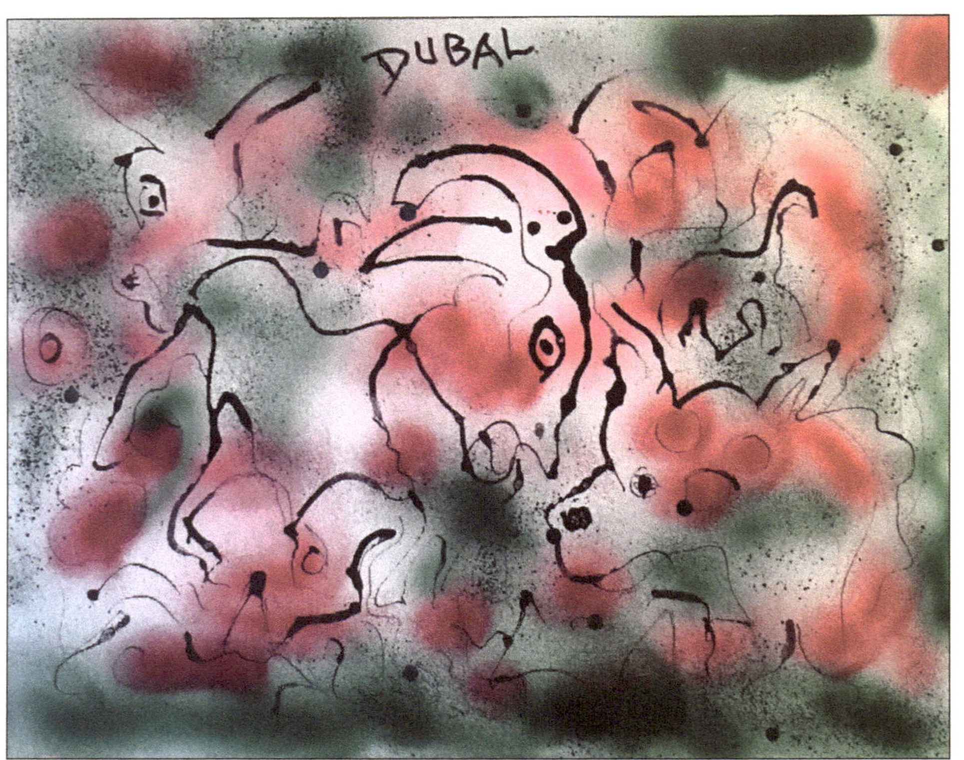

Cave Painting I.
20 x 16. Spray paint and black watercolor. 2017.

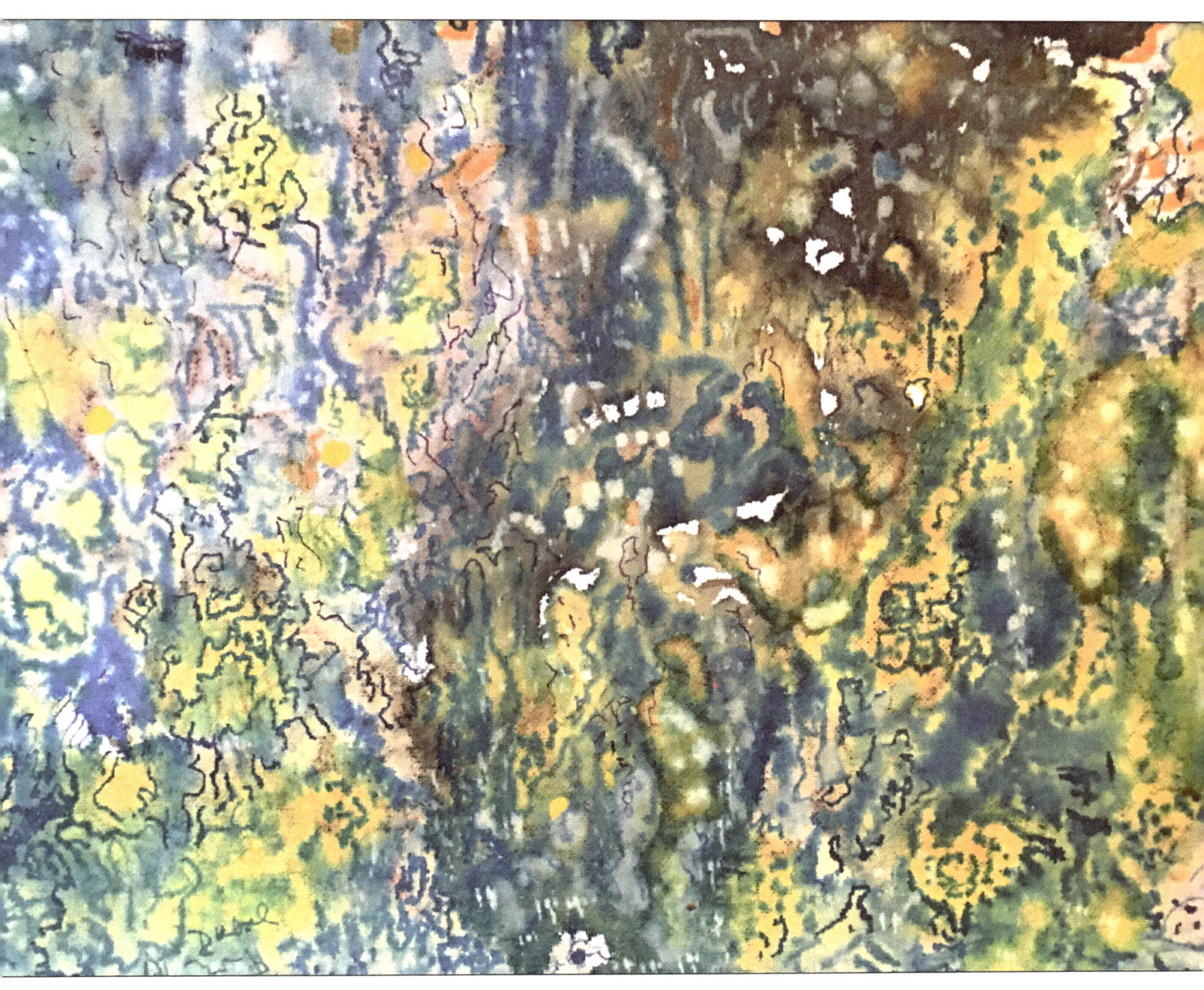

My Jungle.
12 x 16. Watercolor on canvas board. 2009.

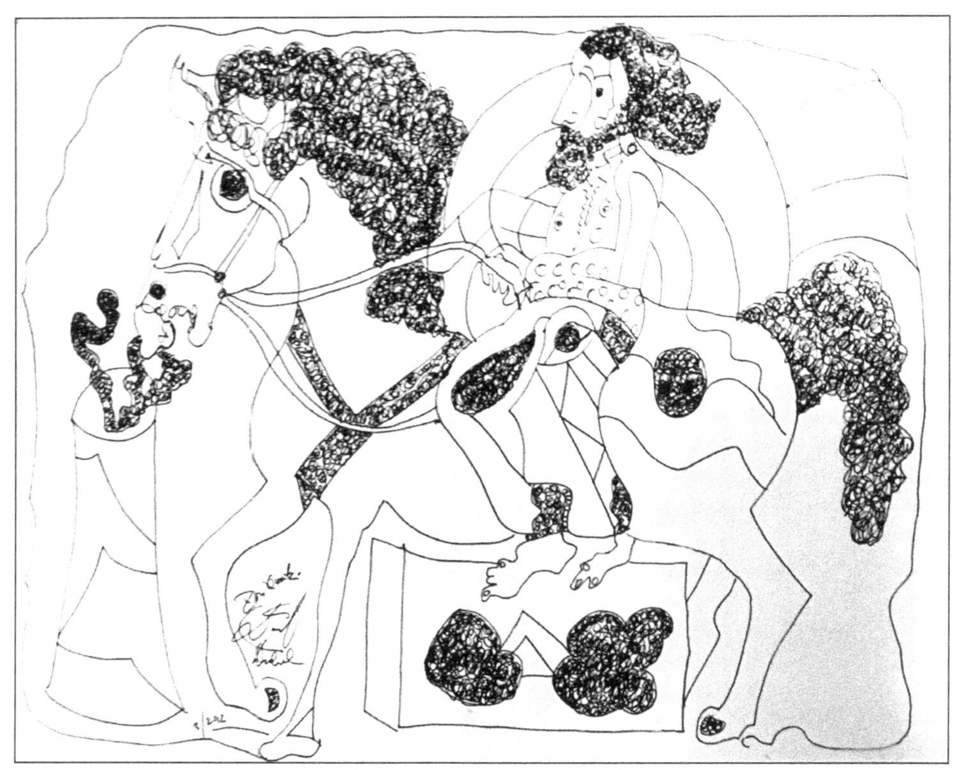

***Don Quixote Feeding
His Horse.***
12 x 17. Pen and ink on
paper. 2002.

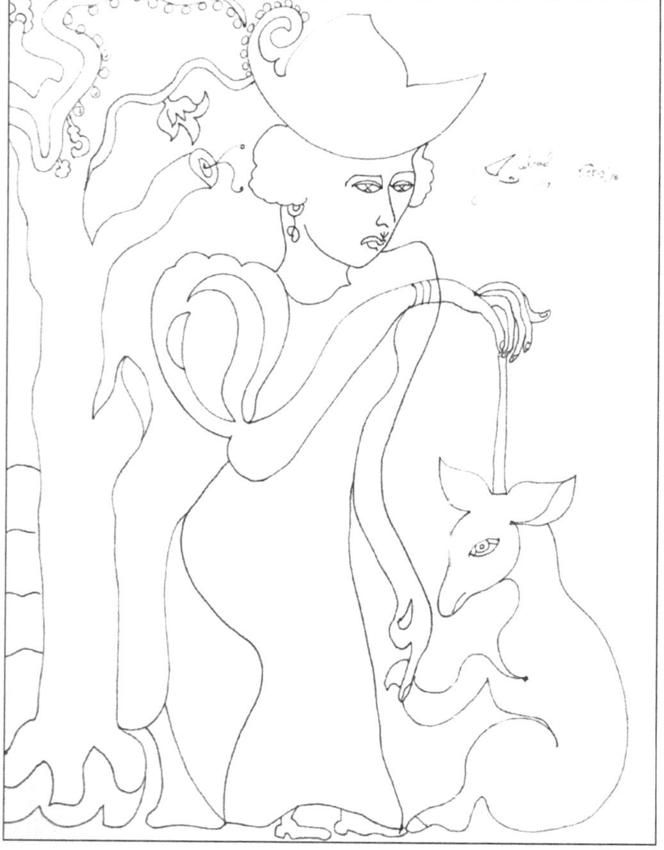

***Daffodil and Woman
Touching Her Animal.***
11 x 14. Pen and ink on
paper. 2000.

     THE PAINTINGS OF DAVID DUBAL

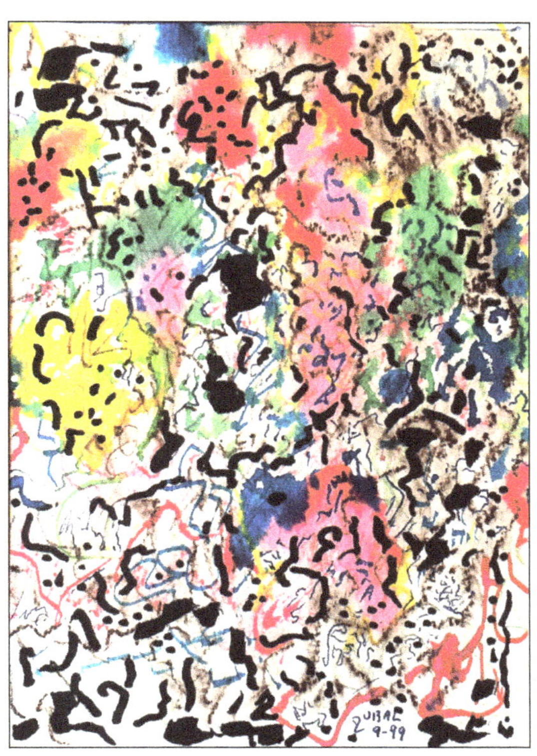

Clumps.
4½ x 6½. Watercolor on paper.
1999.

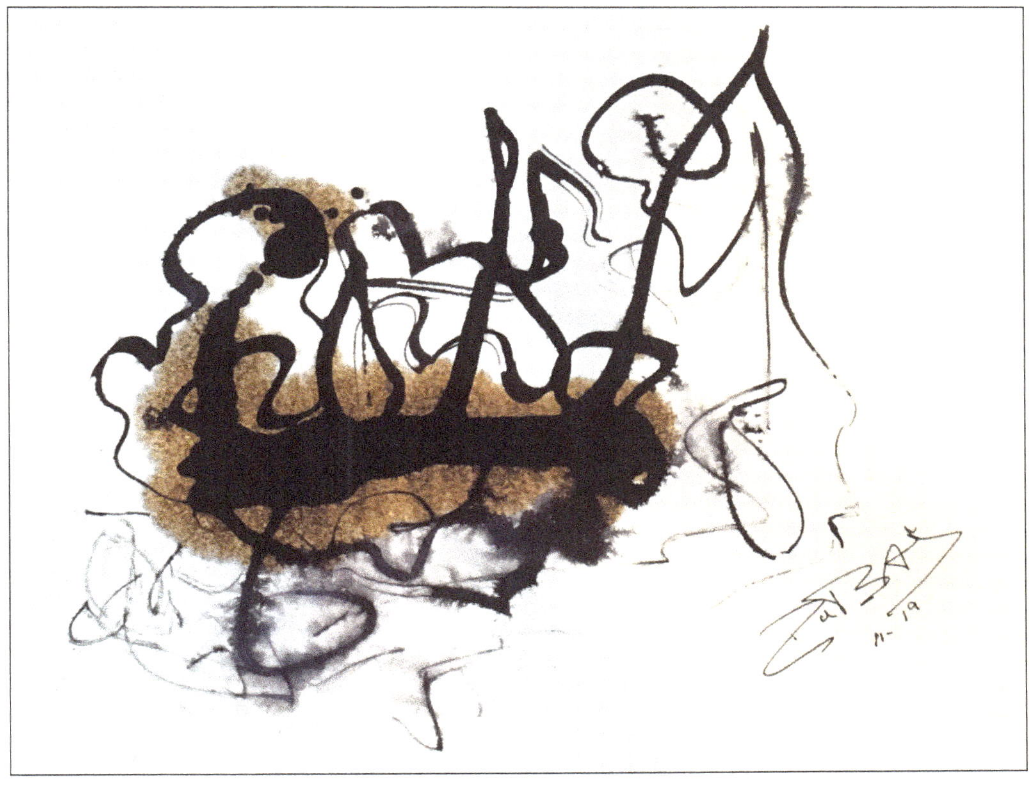

The Virtuoso.
11 x 14. Ink and brown watercolor on paper. 1999.

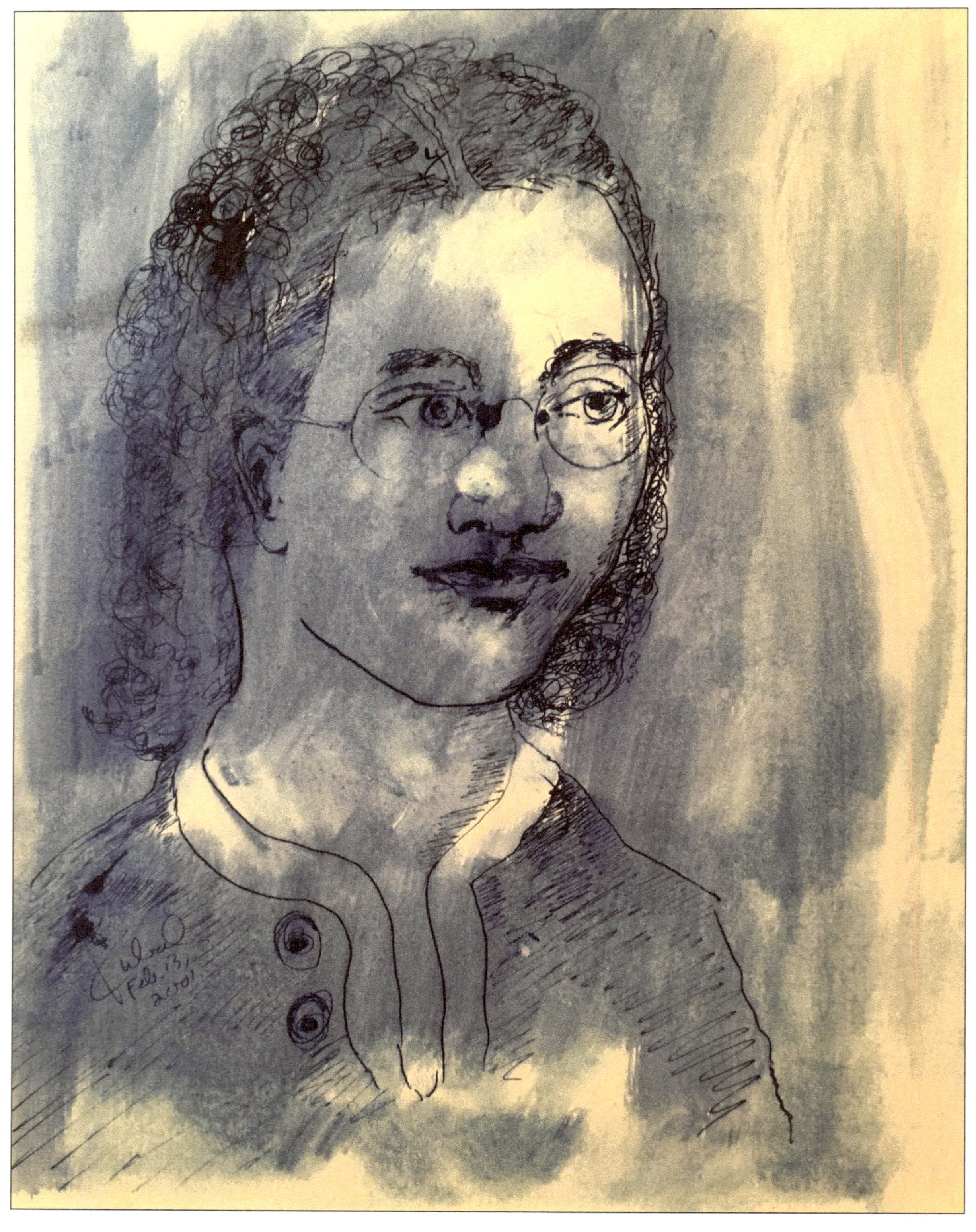

Young Girl in Blue.
11 x 14. Pen and ink and blue watercolor. 2001.

THE PAINTINGS OF DAVID DUBAL

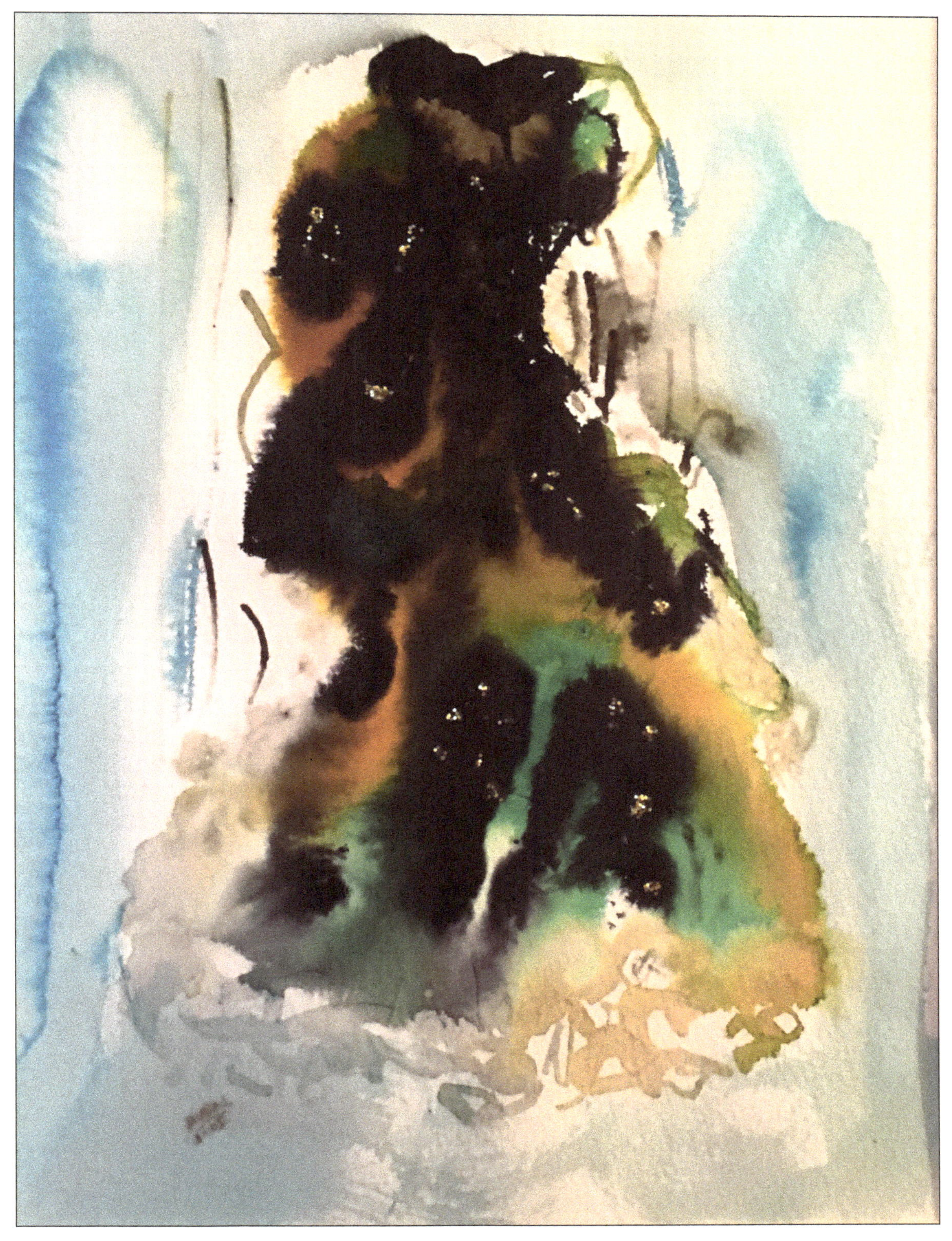

Out of the Blue.
14 x 11. Watercolor on paper. 2001.

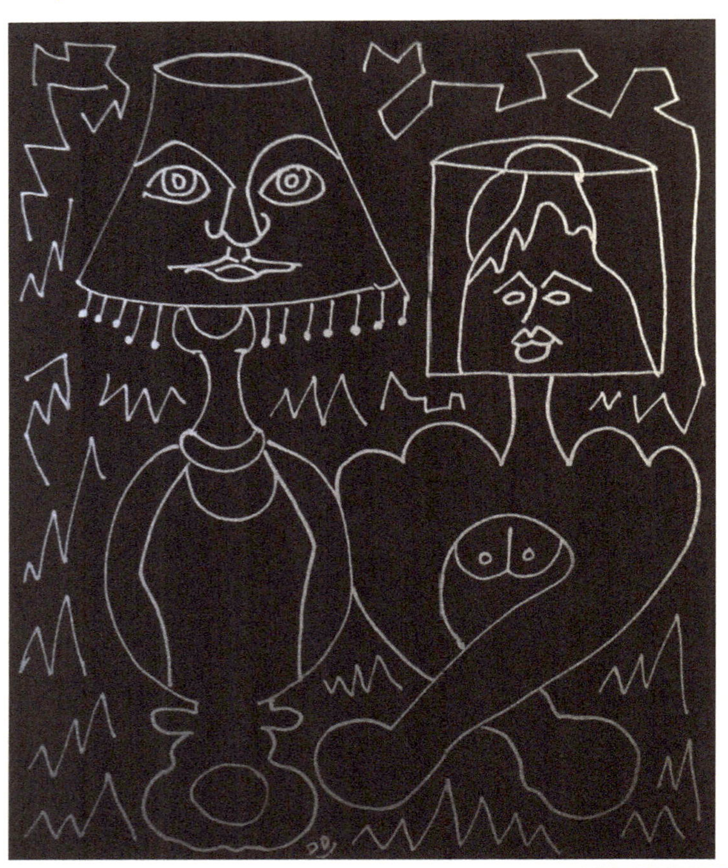

Lamp Lovers.
10 x 8. Silver ink on black board.
2009.

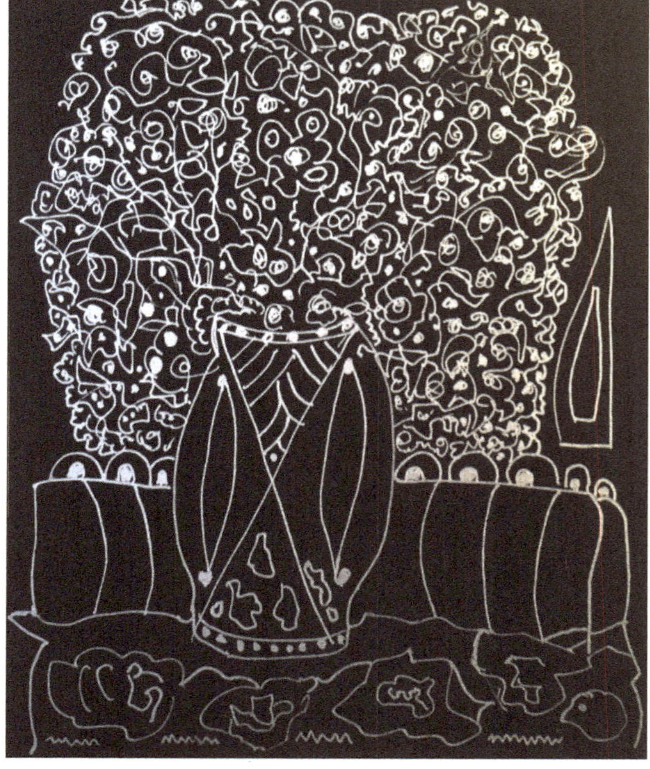

Vase with Flowers.
10 x 8. Silver ink on black board.
2009.

THE PAINTINGS OF DAVID DUBAL

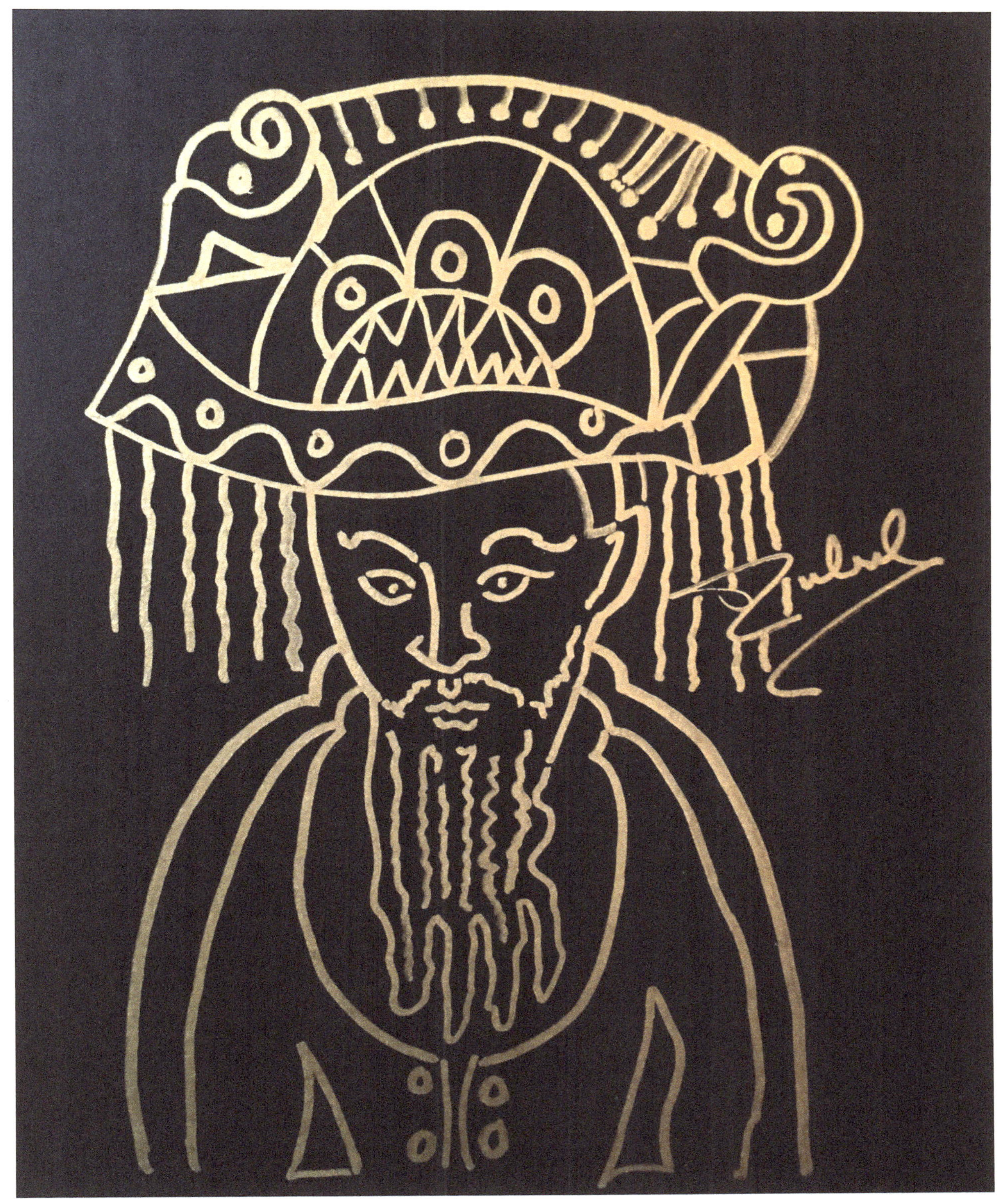

Chinese Fellow on Holiday.
10 x 8. Gold ink on black board. 2008.

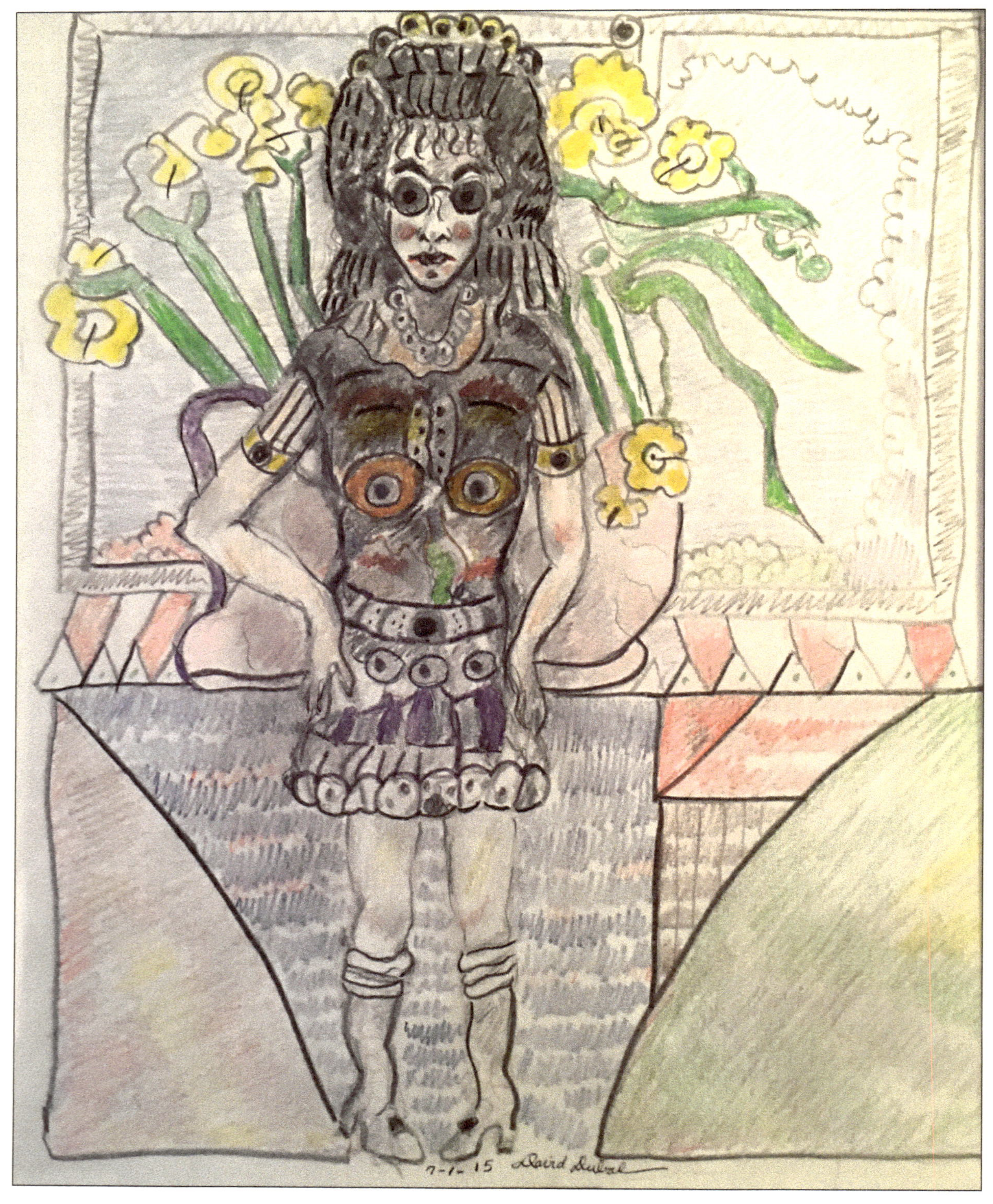

Quite a Girl!

14 x 11. Colored pencils. 2018.

THE PAINTINGS OF DAVID DUBAL

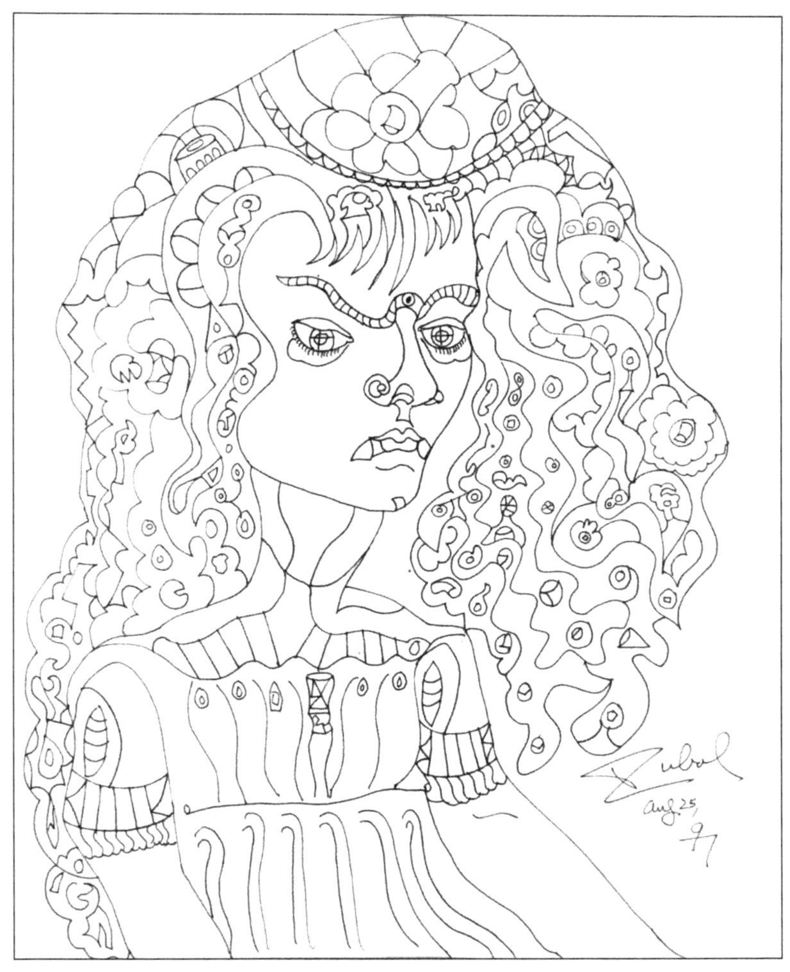

A Real Dreadful.

24 x 11. Pen and ink on paper. 1997.

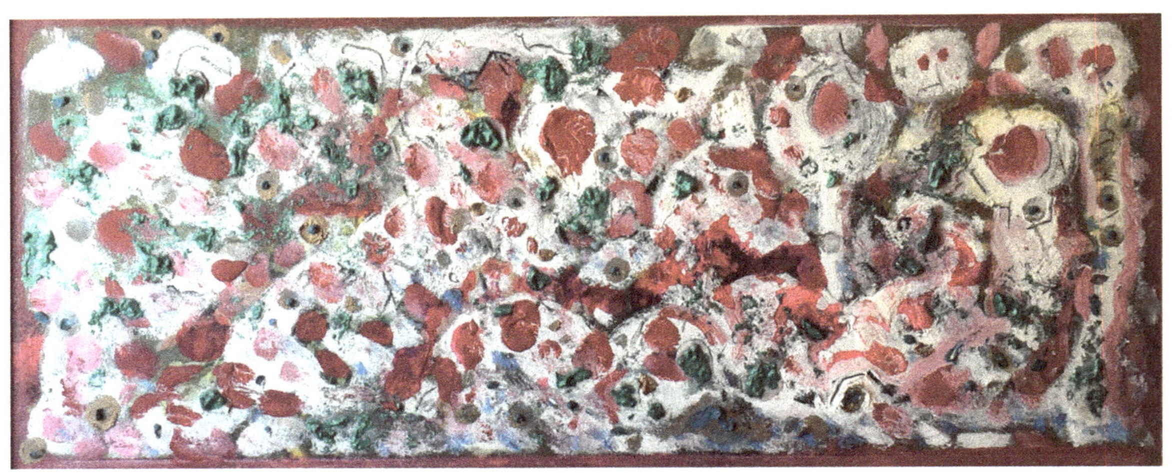

In the Hotbed.
14 x 36. Mixed media. 2010.

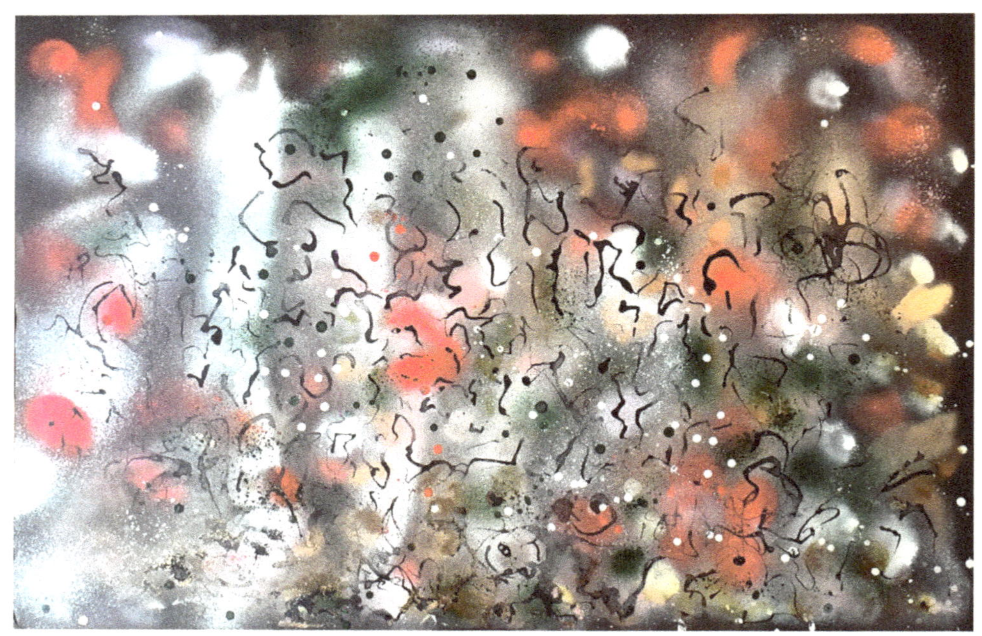

Glory on Black Board.
20 x 30. Spray paint. 2013.

     THE PAINTINGS OF DAVID DUBAL

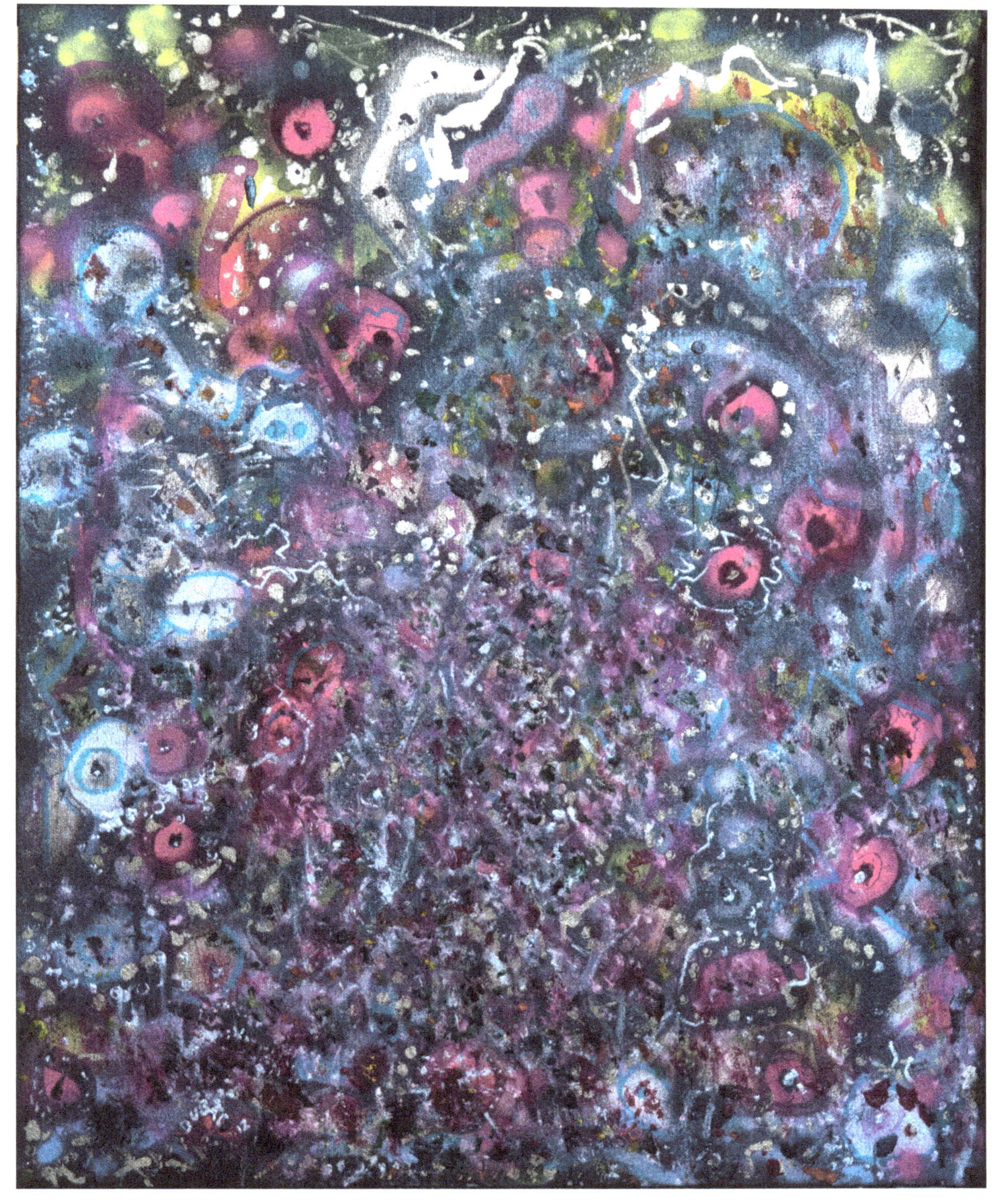

Your Eden.
20 x 16. Oil on canvas. 2012.

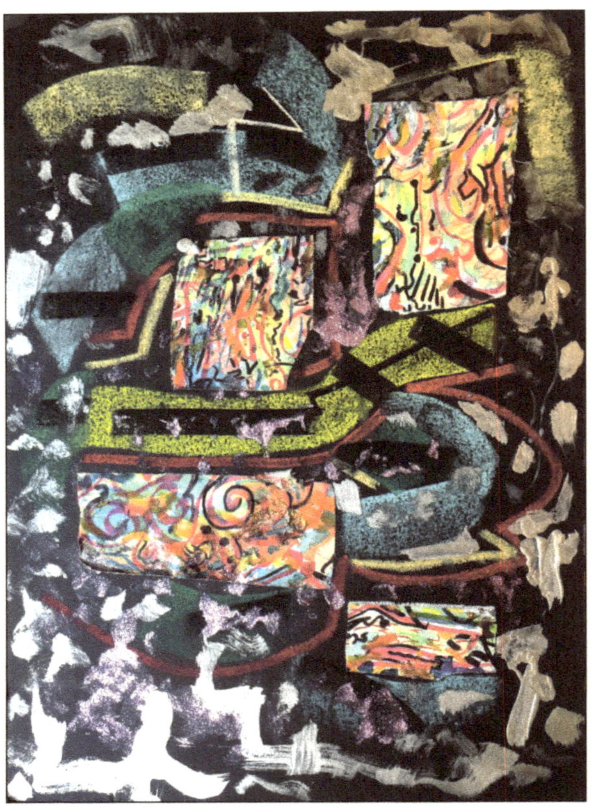

Untitled Collage.
20 x 30. Mixed media. 2015.

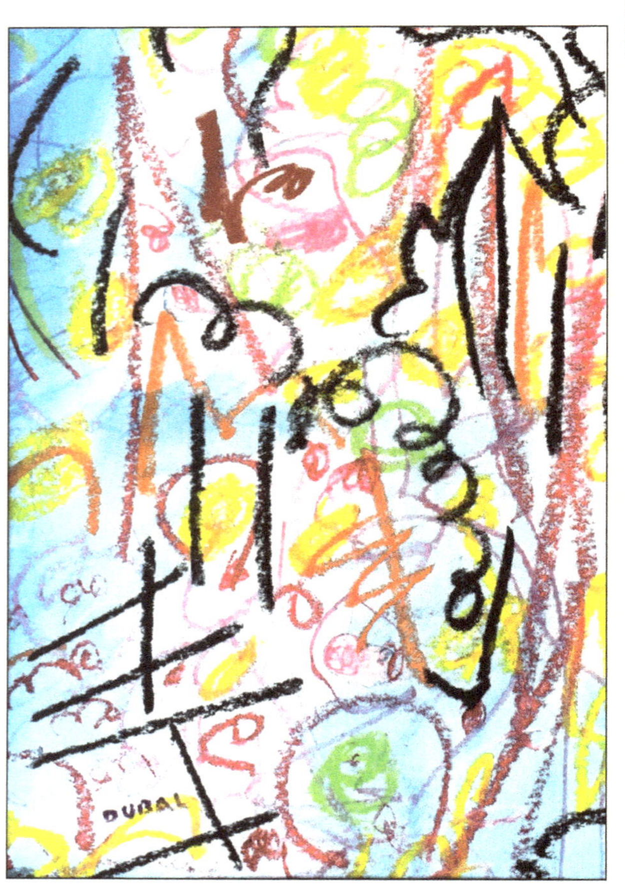

Untitled.
7 x 4½. Watercolor. 1999.

THE PAINTINGS OF DAVID DUBAL

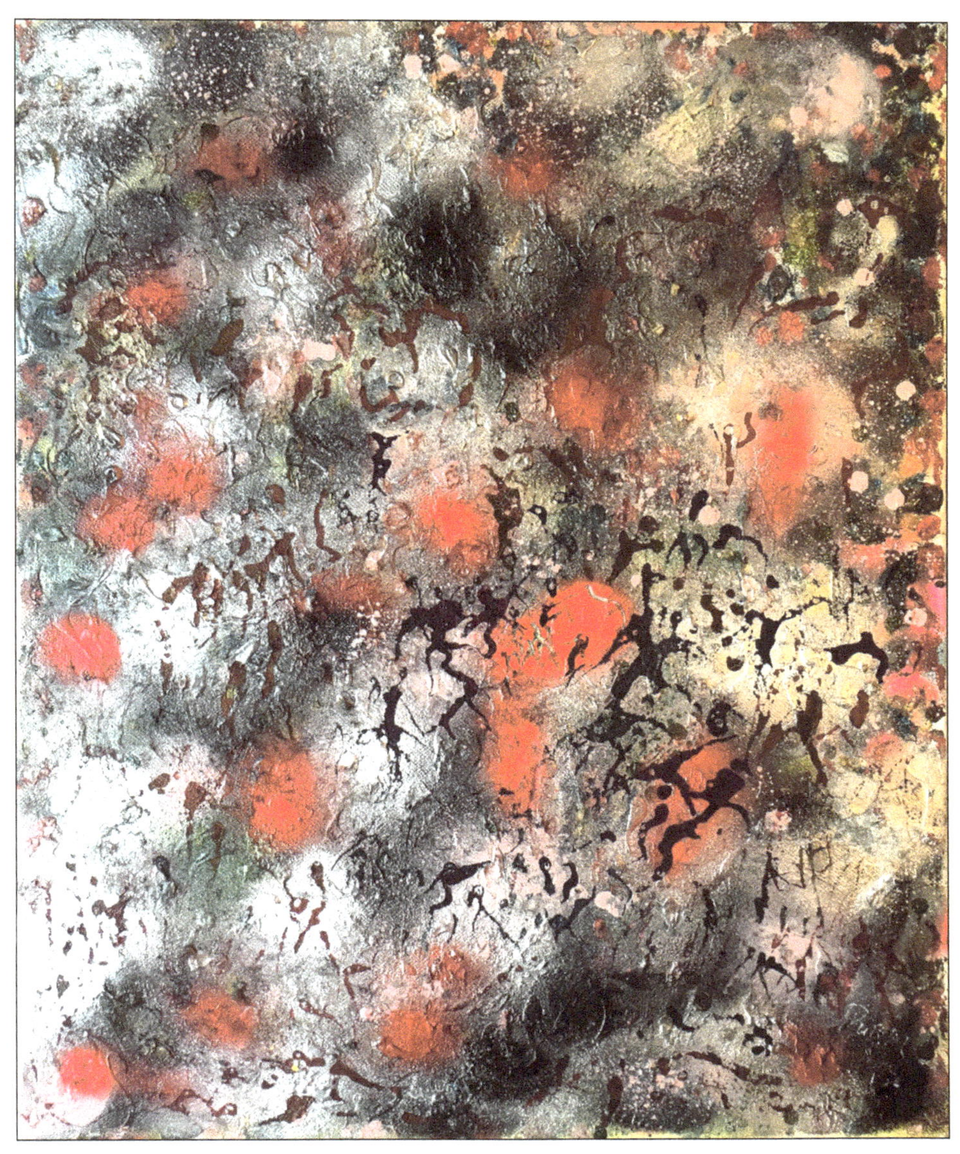

Highly Textured.
20 x 16. Paste, spray paint and India ink on canvas. 2016.

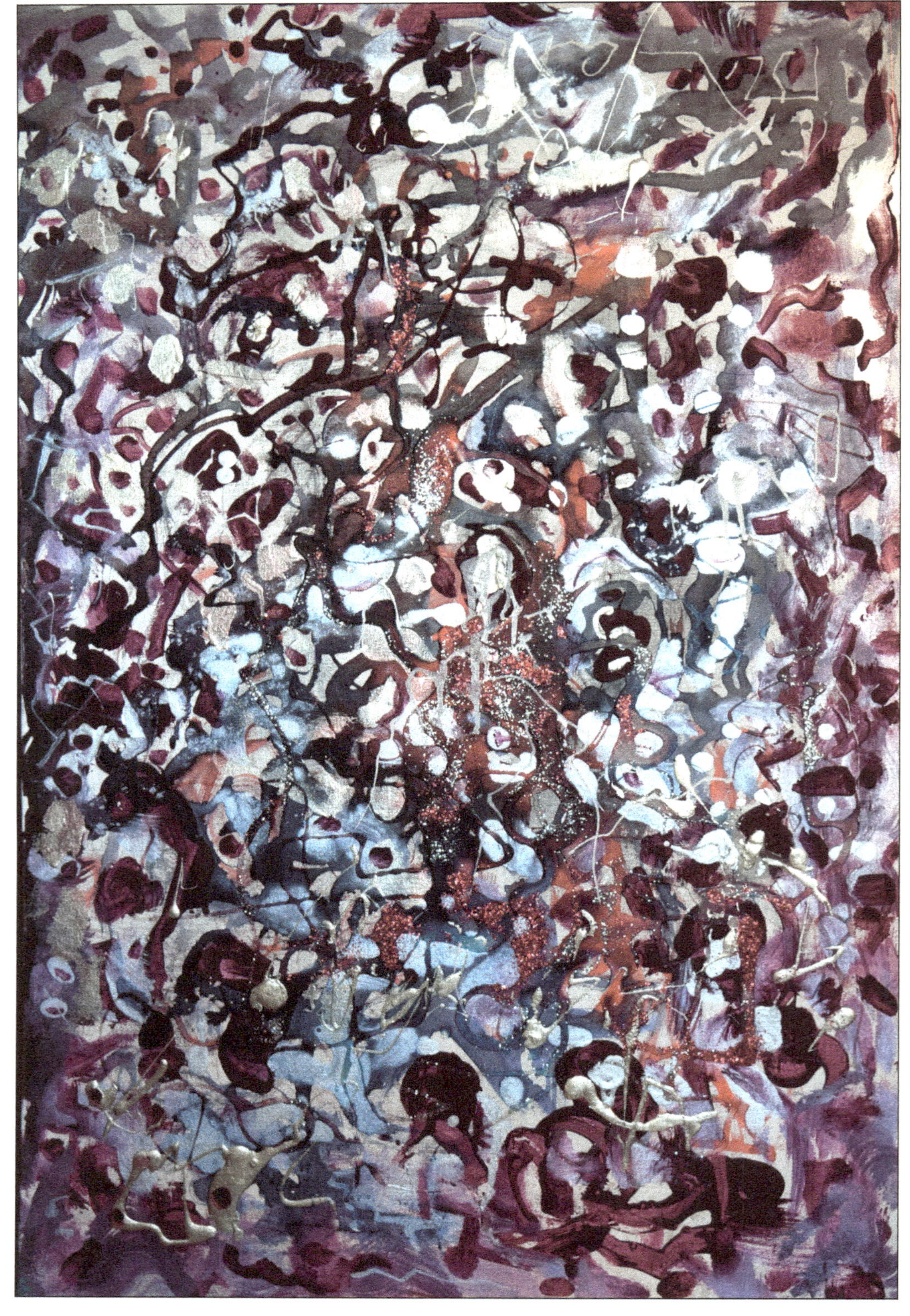

It Tells a Secret.
36 x 24. Mixed media on canvas. 2011.

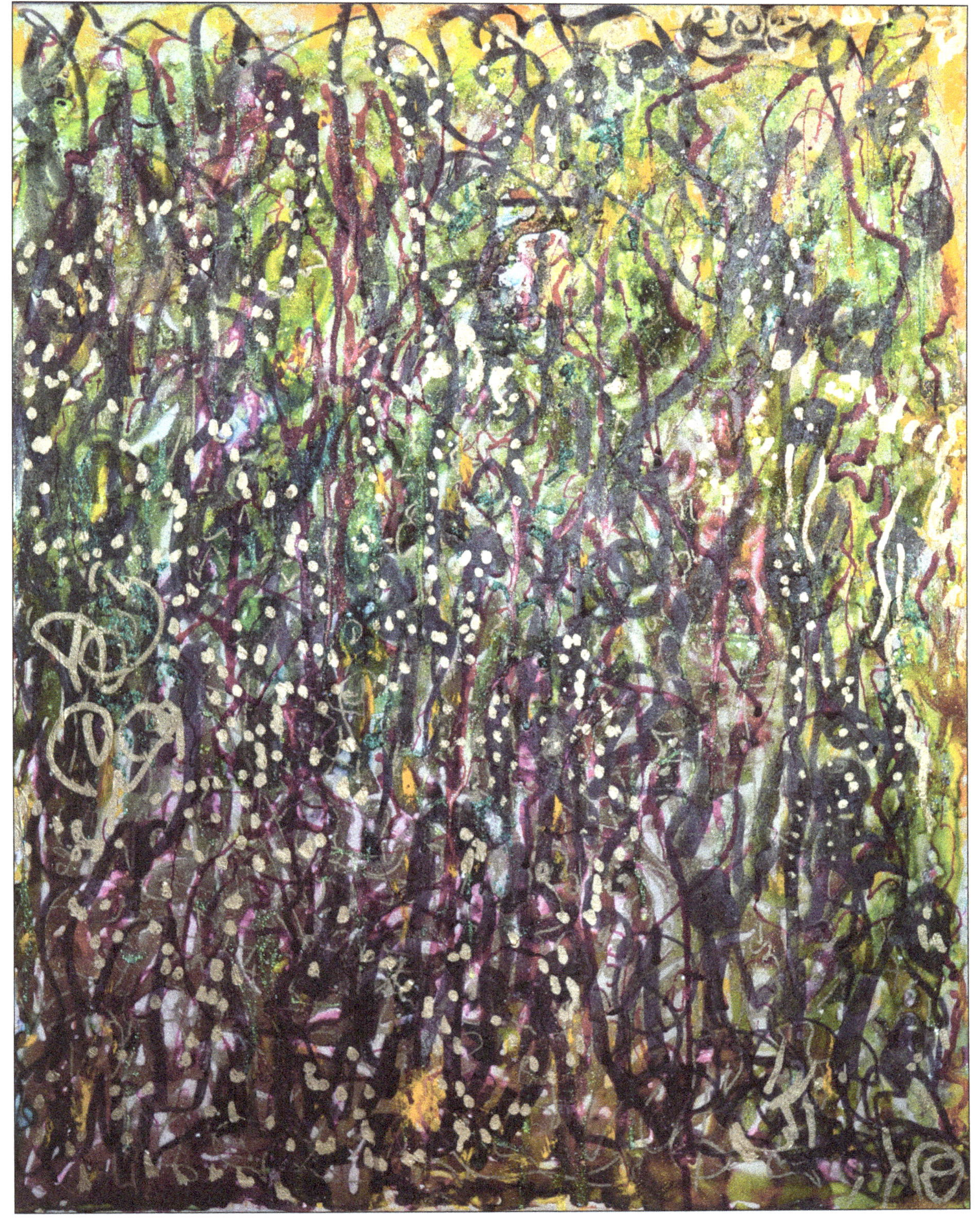

In Burma.
24 x 22. Mixed Media on canvas. 2011.

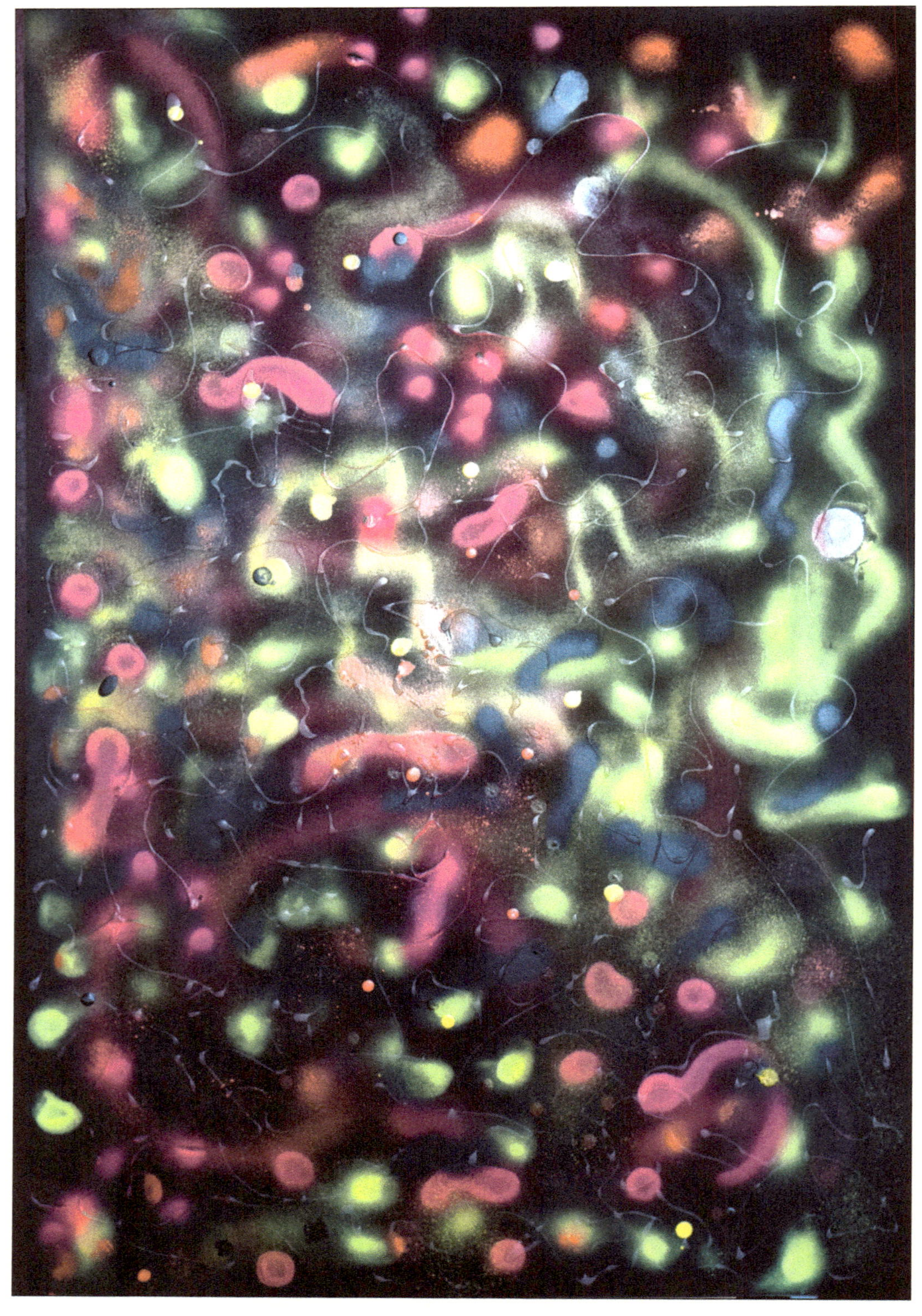

People See Differently.
24 x 30 Spray paint. 2010.

THE PAINTINGS OF DAVID DUBAL

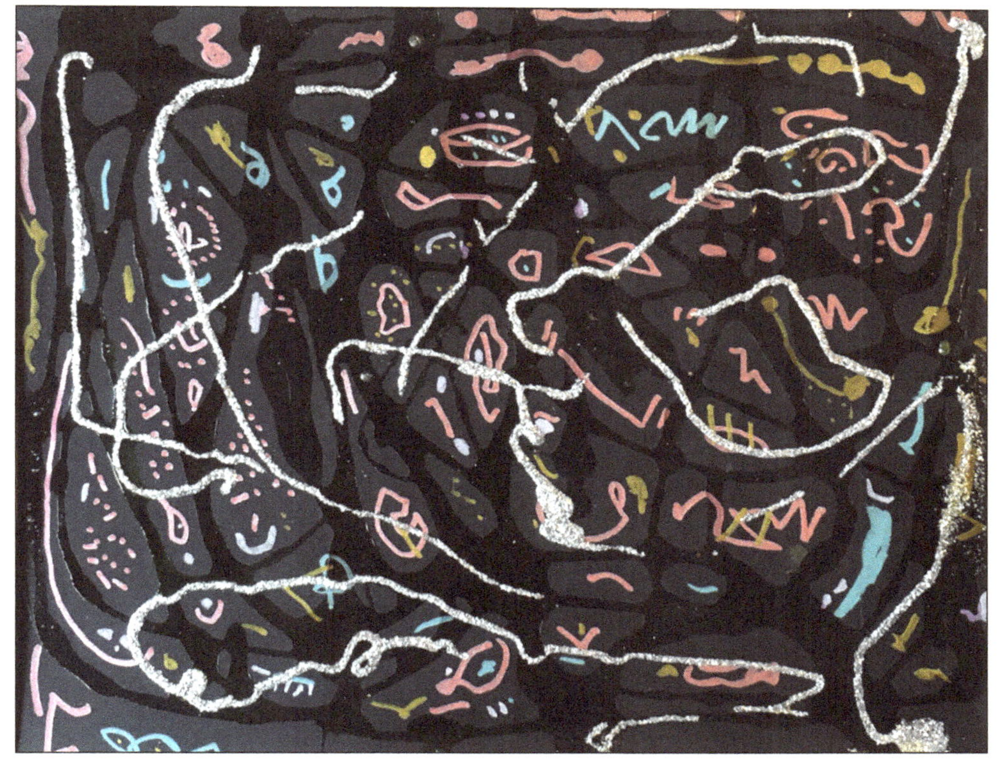

Untitled.
White paint on black board. 2016.

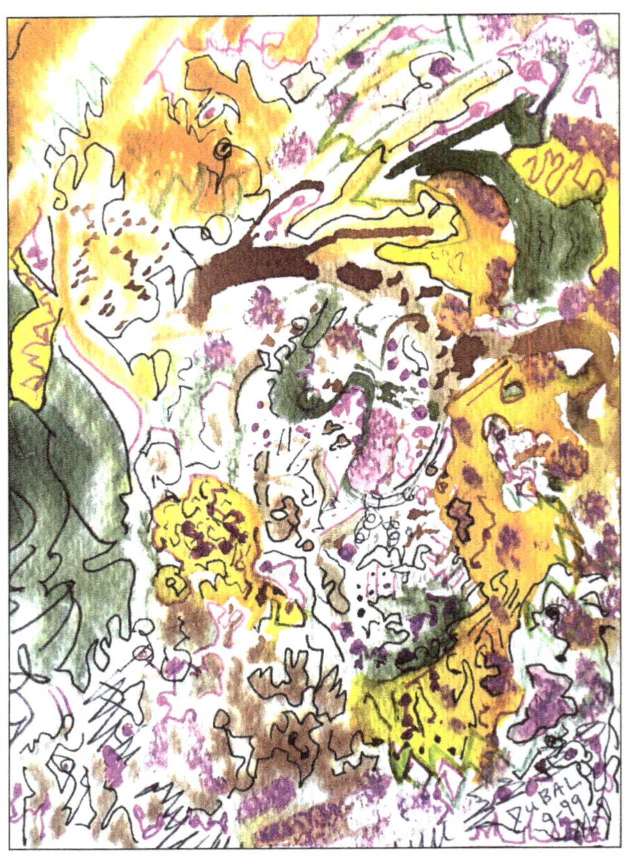

Abstract 14.
4 x 6½. Watercolor on paper.
1999.

Abstract 37.
4 x 6½. Watercolor. 2000.

THE PAINTINGS OF DAVID DUBAL

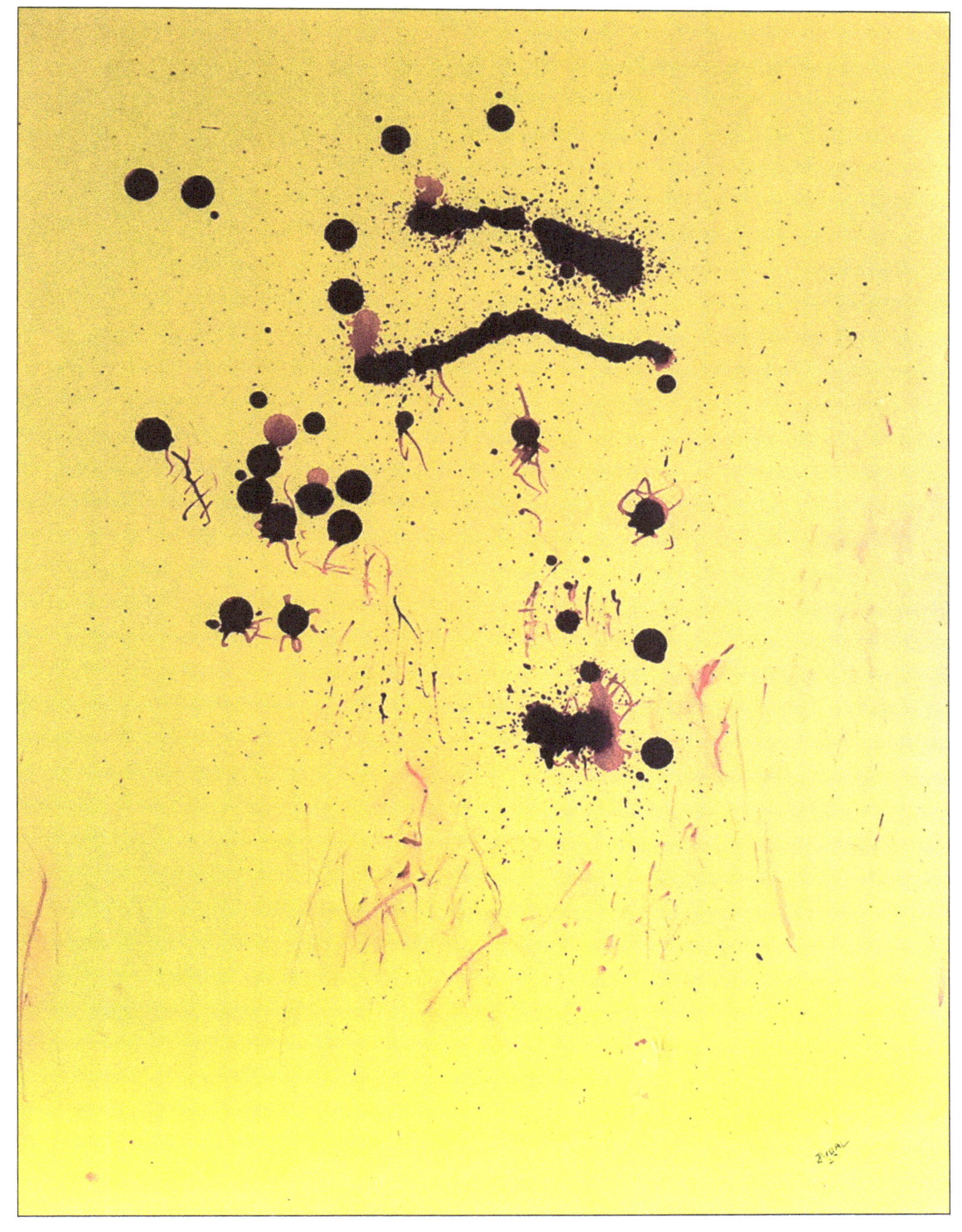

Yellow Burst.
20 by 30. Watercolor on board. 2020.

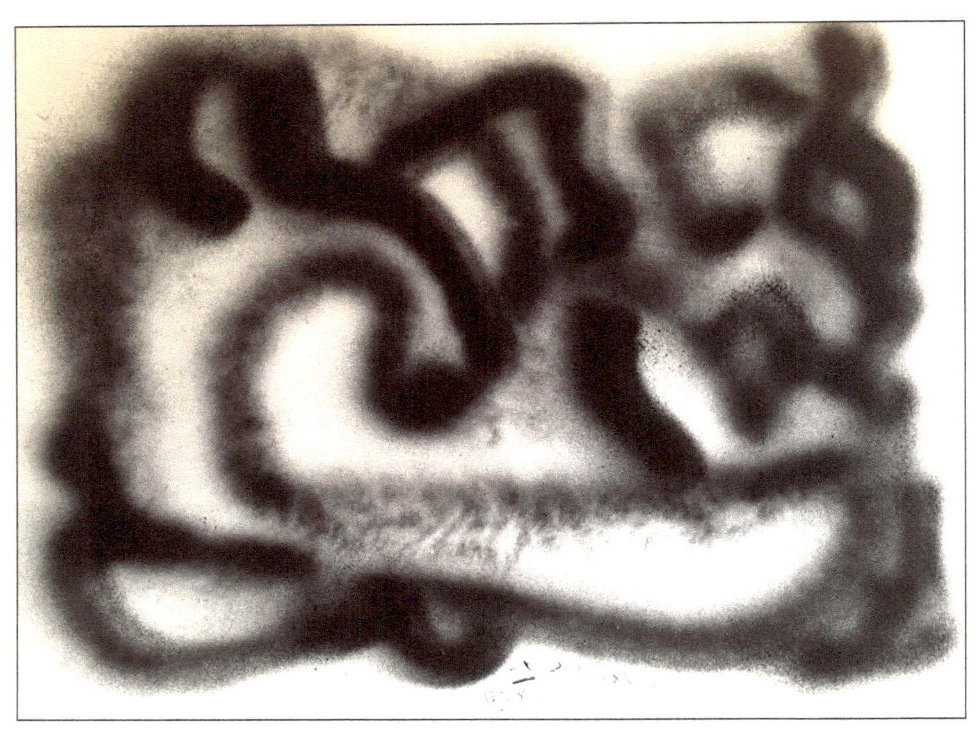

Black Camphor.

22 x 28. Black spray paint. 2018.

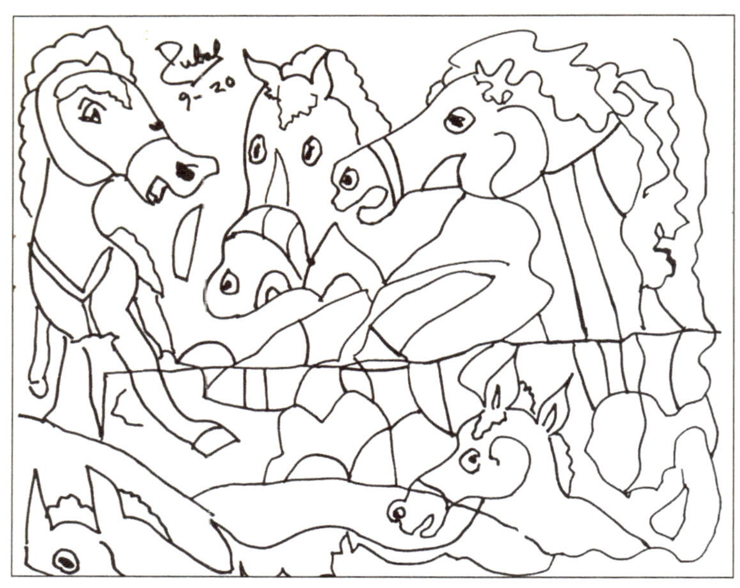

The Carousel.

20 x 24. Ink on white board. 2020.

                          THE PAINTINGS OF DAVID DUBAL

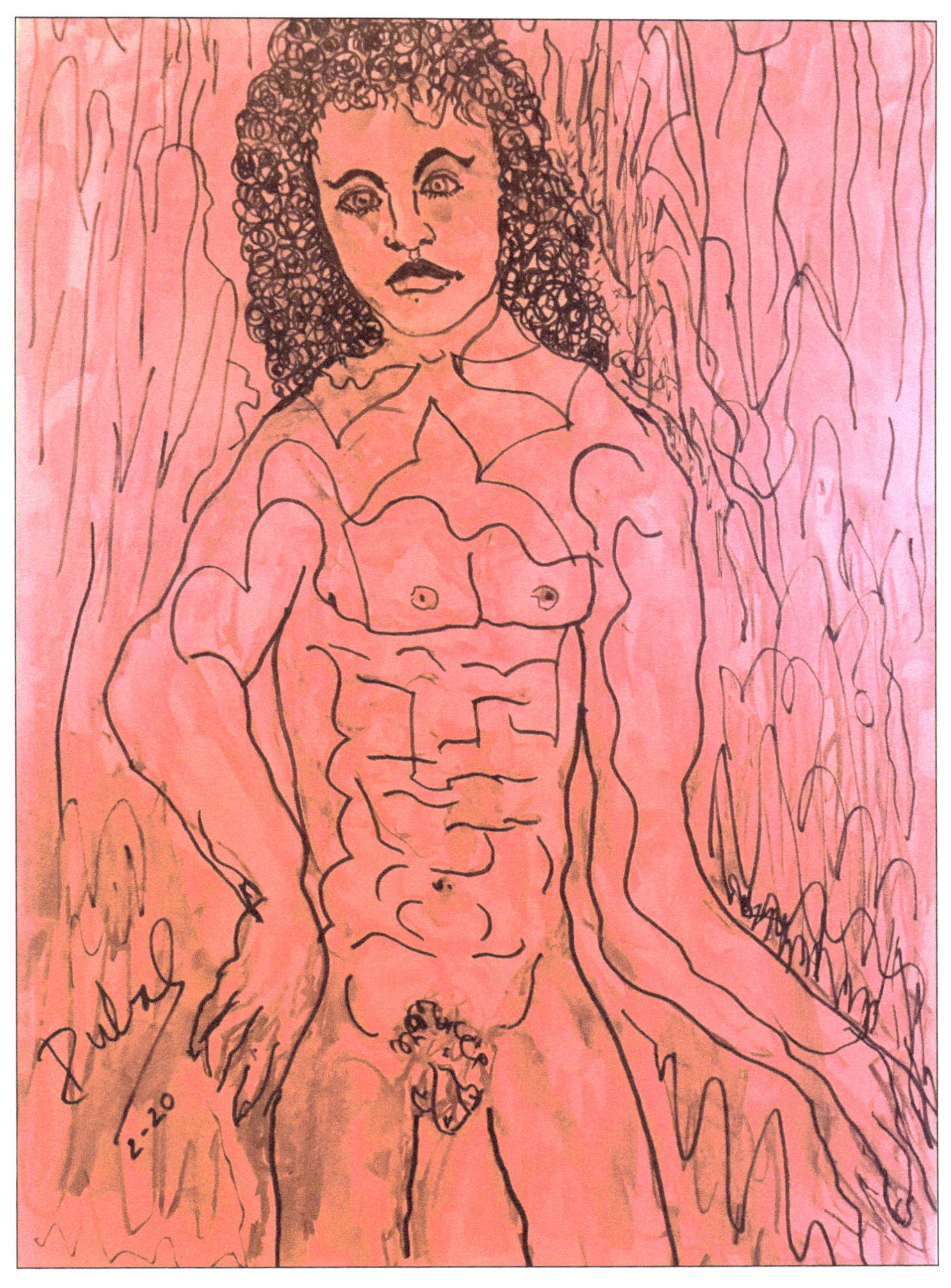

Adam, the First Man.
20 x 30. Charcoal on board. 2020.

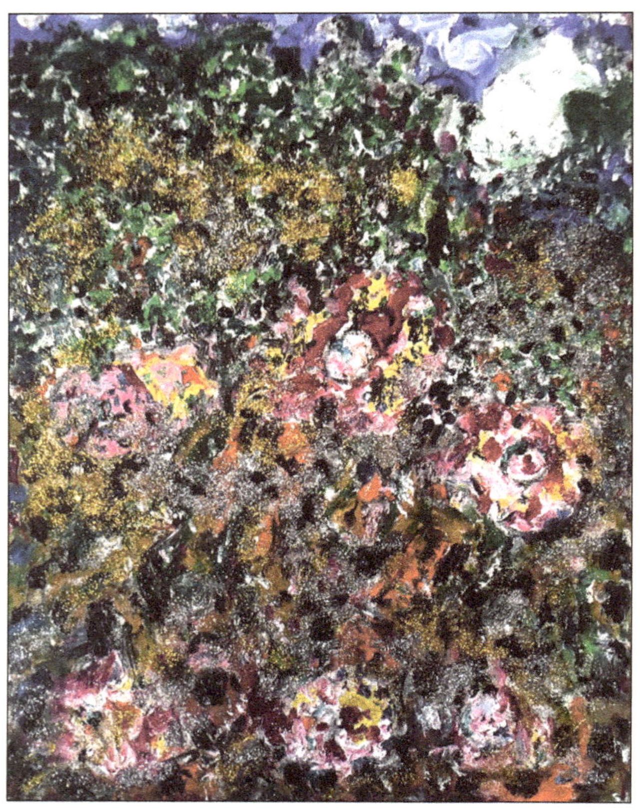

In the Hudson Valley.
17 x 21. Oil on canvas with glitter.
2014.

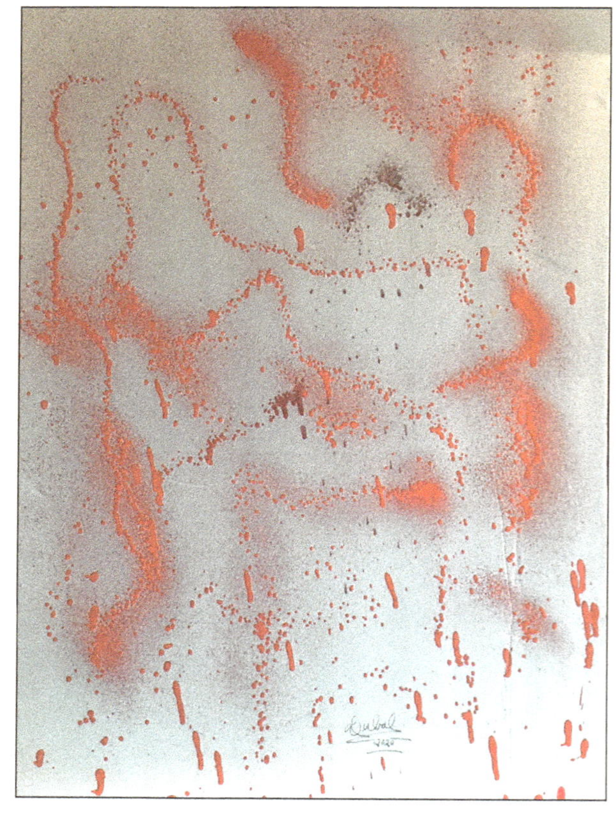

The Ghost Machine.
20 x 30. Spray paint on board.
2020.

THE PAINTINGS OF DAVID DUBAL

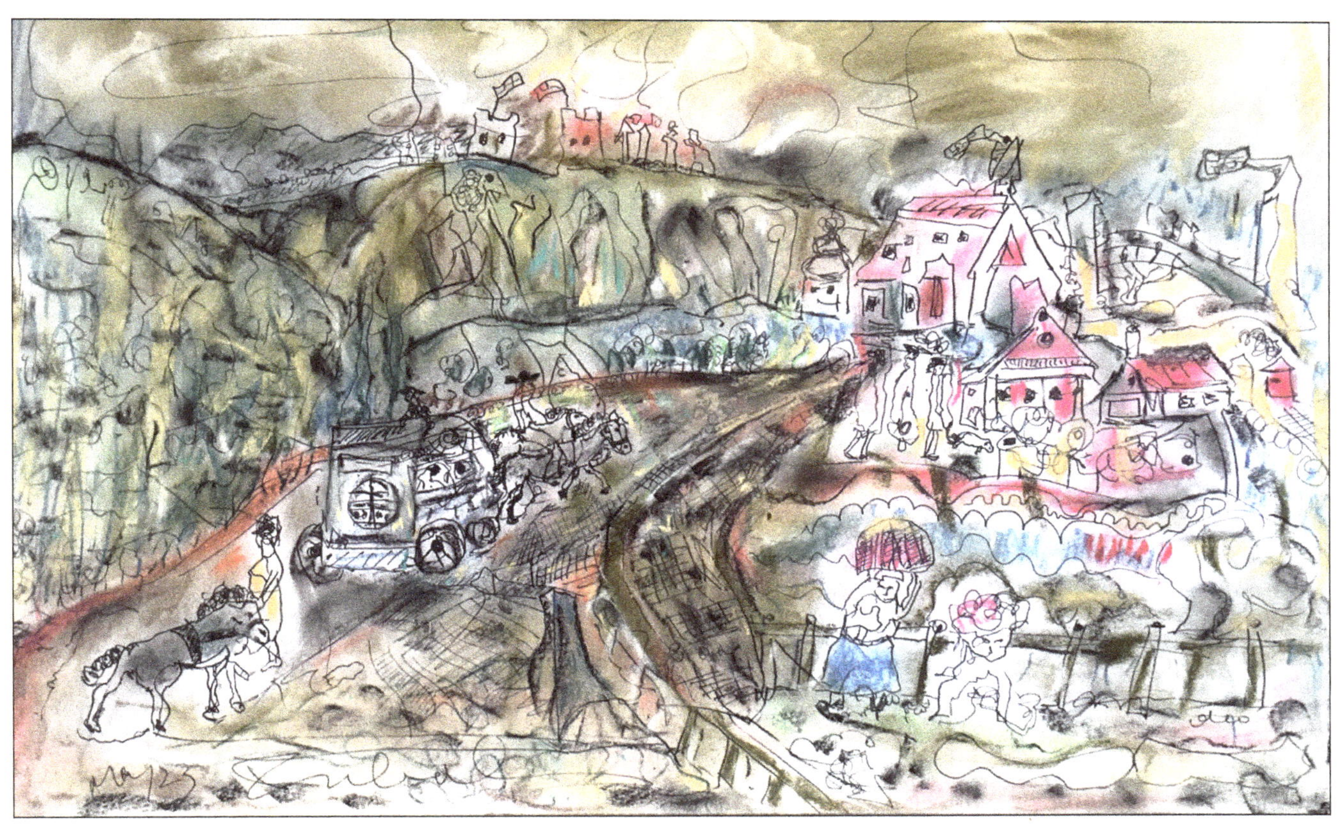

The Last Stage Coach Ride.
14 x 22. Mixed media. 2020.

www.ingramcontent.com/pod-product-compliance
Lightning Source LLC
Chambersburg PA
CBHW041030050726
47599CB00018B/1913